Saint Patrick Catholic Community

Scottsdale, Arizona

W9-BFS-771

Dear Readers,

St. Patrick Catholic Community is a spirit-filled community that was established in north Scottsdale, Arizona in 1980. We have always been known as a Roman Catholic community that challenges itself to be a family of hospitality and life-giving worship. St. Patrick exudes a spirit of hospitality, making people feel welcome and giving them dignity and respect. As we examine and treasure with pride the accomplishments and trials of the past in our diocese and parish, we look forward to what the future promises in challenges and the gift of stead fast faith.

Throughout the history of St. Patrick Catholic Community, there have been four foundational areas emphasized in all we do: Good Liturgy Builds Faith, Hospitality, Stewardship and Social Justice. Liturgy is the way we bring Christ to one another in our singing, praying and worshipping. Hospitality in the way we offer an attitude of welcoming to all, taking everyone where they are in life as they build a stronger foundation centered on Jesus Christ. Stewardship implores us to share what God has given us with others in the form of gifts of time, talent and treasure. Social Justice calls our parish to commit both energy and resources to bring about justice in response to what the Church teaches and the Gospel calls us to.

Together we look to the future in the belief . . .
"The Mass Must be Lived, Go Forth to Love and Serve the Lord."

Peace in Christ,
Fr. Eric Tellez, Pastor

Fr. Eric Tellez

St. Patrick Catholic Community
10815 N. 84th Street Scottsdale, AZ 85260
Phone: (480) 998-3843 Fax: (480) 998-5218
Website: www.stpatricksScottsdale.org

Acknowledgments

Authors
Rev. Steven M. Avella, General History
John Hanley, Parish History

Advisors
Rev. Timothy Davern, J. C. L.
Rev. Michael L. Diskin, Assistant Chancellor
Rev. Peter P. Dobrowski, Pastor
Rev. Msgr. Richard Moyer
Robert DeFrancesco, Editor, *The Catholic Sun*
James Dwyer, Public Information Officer

Project Directors
James Neal, Archivist
Sr. Jean Steffes, C. S. A., Chancellor

Publisher
Éditions du Signe
B.P. 94
67038 Strasbourg - France
Tel: 011 333 88 78 91 91
Fax: 011 333 88 78 91 99
Email: info@editionsdusigne.fr

Publishing Director
Christian Riehl

Director of Publication
Joëlle Bernhard

Publishing Assistant
Audrey Gilger

Photography
John Glover

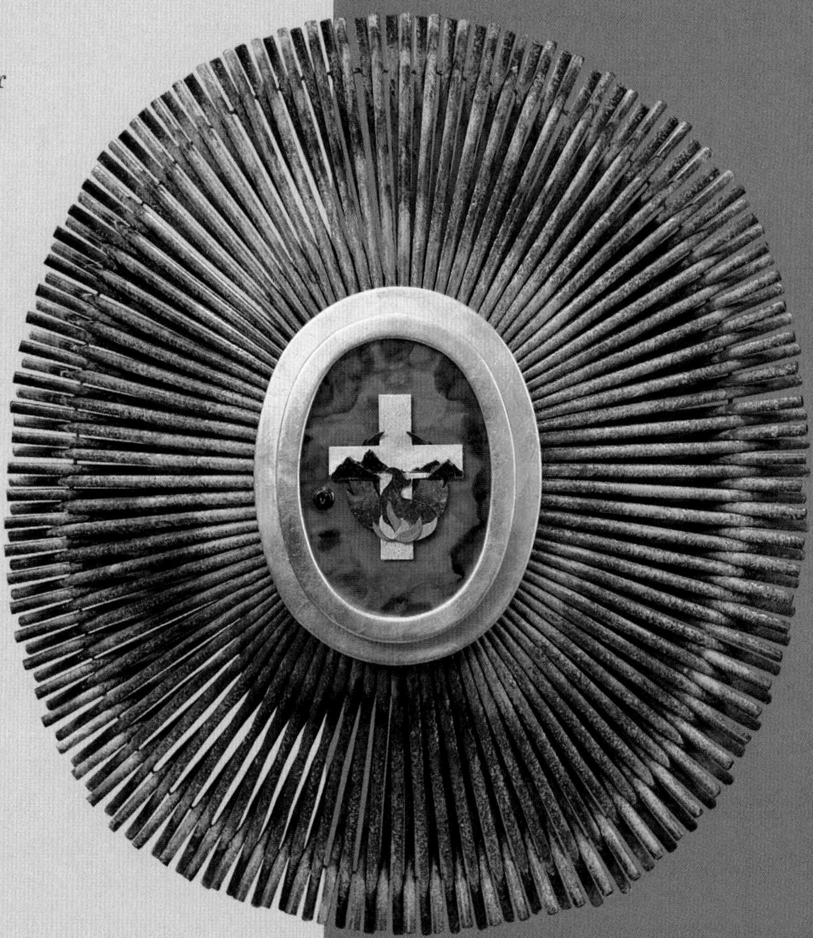

ISBN: 978-2-7468-2211-5
Printed in China

We wish to express special thanks to all the photographers whose work appears in this book. Photographs included in this book were taken from the diocesan archives and *The Catholic Sun*. Additional photographs used in this book were allowed courtesy of the following collections:
Archives of the Archdiocese of Santa Fe, Archives of the Sisters of Charity of the Blessed Virgin Mary, Archives of the Roman Catholic Church of the Diocese of Tucson, *The Arizona Republic*, *Catholic Advance* (Diocese of Wichita), Office of Catholic Mutual, Marquette University Archives, Phoenix Public Library, Phoenix Museum of History, and Tempe Historical Museum.

We regret any errors or omissions in the text, captions and acknowledgments.

My Dear Brothers and Sisters in Christ,

How blessed we are to be members of a Church that has graced our world with the saving message of Jesus Christ for over two millennia. As we celebrate the 40th Anniversary of the Diocese of Phoenix, we may at first question how significant this event is in view of the history of the Church. But, as you read the history that is contained in this anniversary book, I hope that you will come to appreciate how the last 40 years is the latest chapter in a story of faith that goes back to the 16th century and beyond.

When I reviewed the history of the Catholic Church in what is now the Diocese of Phoenix, I was struck by a common thread. If faith is a gift, and we believe it is, then for us it is a gift that has been brought to us on the shoulders and from within the hearts of dedicated priests, religious and laity who exemplify the universal nature of our Catholic Church.

Those who first brought the message of faith to the native peoples of our state were Spanish Franciscan and Jesuit missionaries. Our Catholic roots go back to Fray Marcos de Niza who accompanied Francisco Coronado on his explorative journey in AD 1539. It was not until the 19th Century that what is now Arizona became part of the United States of America.

In 1850, Father Jean Baptiste Lamy was appointed as Vicar Apostolic of Santa Fe. His territory included what are now the states of Colorado, Utah, New Mexico and Arizona. As bishop and later archbishop, Archbishop Lamy relied heavily on French priests to minister to the Catholic populations that were spread throughout his territory. Followed by Bishop (later Archbishop) Jean Baptiste Salpointe, the first Vicar Apostolic of Arizona, then by Bishop (later Archbishop) Peter Bourgade who became the first Bishop of Tucson, and by Bishop Henry Regis Granjon a tremendous debt of gratitude must be given to the French clergy who bore the weight of the tremendous challenges that existed during the time of their faithful service. It wasn't until 1923 that the first American was appointed as Bishop of Tucson, Bishop Daniel J. Gercke of Philadelphia.

The period of tremendous growth in Arizona that took place after World War II is marked by the recruitment of some 60 priests from Ireland. These men were responsible for the development of many of the parishes and schools that serve the metropolitan Phoenix area. Women religious also came from Ireland. Without their presence, it is unlikely that our present Catholic school system would exist as it does. The contribution of these women and men cannot be adequately measured or appreciated.

Today, our Diocese continues to be marked by the arrival of priests from other nations. Religious communities from Africa and South America have assumed the pastoral care of parishes in the Diocese. The Diocese has also been blessed with priests from Vietnam, South Korea, the Philippines and other nations, some of whom have been incardinated here. The unique nature of our Catholic Church is reflected in the multi-national make up of both the clergy and religious who have ministered and continue to minister here.

The Diocese of Phoenix has also been blessed by the sacrificial service of countless lay men and women, most of whom came to Arizona from other regions of the United States, as well as from foreign countries, to share their unique talents and vision with love and devotion. As faithful stewards of God's gifts, their initiative is seen in the development of many organizations and agencies that witness to the two great commandments: love of God and love of neighbor. Faithful to their baptismal call, it is primarily through the initiative of the laity that our Diocese has been blessed by the St. Vincent de Paul Society, the Knights of Columbus, the Catholic Community Foundation, Maggie's Place and Crisis Pregnancy Centers to identify just a few. By chairing the annual Charity and Development Appeal, serving on Diocesan boards and commissions, exercising leadership on parish councils, finance councils and school boards and as parish catechists and liturgical ministers, the mission of the Church is carried forward.

It is my hope that, as you read the pre-history and history of our Diocese, you will join me in a prayer of gratitude for how abundantly God has blessed the Diocese of Phoenix.

Sincerely yours in Christ,

Thomas J. Olmsted

+ *Thomas J. Olmsted*
Bishop of Phoenix

Encountering the Living Christ

■ Introduction

This overview of the Diocese of Phoenix is only the beginning of what will one day be a longer and more substantive study. Commissioned as a 40th Anniversary Project, this brief history provides a glimpse into the origins of the Catholic Church in this beautiful part of Arizona. This narrative not only celebrates and chronicles the events, people and issues that have defined the Catholic Church in Arizona over the years, but it is also a testimony to the activity of God among His people. Since a number of people described in this book are still alive, the last chapter of their lives and the impact of their decisions are not yet known. Time and its accompanying blessing, perspective, will allow a future historian to explore and evaluate what is not here.

In compiling this history, I relied heavily on printed materials: parish histories, Catholic newspapers and periodicals, and oral history. I interviewed a number of people who played key roles in the history of the diocese–including a few who were there "in the beginning." I thank especially Rev. Msgr. Richard Moyer, Mr. Frank Barrios, Mr. Harvey Newquist, Sister Anthony Poerio, Father Fredrick Adamson, Father Timothy Davern, Bishop Thomas O'Brien, and Bishop Thomas Olmsted for their helpful insights. Father Vernon Meyer's excellent doctoral dissertation (*This Far by Faith: A History of Black Catholics in Phoenix, 1868-2003* (University of Dayton, Ohio, 2004) was a great help–well researched, superbly written and challenging. I also benefitted from Bradford Luckingham's *Phoenix: History of a Southwestern Metropolis* (University of Arizona Press, 1995). Father Chuck Kieffer, my gracious host during a visit to Phoenix in August 2008, helped me make sense of a lot of things. James Neal, the meticulous and hard-working archivist of the Diocese of Phoenix, was instrumental in bringing this book to fruition.

The Diocese of Phoenix is in the American Southwest. That simple fact imposes a particular framework on the Catholic experience in Arizona. This part of the United States is growing rapidly, and the Catholic Church is working to meet the needs of a large and culturally diverse population–all hungry for the Bread of Life. Those who rise daily to meet the challenges imposed by that growth and the unique demands of the local culture must find themselves enthused by the new opportunities to proclaim the Lord Jesus. At times they must often feel weary and frustrated by the demands and trials it brings. However, inspired by their daily encounter with the living Lord of all history, I am certain that the present generation of Arizona Catholics will go forward in hope to do the work of the Gospel just as their forebears did. For indeed, every generation of believers arises like the Phoenix, a symbol of the Risen Christ, to meet the challenges of every age. "To Him whose power now at work in us can do immeasurably more than we can ask or imagine–to Him be glory in the church and in Christ Jesus through all generations." (Eph. 3:20)

Steven M. Avella
June 29, 2009, Feast of the Apostles Peter and Paul

TABLE of Contents

Acknowledgments .... p. 2

Bishop's letter .... p. 3

Introduction .... p. 4

PART I: HISTORY OF THE DIOCESE OF PHOENIX .... p. 7

Chapter 1: The Diocese of Phoenix: Historical Prelude .... p. 8

Chapter 2: The McCarthy Years (1969-1976) .... p. 34

Chapter 3: The Rausch Years (1977-1981) .... p. 56

Chapter 4: The O'Brien Years (1981-2003) .... p. 68

Chapter 5: The Olmsted Era (2003-   ) .... p. 98

PART II: PARISHES OF THE DIOCESE OF PHOENIX .... p. 113

PART III: MISSIONS, CAMPUS MINISTRIES, HIGH SCHOOLS OF THE DIOCESE OF PHOENIX ... p. 209

Missions .... p. 210

Campus Ministries .... p. 214

High Schools .... p. 215

HISTORY

THE DIOCESE
of Phoenix

CHAPTER 1

The Diocese of Phoenix:
Historical Prelude

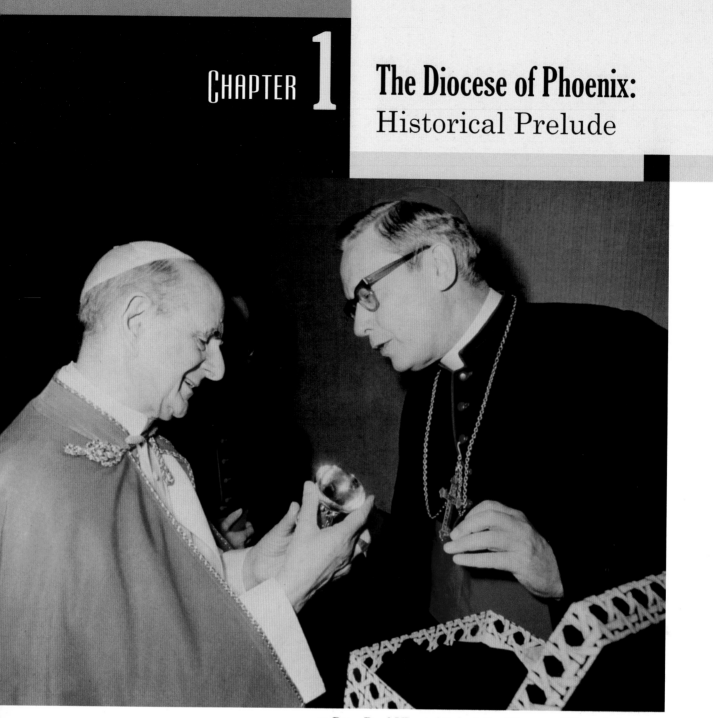

» *Pope Paul VI established the Diocese of Phoenix in 1969.*
Bishop Edward Anthony McCarthy was the first bishop.

Pope Paul VI officially established the Diocese of Phoenix on December 2, 1969, and appointed Bishop Edward Anthony McCarthy, a former auxiliary of Cincinnati, as its first bishop. The friendly and hard-working McCarthy had his work cut out for him: creating a diocesan structure to meet the needs of the People of God in this fast-growing area. McCarthy labored to secure additional human and financial resources to serve the new diocese and to forge a sense of common identity for the Catholics in the four counties under his care–Coconino, Maricopa,

Mohave and Yavapai. However, unlike some of his predecessors in Arizona, he did not have to begin from scratch. Before he arrived, there was already a well-developed network of churches, schools and generous clergy, religious and laity. Catholics, motivated by faith, and drawing on time-tested methods of Catholic evangelization and institutional development, had already carved a niche for themselves in Arizona. Understanding this "prehistory" helps us make sense of what later followed.

Early Catholicism: Missions and Borderlands

Arizona's native peoples included Apache, Papago (Tohono O'odham), Hohokam, Navajo, Pima and other tribes—all of whom created stable communities bound by language, tradition and culture. Each had their own religious system, which sought to explain the origins of the world, the reality of evil, helped "tame" the somewhat capricious acts of nature, and ritualized life's transitions from birth to death. European settlers came upon these native peoples, and in the encounters that followed learned much from them and also imparted some of their own culture and material goods. One aspect of this exchange was religion.

» *Mission of San Jose de Tumacacori, founded by Father Eusebio Kino about 1701.*
Credit: Phoenix Public Library

Catholic origins stretch back to the 16th century when Franciscan and Jesuit missionaries first attempted to convert native peoples. Fray Marcos de Niza arrived in this region in 1539 in company with Francisco Coronado whose search for the fabled Seven Cities of Cibola eventually led him through the Southwest to the heart of the Great Plains. In 1629 Fray Francisco de Porras and two other Franciscan missionaries arrived from Santa Fe to minister to the Hopi pueblo of Awatovi in northern Arizona. The Pueblo Revolt of August 1680 terminated this early mission, and the Franciscans were driven out of the Southwest for 12 years. In 1691 Jesuit Father Eusebio Kino and the Jesuits arrived and established missions in northern Mexico and southern Arizona: Los Arcangelos de Guevavi, San Cayetano de Tumacori and San Xavier del Bac. Kino died in 1711 after founding 24 missions. His name and reputation became inextricably linked with the early history of Arizona.

In 1767 the King of Spain expelled the Jesuits from his domains—thus ending their mission work. With the removal of the Jesuits, the Franciscans renewed their efforts in Arizona. Fray Francisco Tomas Garces arrived in San Xavier del Bac and moved northward in search of converts until he was killed in 1781. For 60 years the Franciscans kept Catholicism alive until the newly-formed Mexican government ejected all European priests in December 1827. Arizona went without any resident clergy for a time, although missionaries from northern Mexico, New Mexico and California visited periodically.

While the objectives of missionary endeavors among the native peoples are sometimes a cause of controversy, they represented the missionaries' honest zeal and unshakeable belief that the native peoples needed Jesus Christ in order to be saved.

The United States Takeover and the Era of the French Bishops (1848-1922)

Border conflicts between the United States and Mexico erupted in war in 1846. In two years of fighting the United States was able to wrest Mexico's claim to the vast lands north of its current border. In 1852 in anticipation of building a southern railroad route, the United States made the Gadsden purchase, rounding out Arizona's southern boundary with Mexico. These land acquisitions by the U.S. meant a change in ecclesiastical organization as well, since Mexican dioceses withdrew their priests from all of the ceded areas. U.S. bishops petitioned Rome to create new ecclesiastical territories headed by bishops proposed by the American hierarchy. At this juncture, Catholic life in the Southwest became the responsibility of a remarkable group of French bishops, priests and nuns who labored long and hard to create a stable Catholic presence. Not only did they learn to adapt to the geography and climate of Arizona, but also to its array of local cultures, which included Indians, Mexicans and a growing number of Anglos.

Archbishop Jean Baptiste Lamy of Santa Fe and the Renewal of the Arizona Missions
....

» *Archbishop Jean Baptiste Lamy, appointed Vicar Apostolic of Santa Fe in 1850, was later created bishop and archbishop. Lamy was one of the founding fathers of Catholic life in the modern Southwest.*
Credit: Archives of the Archdiocese of Santa Fe

Father Jean (John) B. Lamy, a French-born priest who had been working in Ohio, was appointed vicar apostolic of Santa Fe in 1850 and given responsibility to administer and expand Catholic life in all of what is now Colorado, Utah, New Mexico and Arizona. Lamy soon after traveled to Europe to recruit priests and religious, particularly from France, to help him provide for the sacramental and educational needs of his widely scattered flock. In 1859 one of those recruits, Father Joseph Machbeuf (later a vicar apostolic himself and first bishop of Denver), was dispatched from New Mexico to Arizona to report on conditions. Here he noted that there were remnants of the Spanish/Mexican churches. In Tucson the Spaniards had built a small chapel in 1777 in honor of St. Augustine, which still stood—albeit in a poor state of repair. Other pockets of Catholic life existed at San Xavier del Bac, Tubac (an old Spanish presidio) and Yuma. Catholics living in these areas had "survived" without the regular ministry of priests—no doubt gathering for prayer on Sundays and practicing home devotions from printed prayer manuals. Machbeuf breathed some life into the Catholic community in Tucson. Later he was called back to Santa Fe and reassigned to Colorado. Other priests visited and attempted to shore up Arizona's Catholic presence, but by 1864 only the mission of San Xavier del Bac remained open.

Arizona had become a territory of the United States in 1863, but sporadic warfare between the American Army and native tribes beset the future state. When Lamy called for clerical volunteers to go to Arizona, three of his priests—Francis Bouchard, Patrick Birmingham and most notably Jean (John) Baptiste Salpointe—volunteered to go, although the threat of danger from Indians delayed their departure.

Salpointe was born February 21, 1825, in Saint Maurice-de-Poinsat, Puy-de-Dôme, France. He was educated for the priesthood under the auspices of the Diocese of Clermont-Ferrand (Lamy's home diocese) and ordained to the priesthood December 20, 1851. Serving for a time in pastoral work and later as an instructor at the preparatory seminary, he arrived in Santa Fe in 1859 and within a year Lamy appointed him Vicar General. In February 1866 he went to Tucson in the company of Fathers Bouchard and Birmingham—and a military guard. Salpointe became pastor in Tucson, assisted by Bouchard. Birmingham went to the Catholic enclave in Yuma.

Bishop Jean Baptiste Salpointe: Vicar Apostolic (1869-1884)

» *Most Reverend Jean Baptiste Salpointe became Archbishop of Santa Fe in 1894.*
Credit: Archives of the Roman Catholic Diocese of Tucson

Bishop Lamy, already burdened by years of long travel, petitioned Rome for a reduction in the size of his ecclesiastical territories. At the Second Plenary Council of Baltimore in 1866, Baltimore Archbishop Martin Spalding wrote on his behalf to the Prefect of the Congregation for the Propagation of the Faith in Rome (the Vatican office overseeing the missions), Cardinal Alessandro Barnabo, petitioning for the creation of a new ecclesiastical jurisdiction in Arizona. Spalding wrote, "The distance of Santa Fe to the Arizona border is from three to four hundred miles; there is no good road and the savages are everywhere. Therefore it is impossible for the Bishop of Santa Fe to visit...since he already has a Diocese half the size of Italy. On the other hand the Arizona territory is increasing in population day by day." (Quoted in Meyer, This Far by Faith: 32-33.) On September 25, 1868, Pope Pius IX created the Vicariate Apostolic of Arizona, which included all of Arizona, southern New Mexico and El Paso County in Texas. Salpointe became the vicar apostolic and was consecrated on June 20, 1869, in his native France. Like Lamy, he used the time abroad to "shop" for priests to serve his territory.

» *Reverend Monsignors Edouard Gerard (on the left) and Peter Timmermans (on the right) standing outside the episcopal residence in Tucson.*
Credit: Archives of the Roman Catholic Diocese of Tucson

For the next 15 years Salpointe served as vicar apostolic of Arizona. He finished St. Augustine Church (later Tucson's cathedral), and he welcomed the Sisters of St. Joseph of Carondelet who opened St. Joseph's, a girls academy, next to it. A mission opened at Florence, Arizona, in 1870, which became a staging ground for other parish communities north of Tucson. Working from the base in Florence, Father Edouard (Edward) Gerard, a French priest, built a chapel in Tempe, and together with Father Joseph Bloise founded St. Mary Church (later Basilica) in Phoenix. Schools for boys opened in Tucson and Florence–as well as in New Mexico and Texas. French priests opened a mission at the Indian village along the Gila River. The territorial capital, originally located on the west side of Granite Creek near a number of mining claims, moved to what is today the city of Prescott. Prescott remained the capital of the Arizona Territory until November 1, 1867,

when it relocated briefly to Tucson. The territorial capital returned to Prescott in 1877, then moved permanently to Phoenix on February 4, 1889. The church of the Sacred Heart in Prescott was begun in 1877–the oldest church in what would become the Phoenix diocese. The Prescott church was a base for the development of the Church in northern Arizona.

City of Phoenix Catholicism

The Catholic presence in Phoenix grew in tandem with the rising fortunes of the upstart city. Phoenix's origins date back to the settlement begun in 1868 by the legendary John W. (Jack) Swilling, one of the very early settlers of what became the city of Phoenix. Swilling was one of the first to note the potential for development in the Salt River Valley by reactivating the ancient Hohokam irrigation system, which had sustained

» *Jack Swilling, an early settler of the Salt River Valley, with an unidentified man.*
Credit: Phoenix Public Library

the agriculture of the early Native Americans for many years. Swilling's early settlement gave way to a more permanent town site, planned by John T. Alsap in the center of the 40 mile long, 15 mile wide valley. By 1871 it had become the seat of newly-formed Maricopa County. Utilizing the developing water resources and federal laws liberalizing land ownership, Phoenix slowly but steadily became the most important city in central Arizona.

The city's growth was accelerated by its linkage to the expanding railroad system. In 1878 the Southern Pacific ran a line through the city of Maricopa, 30 miles south of Phoenix. Although later rail lines would come directly into Phoenix, this first connection was vital to its subsequent development into Arizona's largest city. In 1880 community leaders moved forward with a plan to incorporate, form a stable city government and make the community, now approximately 1,700 people, respectable. A series of public and private projects energized the economic and social development of the city.

Catholic life was already active in the Mexican families of early Phoenix. No doubt the cultural heritage of their religious upbringing–religious practices at home, devotions to saints and the Virgin Mary–sustained them between the infrequent visits of traveling priests. Father Andre Eschallier held the first recorded Mass in the Swilling home in 1870. Father (later Monsignor) Edward Gerard traveled from Florence to celebrate Mass in the home of Jesus Otero on First Avenue and Washington Street. On land donated by Mexican Catholics, a "Gothic style adobe" church was raised and named St. Mary's. Bishop Salpointe dedicated St. Mary's on June 24, 1881. In 1882 Father Joseph Bloise became its first resident pastor.

The development of Phoenix continued apace. Mesa, to the east, was incorporated in 1883, Tempe in 1894. In 1911 the Roosevelt Dam was completed at the confluence of the Salt River and Tonto Creek, 65 miles north of Phoenix. This dam together with the re-working of a privately owned network of canals provided, as historian

» *Salt River Railroad Bridge (c. 1887)–The Salt River Bridge spanned the Salt River for the Maricopa and Phoenix Railroad. The railroad contributed to Phoenix's subsequent growth.*
Credit: Phoenix Museum of History

» *The Roosevelt Dam was dedicated on March 19, 1911, and played an important role in the prosperity of the Salt River Valley.*
Credit: Phoenix Public Library

» *The Arizona State Capitol building in Phoenix.*
Credit: Phoenix Museum of History

Bradford Luckingham notes, "vital stability to the water supply...irrigation control and assured agricultural growth in the valley." (Luckingham, Phoenix, History of a Southwestern Metropolis: 47.)

Phoenix steadily improved its direct links to the railroad, bringing about a quickening of commercial life. By 1887 a branch line extending through Tempe connected Phoenix with the large Southern Pacific system. Subsequent rail lines linked the growing city with the east-west transcontinental line, the Atchison, Topeka and the Santa Fe. The railroad brought prosperity to Phoenix and increased the number of Anglos who migrated to Arizona, steadily pushing aside the existing Mexican population. As noted earlier, in 1889 Phoenix snatched from Prescott the honor of being the territorial and later the state capital. The city developed a prosperous downtown, and residential neighborhoods began to appear.

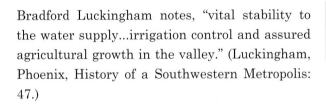

Northern Arizona Catholicism

Prescott was an important early hub of Catholic life in Arizona. The first priest, Fray Francisco Garces, had visited the area in 1776. Bishop Lamy of Santa Fe paid a visit to Prescott in December 1863, saying Christmas Day Mass there in a miner's eight-feet square cabin. In 1877 Irishman Father Michael Murphy became the first priest assigned to Prescott; however, he died shortly thereafter of consumption. In 1878 Father F. C. Becker arrived and secured a small house on North Marina Street in which he set up a chapel dedicated to the Sacred Heart. That same year, three Sisters of St. Joseph of Carondolet arrived and began a school in their residence. After Father Becker left in 1879, a series of short-term priests served local Catholics. In 1899 Bishop Peter Bourgade of Tucson came for Confirmations and assigned Father Alfred Quetu, who built the

» Jubilee celebration for Monsignor Edouard Gerard at Prescott (1927). Bishop Daniel Gercke is in the middle.

Credit: Archives of the Diocese of Phoenix

first permanent church–the Gothic style Sacred Heart–which Bishop Bourgade dedicated on February 1, 1896. During Father Quetu's years in Prescott, he also built a mission at the mining camp of Jerome (later a parish) in 1897. He and his assistants covered a vast territory, ministering to Catholics along the Santa Fe railroad from Flagstaff all the way to Barstow, California, and reaching down south as far as Wickenburg. Sacred Heart would become the mother parish for a number of communities from Wickenburg to far off Fort Yuma.

Railroads also stimulated the growth of the Church farther north as missions were created along the path of the Atlantic and Pacific Railroad. In 1876 the city of Flagstaff was founded and served by a growing local economy of timber, sheep and cattle. By the 1890s Flagstaff was one of the busiest rail stops between Albuquerque and the Pacific Coast. Already in 1887 Flagstaff Catholics like Michael R. Riordan petitioned Catholic authorities for a church. On land donated by P. J. Brannen, Father Carlo M. Ferrari, S.J., built a new church, which had its first Mass on Christmas Day 1888 and was named the Church of the Nativity. In 1893 a small Catholic school was begun staffed by lay people. In 1899 the Sisters of Loretto of Nerinx, Kentucky, opened a parochial school. Flagstaff continued to grow, and more Catholic parishes would follow.

In 1882 the railroad helped create the city of Kingman in Mohave County, and Catholic missionaries began visiting that community. Already in 1901 Father Cypriano Vabre pressed for the creation of a parish in the area. Finally in 1906 Vabre laid the cornerstone for St. Mary Church, built of volcanic tufa stone from a nearby quarry. In 1914 Father Edward Albouy was appointed as its first resident pastor, and priests from Kingman ministered to surrounding missions. In 1944 Dominican Sisters from Adrian, Michigan, opened a school. Although under the jurisdiction of the Diocese of Gallup for a time, the Kingman church was one of the oldest churches in the Diocese of Phoenix when the diocese was created. As settlement in the region grew, so did the number of priests. There were three priests in Arizona when Salpointe arrived in Tucson in 1866.

In the meantime, Santa Fe was raised to the status of an archdiocese in 1875, and Lamy was elevated to an archbishop. In April 1884 Bishop Salpointe was appointed coadjutor to Archbishop Lamy. Salpointe's replacement in Tucson, Father Peter Bourgade, built on the firm foundation laid by his predecessor. Salpointe served in Santa Fe for a mere nine years before stepping down in January 1894. He returned to Tucson where he lived until his death in 1898.

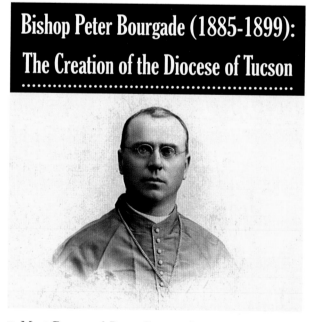

Bishop Peter Bourgade (1885-1899): The Creation of the Diocese of Tucson

» Most Reverend Peter Bourgade.

Credit: Archives of the Roman Catholic Diocese of Tucson

Peter Bourgade was appointed to the vacant vicariate on February 7, 1885, and Archbishop Lamy (assisted by Salpointe and Machbeuf) consecrated him on May 1, 1885. Born October 17, 1845, in Vollore-Vill, Puy-de-Dôme, in the Diocese of Clermont, Bourgade was educated in Billom, France. He volunteered for the Santa Fe diocese and was ordained by Lamy on November 30, 1869. Bourgade served in a variety of places in the far-flung diocese, including posts in Arizona, Texas and New Mexico.

Bishop Bourgade was fortunate to have his territory reduced when in 1892 Rome detached the El Paso County, Texas, portion of his jurisdiction. Five years later, on May 8, 1897, Pope Leo XIII created the Diocese of Tucson—which still included all of Arizona and Dona Ana, Grant, Otero and Eddy counties as well as part of Sierra County in New Mexico. Bourgade headed the Tucson diocese for only two years, until he, like his predecessor, was selected to lead the Archdiocese of Santa Fe in 1899. The area's first leaders came from the early industries—mining and cotton farming, which flourished in the region.

In 1886 Father Francois Xavier Jouvenceau became pastor of St. Mary's in Phoenix. Father Jouvenceau retired in 1895, and the Franciscan friars of the Sacred Heart Province in the Midwest arrived to serve St. Mary's. Bishop Bourgade welcomed Fathers Seraphim Lampe and Jose Godiol to St. Mary's. Later Father Novatus Benzing joined them together with Brothers lldefons Lethert, Adrian Wewer, Eugene Obert

» *Reverend Francois (Francisco) Jouvenceau, one of the founders of St. Mary's Church (later Basilica), Phoenix.*
Credit: *Archives of the Roman Catholic Diocese of Tucson*

and Robert Rechsteiner. St. Mary's became the hub from which the friars launched missions in Tempe, Wickenburg (a mining town 65 miles from Phoenix) and places now with thriving parishes such as Glendale, Tolleson, Goodyear and Mesa. Indian missions at Gila Bend, Guadalupe and the Salt River Reservation also originated from St. Mary's in Phoenix.

Early Religious Sisters in Phoenix

» *Early Sisters of Mercy with young girls at their academy.*
Credit: *Archives of the Diocese of Phoenix*

On September 5, 1892, the Sisters of Mercy opened Sacred Heart Academy—a predecessor of St. Mary High School. The sisters had come to Arizona in 1880 at the invitation of Bishop Salpointe. Mother Mary Paul O'Grady had earlier attempted schools in Florence (a school originally opened by the Sisters of St. Joseph) and in Yuma. In Phoenix, Sacred Heart Academy offered special courses in French, instrumental music, painting and drawing. At the same time a separate school, named for St. Anthony and located in a house, opened for Mexican students in Phoenix. Father Benzing, who succeeded Father Lampe as pastor of St. Mary's, was anxious to centralize authority in the parish and bargained with the Sisters of Mercy to gain control over the school, which the sisters held in their name. After he had accomplished this task in 1897, he remodeled Sacred Heart Academy into St. Mary parochial school and built a new brick schoolhouse for the Mexican students.

» *Two views of St. Joseph Hospital.*
Credit: Archives of the Diocese of Phoenix

The Sisters of Mercy continued to staff both schools, but they also built a new convent and academy. Eventually, the Sisters of Mercy left the school and moved into health-care work. In February 1903 the Sisters of the Precious Blood from Dayton, Ohio, agreed to purchase the convent of the Sisters of Mercy and to teach in the school.

» *Sisters of the Precious Blood with students.*
Credit: Archives of the Diocese of Phoenix

St. Mary High School for girls began in the old Sacred Heart Academy. One block away, St. Mary High School for boys opened in 1937, run by the Franciscan friars. In 1958 the two schools merged into a coeducational school on Polk and Second streets.

The Sisters of Mercy filled an important need in these early days when they chose to tend to the many health seekers who flocked to the sunny and dry climes of Arizona. Of particular concern were those chronically ill with the "white plague" tuberculosis. Moved by the plight of uncared-for tubercular patients, the sisters raised money to rent a six-bedroom, brick cottage on Polk Street, which they called St. Joseph Sanitarium (later to become St. Joseph Hospital). By March 19, 1895, the sisters had raised additional funds to build a two-story, brick building with 24 private rooms. Subsequent expansions and continual professional upgrading attended every phase of the hospital's development. In 1910 the sisters opened the state's first nursing school.

Early Ministry to the Native Americans

Missionary efforts to minister to native peoples were renewed in the 19th century. Changes in federal Indian policy contributed to the creation of the reservation "system"–a policy of creating separate territories for Indians, which were often synonymous with ancestral holdings, but sometimes not. In Arizona from 1859 to 1978 twenty Indian reservations were established, beginning with the Gila River Indian Reservation. On some of these reservations, Catholic leaders attempted to carry on their ministry to Catholic members of the tribes.

French missionaries laid the groundwork for mission life. Franciscan Father Severin Westhoff visited a number of the Pima Indian settlements at the Gila River Reservation, south/southwest and southeast of Phoenix. With the help of the Sisters of St. Joseph of Carondelet, Father Justin Deutsch opened a day school in 1901–St. John the Baptist in Komatke (Laveen), which represented

» *Fr. Severin Westhoff, O.F.M., with St. Mary Mission (Tempe) Yaqui Indians and Hispanic community (c. 1900).*
Credit: Tempe Historical Museum

» *First Communion Class St. John The Baptist Church.*
Credit: Marquette University Archives

» *Sister Mary Joseph, St. John The Baptist Church.*
Credit: Marquette University Archives

one of the first permanent Catholic commitments to the Pima people. The next year Father Deutsch founded a boarding high school that lasted until 1970. A Catholic grade school at St. Peter mission in Bapchule, run by the Franciscan Sisters of Charity from Manitowoc, Wisconsin, still exists. From these centers, Catholic missionaries fanned out through the entire Pima territory and even down into northern Papago country.

The present Diocese of Phoenix has responsibility for the main ministry on four Indian reservations: the Gila River Indian Reservation is today the largest in the Diocese of Phoenix. This reservation consists of Pima and Maricopa communities and is served by six churches. To the south and west of Phoenix is the Ak-Chin Reservation, where many tribes live, such as the Maricopa and Pima. West of Phoenix is the San Lucy Indian Reservation, consisting of the Papagos (Tohono O'odhams) and having one church. To the east of Phoenix in Scottsdale is the Salt River Pima-Maricopa Indian Reservation with St. Paschal Baylon Chapel and St. Francis of Assisi Mission. Reservations along the Grand Canyon, the Colorado River near the California border, near Prescott and the Prescott Valley, Camp Verde and the Fort McDowell Indian Reservation near Scottsdale also have Catholic Native people. The Yaqui Indians migrated from the Yaqui River Valley in Sonora to Arizona during a period of unrest in Mexico late in the 19th century. They established several villages in Arizona, including St. Mary Mission in Tempe and Guadalupe outside of Phoenix where they built a church. With the help of the Bureau of Indian Catholic Missions, the Catholic Church Extension Society, and the American Board of Catholic Missions, each reservation built mission stations. This enabled them to provide catechetical instruction and assist the Native people with their social welfare and health needs.

The Last of the French Bishops:
Henry Regis Granjon (1900-1922)

» *Most Reverend Henry R. Granjon.*
Credit: Archives of the Roman Catholic
Diocese of Tucson

Bishop Bourgade's successor was the last of Arizona's French-born bishops. Henry Regis Granjon was born in St. Etienne, Loire, France. He studied in France and in Rome and was ordained to the priesthood on December 17, 1887, in his native Lyons. He worked for three years in the Lyons diocese, and in 1890 volunteered for service in Arizona. In 1897 he was chosen to become the assistant director of the Society for the Propagation of the Faith in Baltimore. Cardinal James Gibbons of Baltimore consecrated him on June 17, 1900. Granjon spent more than 22 years as the head of the Tucson diocese. In 1912 Arizona entered the Union. In 1914 a shift in territorial boundaries brought all of Arizona under his pastoral care, but detached the portions of the diocese extending into southern New Mexico. Granjon, according to historian Fr. Charles W. Polzer, S.J., "had high hopes for educating the populace of the diocese." By the time Granjon died in 1922, the Diocese of Tucson had 19 parishes, 35 priests and Holy Hope Cemetery had been established.

Division in Phoenix:
Anglos versus Mexicans

Bishop Granjon was on hand to witness the large migrations of Mexicans who began to flood into Arizona and other parts of the Southwest, fleeing revolutionary upheaval in their homeland. It was during his watch that a serious rupture took place between Mexican and Anglo parishioners of St. Mary's in Phoenix.

» *School children at Immaculate Heart of Mary Parish, Phoenix.*
Credit: Archives of the Diocese of Phoenix

Catholic Dignitaries Dedic.
Mexican Cathedral In Phoe

Impressive Rites Heard By Hundreds

While hundreds stood with bowed heads Rt. Rev. Daniel J. Gercke, bishop of the Tucson diocese, blessed and dedicated Phoenix' new Mexican Catholic church, "Santuario del Corazon de Maria," yesterday morning. Church dignitaries from Mexico, California and Arizona aided in the ceremonies and the church was filled to the doors for the solemn pontifical mass which followed the dedicatory procession and blessing.

Opening with procession at 9 o'clock in the morning the dedicatory program was continued until late last night, a festival being held in the Parochial school concluding the activities. A banquet was held in the rectory at noon which was attended by approximately 40 church dignitaries with Mayor F. J. Paddock as guest of honor.

Knights in Uniform

Bishop Gercke, Rt. Rev. Juan Navarrete, bishop of Sonora, Mexico, Rt. Rev. Augustin Aguirre Y Ramos, provincial of Sinaloa, Very Rev. A. Ross, provincial of the Congregation of Missionary Fathers in the United States and Canada were among those heading the procession which marked the opening of the ceremonies.

Carmelites of Tucson, Jesuit priests from the Brophy College, Franciscan Fathers of St. Mary's church here and priests from the Congregation of Mission Fathers of Los Angeles, San Gabriel and Compton in California and from Yuma, Jerome and Prescott followed. A delegation of Fourth degree Knights of Columbus in full regalia, added to the procession.

After the blessing of the cornerstone and the edifice by Bishop Gercke the procession entered the church and mass was celebrated.

Bishop Gercke Officiates

Bishop Gercke was the celebrant. Rev. Manuel Milagro, O. F. M., and Rev. Angel Esteos, O. C. D., were deacons of honor; Rev. Gerard Brenneke, O. F. M., was deacon of the mass and Rev. James E. Maloni, subdeacon. Rev. Antino Nebrada, C. F. M., was assistant priest and Rev. Juan Arans, C. F. M., master of ceremonies.

The mass was sung by three parochial choirs, augmented by St. Villa's choir of the Plaza church in Los Angeles with the priests assisting. Bishop Navarrette then preached a sermon.

A banquet was held in the rectory at 1 o'clock. W. J. Burns was toastmaster and introduced Mayor Paddock, J. T. Whitney, M. Oria, Rev. A. G. Nebreda and Bishop Gercke.

Bishop Gercke gave the principal address. He told of the wonderful work accomplished by Father Nebreda, pastor of the new church, in bringing about its construction. He commended the leaders of the church on the support which they have shown and then talked at

(Continued on Page Two)

(Continued from Page
length upon bringing ab
thorough understandin
non-Catholics as to the
of the church.

Paddock Lauds W
Mayor Paddock in his
gratulated the congregat
work it has accomplish
in bringing another
building to the city but t
good the church has d
the people in general.

Father Nebreda spoke
his appreciation in en
parish in its new home.
the struggle encountere
ing about the financing
ject and of the wonderfu
tion of one and all in its

Orta, the contractor, ar
representative of the
Columbus, each gave sh

Vesper service t to be
the day and at 8 o'clock
of music and dramatics
on in the school auditor

Drama Enacte
A feature of the prog
drama, "Miracle of the
Guadalupe," played by a
actors from Los Angeles
dero, known as "The M
uso," sang several select
ular Mexican numbers.

Gayou delivered an addr
J. Rius recited a short s
Two other short drama
ware also on the progr
who took part were J
Nino, Reinaldo Bar on,
Frank Romero, Heronim
Frank Ramos, and Lorete

The new buildings ad
beauty spot to the city. Th
most of the block ext
Washington street betw
and Tenth streets. All
inforced concrete with a c
ed finish on the exterior,
three distinct building
group, the school, para
the church.

Seats 1,200 Pers
The building dedicated
is located at the Ninth
ner. It has a seating c
approximately 1,200 pe
appointments are along
modern architectural l
main altar was beautiful
ed with flowers adding to
of its permanent orname

There are small altar
side of the main altar.
The pulpit is located a
side of the auditorium.
dows are all of stained g
blue and light tan colo
carried out throughout th
Many beautiful statue
ings add to the interior

» *The dedication of Immaculate Heart Church in Phoenix was a cause for great celebration among Latino peoples in the state capital.*
Credit: Archives of the Diocese of Phoenix

Local historian Frank Barrios notes that Mexican Americans and Anglos mixed easily in early Phoenix and in other parts of the state. Some Mexican Americans were prominent businessmen and landowners. As Arizona gained more and more Anglos and the percentage of Hispanics living in the state declined (in Phoenix alone numbers dropped from 52 percent in 1870 to 14 percent in 1900), the Mexican American's social position noticeably diminished. Those who felt the Spanish-speaking did not fit with the vision of a new and dynamic Phoenix openly expressed anti-Hispanic sentiments. Increasing numbers of Hispanics became marginalized from "mainstream" Arizona life, both socially and spatially. In Phoenix many, though not all, Hispanic families relocated to barrio areas south of Van Buren Street, which developed names such as Golden Gate, Cuattro Milpa, Grant Park and El Campito. While they cultivated a lively subculture that sustained them—a bitter conflict broke out over their place within the Catholic Church, an institution central to their religious and cultural lives, and one in which they believed they had a particular stake. An acrimonious contest over space in the city's only parish, St. Mary's, brought this struggle into focus.

Missionaries to Arizona had always had to adjust to the particular circumstances there. Perhaps none more so than the German-speaking friars, who came from a Midwestern Catholic Church with well-built, solid brick churches, elaborately decorated within. Their reaction to the simple adobe St. Mary Church, which the friars uncharitably commented "resembled a barn rather than a place of worship," was to be expected. The old adobe church was torn down, and fund raising began for an imposing mission-style church. Once the lower section of the church was completed, more money was saved and in 1914 a handsome upper church was erected and decorated with fine altars, statuary and exquisite stained glass. Anglo and Hispanic parishioners had both contributed to the church; however, to the consternation of many, Father Benzing announced that Hispanic parishioners would continue to have their services in the basement, while the nicer and more elaborate upper church

would be for the English-speaking. In his defense Benzing had not absolutely excluded Hispanics from attending Mass upstairs; nonetheless, the sermons there would be delivered in English. The reaction was one of outrage and shock. Moreover, when Hispanics asserted that they had donated the land for the church, Benzing conducted his own land-title search, which seemed to dispute their claims. Although besieged by complaints, the priest stubbornly refused to yield. Bitterness over this decision has rankled the collective memory of Hispanic Phoenicians to the present time. Bishop Granjon was unable to resolve the matter. When he died unexpectedly in 1922 at the age of 59, the matter was turned over to his successor, Bishop Daniel Gercke.

American Bishop Takes the Reins: Daniel Gercke (1923-1960)

» *Most Reverend Daniel J. Gercke.*
Credit: Archives of the Roman Catholic Diocese of Tucson

Father Daniel James Gercke was chosen to head the Tucson diocese on June 21, 1923, and was consecrated in Philadelphia on November 6, 1923. Gercke was born October 9, 1874, in Holmesburg, Pennsylvania. The fifth of 14 children, he studied for the priesthood in the archdiocesan seminaries

» *St. Mary's Church (later Basilica), Phoenix.* Credit: Archives of the Diocese of Phoenix

of Philadelphia and was ordained on June 1, 1901. Between 1903 and 1905 he was a missionary in the Philippines where he worked with his future Ordinary, Bishop (later Cardinal) Denis Dougherty, in the Diocese of Jaro. Gercke would administer the affairs of the Tucson diocese until his resignation in 1960.

Bishop Gercke immediately attempted to deal with the ongoing turmoil at St. Mary's. Even though Father Benzing had left and a Hispanic pastor was in place, the upper-/lower-church controversy still raged. The result was the creation of a second parish in Phoenix, Immaculate Heart of Mary, which formally began on December 12, 1924. Immaculate Heart's first pastor, Father Antimo G. Nebreda was a member of the Claretian Fathers, who had been in Arizona for some time, and had assumed ministry to the Spanish-speaking of Maricopa County. After intense fund-raising, Nebreda gathered enough to build a church. On January 10, 1928, the parish broke ground, erecting a church, school and

rectory. Immaculate Heart remains to this day a touchstone for the Hispanic community.

In Flagstaff a similar kind of segregation took place. The original Nativity Church had been abandoned in 1911, and parishioners relocated to the hall of the parish school on the corner of Cherry Avenue and Beaver Street. Plans were made to build a new church on Cherry Avenue between Beaver and Humphreys streets where the parish had earlier purchased land. By this time, Flagstaff had a growing Hispanic population who shared space with Anglo parishioners. Growing tensions between the two groups led pastor Father (later Monsignor) Edward Albouy in 1926 to build a new church for the Hispanics, Our Lady of Guadalupe, which celebrated its first Mass on December 12, 1926. Four years later, a new Nativity Church was built (now known as the Nativity of the Blessed Virgin Mary), and it became the church of the Anglo parishioners. In a variety of ways it was made known, Hispanics were not welcome as members. Although the two churches served their

» *Father (later Monsignor) Edward Albouy,*
a pastor in Flagstaff in the 1920s.
Credit: Archives of the Roman Catholic Diocese of Tucson

Route 66. The small community served a thriving tourist populace with hotels and restaurants and gift shops. St. Joseph's (originally known as Sacred Heart) was begun in 1895 as a mission of Flagstaff and tended by visiting priests. Its first church was built in 1896, and from 1914 to 1916 Father Edward Albouy administered the mission. In 1928 it was raised to parochial status, and Father Joseph Tremblay became the first resident pastor and remained until 1940.

Arizona and the Great Depression/ A New Diocese and Parish Growth

The effects of the Great Depression in the decade between the 1930s and 1940s hit Phoenix more slowly than other parts of the industrialized United States. However, mining and farming, the economic mainstays of the state, eventually declined. The city tried to bolster its local economy by enhancing its reputation as a place for tourism and health. In 1934 a local advertising firm began marketing the Phoenix area as the "Valley of the Sun."

parishioners well, Hispanic Catholics were angry at the treatment they received from their Catholic brethren. As a result, Our Lady of Guadalupe Church was an even more important symbol of their place in Flasgstaff Catholic life.

» *Laying of the cornerstone,*
Church of the Nativity, May 1930.
Credit: Archives of the Diocese of Phoenix

The formation of the parish of St. Joseph in the city of Williams in Coconino County was accomplished with less contention. Williams, 6,800 feet above sea level, is strategically located 40 miles south of the South Rim of the Grand Canyon and for many years sat astride the famous

» *The Grand Canyon of Arizona from*
Hotel El Tovar (1902). Tourism brought
thousands of people to Arizona every year.
Credit: Phoenix Public Library

Even during the Great Depression, Rome made boundary changes in the Diocese of Tucson. On December 16, 1939, the Diocese of Gallup, New Mexico, was established, and Bishop Bernard T. Espelage, O.F.M., served as its first bishop. At this time the northern section of the future Diocese of Phoenix became part of the newly-created Diocese of Gallup. Coconino, Mohave and Yavapai counties would be attached to the Diocese of Phoenix 30 years later. Some have argued that the remoteness of these counties from the center of diocesan life in New Mexico and the comparatively few times the priests and parishioners living there saw their bishop may have contributed to a sense of isolation and a feeling of neglect. These feelings were still very much alive when the Diocese of Phoenix was created in 1969.

Still the division with Gallup brought some relief to Bishop Gercke, who now did not have to travel to the far north of Arizona. He also surrendered the diocesan holdings in southern New Mexico, which were given to the Archdiocese of Santa Fe. Under Gercke, parish growth in Phoenix expanded out from St. Mary's to include the new parish for Hispanics, Immaculate Heart of Mary, and St. Francis Xavier, which opened in 1928. Suburban Phoenix was poised for later dynamic development with the opening of parishes in Tempe, Mesa and Chandler. By 1939 growth within the city limits of Phoenix led to the creation of St. Matthew Parish. This new parish was one of the first created by the urban and suburban expansion that began during World War II.

Early Parish Development (1877-1939)

Year established	Parish	City	County
1877	Sacred Heart	Prescott	Yavapai
1881	St. Mary (formerly Immaculate Conception; later the Basilica)	Phoenix	Maricopa
1888	Nativity of the Blessed Virgin Mary (formerly Church of the Nativity)	Flagstaff	Coconino
1906	St. Mary	Kingman	Mohave
1908 (closed 2004)	Holy Family	Jerome	Yavapai
1924	Immaculate Heart of Mary	Phoenix	Maricopa
1926	Our Lady of Guadalupe	Flagstaff	Coconino
1928	St. Francis Xavier	Phoenix	Maricopa
1928	St. Joseph (formerly Sacred Heart)	Williams	Coconino
1932	Our Lady of Mount Carmel	Tempe	Maricopa
1934	Queen of Peace (formerly Sacred Heart)	Mesa	Maricopa
1937	St. Mary	Chandler	Maricopa
1939	St. Matthew	Phoenix	Maricopa

World War II and Its Aftermath

World War II stimulated an even more dynamic and fast-growing economic life for the state. The voracious demands for minerals, cotton and agricultural products energized Arizona's flagging economy. Like the rest of the American West, Arizona did very well during the war. Although it could be terribly hot in the summer months, Phoenix's mild fall and winter weather and clear skies were desirable for flight training and air bases. Military installations popped up in the region–Luke Airfield west of Glendale, Williams Field east of Chandler, Thunderbird II north of Scottsdale and Litchfield Naval Air Facility–all preparing pilots for eventual combat over the skies of Germany and in the Pacific campaigns. Training camps for desert warfare were established in western Arizona: Camps Bouse, Horn and Hyder. A government-owned Goodyear plant opened in 1941, employing 7,500. An Alcoa plant in southwest Phoenix and AiResearch at Sky Harbor Airport employed thousands. After the war, in 1949 Motorola opened its Military Electronics division, which employed 5,000 by 1960. More than 700 other firms settled in the burgeoning metropolitan area. The perfection of air conditioning overcame a major obstacle to Phoenix's growth. It was now easier to live there during the torrid summer months.

Manufacturing soon rivaled mining as Arizona's chief money maker. Agriculture fell farther and farther behind. Historian Thomas Sheridan writes that 70 percent of the manufacturing plants were located in Phoenix and 14 percent in Tucson. This brought growth to both cities–but Phoenix went from 65,414 inhabitants in 1940 to 106,818 in 1950 and 439,170 in 1960, making it the fastest growing big city in the country and rising in rank from the 99th largest city in 1950 to the 29th largest in 1960.

When the guns of World War II began, Glendale, Tempe, Mesa and Scottsdale were still small "satellites from the metropolis," separated by cotton and citrus fields. These areas soon began to fill in as population in the Phoenix metropolitan area increased. After the war, thanks to an active congressional delegation, military spending increased. New employees in these industries expanded Arizona's population. From 1950 to 1960 Arizona jumped from 749,587 to more than 1.3 million. The fastest growth was in Maricopa County, which burgeoned from 331,770 in 1950 to 663,510 by 1960. Bishop Gercke moved decisively to build up the local Church. There were more than 304,000 Catholics in the Diocese of Tucson by the time of his retirement in 1960.

New Parishes for a New Era

» *Monsignor Robert Donohoe (on left) and Bishop Francis Green (on right) at the 25th anniversary of the founding of St. Agnes Parish in Phoenix.*
Credit: Archives of the Diocese of Phoenix

This dramatic spike in Phoenix's population resulted in the creation of new parishes. In 1940 Bishop Gercke sent one of Phoenix's most famous clergymen, 27-year-old Father (later Monsignor) Robert Donohoe, to found St. Agnes Parish. Donohoe was born October 31, 1912, in Williamsburg, Iowa, where his father was a plumbing contractor. He arrived in Phoenix as a lad of 15 and went to school at the Jesuit-run Brophy College Preparatory before it closed. His studies for the priesthood took him to St. Patrick's Seminary in Menlo Park, California, and Kenrick Seminary in St. Louis. Upon his 1937 ordination, he was assigned to Sacred Heart Parish in Nogales and later St. Patrick's in Bisbee. He spent a little time at Tucson's Ss. Peter and Paul with future bishop Francis Green before he was selected to go to Phoenix. The first St. Agnes Church was located in a building at 2533 N. 16th Street, provided rent free for a year by the Arizona Grocery Company until Gercke secured acreage at 24th Street and Palm Lane. Subsequent parochial growth followed.

Under the Diocese of Gallup, Flagstaff's parochial development took place as well. In 1958 St. Pius X Parish was established to serve Catholics in east Flagstaff. The parish moved from its original site ten years later to a new location. Our Lady of Guadalupe Church opened a school in 1953–another sign of Catholic growth.

In Mohave County, federal water projects along the Colorado River and later the expansion of gaming in nearby Laughlin, Nevada, caused a surge in population in northwestern Arizona. In 1947 St. Margaret Mary Mission opened in Bullhead City and later was raised to parochial status. Water sports, tourism and the investment of the McCulloch Chainsaw Company in the area led to the creation of Our Lady of the Lake at Lake Havasu City in 1965–elevated to the status of a parish in 1969.

As the chart suggests, parish development continued at a rapid rate during World War II and its aftermath to the eve of the founding of the Diocese of Phoenix.

Parish Development 1940-1969

* Created under the auspices of the Diocese of Gallup, New Mexico.

Year established	Parish	City	County
1940	St. Agnes	Phoenix	Maricopa
1940	St. Francis*	Seligman	Yavapai
1941	St. Anthony of Padua	Wickenberg	Maricopa
1943	St. Anne	Gilbert	Maricopa
1943	St. Anthony	Phoenix	Maricopa
1946	St. Mark	Phoenix	Maricopa
1947	St. Margaret Mary*	Bullhead City	Mohave
1947	St. Catherine of Siena	Phoenix	Maricopa
1947	St. Gregory	Phoenix	Maricopa
1947	Our Lady of Perpetual Help	Glendale	Maricopa
1948	Our Lady of Perpetual Help	Scottsdale	Maricopa
1950	St. Peter	Bapchule	Pinal
1950	St. Thomas the Apostle	Phoenix	Maricopa
1950	St. John the Baptist	Komatke (Laveen)	Maricopa
1951	Most Holy Trinity	Phoenix	Maricopa
1953	Ss. Simon and Jude (later the Cathedral)	Phoenix	Maricopa
1953	Blessed Sacrament	Tolleson	Maricopa
1955	St. Theresa	Phoenix	Maricopa
1956	St. Pius X (formerly St. Monica)	Phoenix	Maricopa
1956	St. Henry	Buckeye	Maricopa

1956	St. John Vianney	Goodyear	Maricopa
1957	St. Vincent de Paul	Phoenix	Maricopa
1958	St. Pius X*	Flagstaff	Coconino
1959	Christ the King	Mesa	Maricopa
1959	St. Francis of Assisi*	Bagdad	Yavapai
1960	El Cristo Rey*	Grand Canyon	Coconino
1961	St. Daniel the Prophet	Scottsdale	Maricopa
1961	St. Joachim and St. Anne	Sun City	Maricopa
1962	Sacred Heart	Phoenix	Maricopa
1962	St. Frances Cabrini*	Camp Verde	Yavapai
1962	St. Louis the King	Glendale	Maricopa
1962	St. Jerome	Phoenix	Maricopa
1963	St. Michael	Gila Bend	Maricopa
1965	St. John Vianney*	Sedona	Yavapai
1966	Immaculate Conception*	Cottonwood	Yavapai
1967	St. Maria Goretti	Scottsdale	Maricopa
1968	Santa Teresita	El Mirage	Maricopa
1968	St. Charles Borromeo	Peoria	Maricopa
1968	Holy Family	Phoenix	Maricopa
1969	Our Lady of the Lake*	Lake Havasu City	Mohave
1969	St. Joseph	Phoenix	Maricopa

After World War II Bishop Gercke began to focus on finding replacements for the aging French clergy. He dedicated Tucson's Regina Cleri Seminary in 1955—a minor seminary for high school age candidates, directed by the Vincentians. But while various and sundry young men volunteered to come to Phoenix from other dioceses and seminaries around the country, one of the main sources of clerical supply were the seminaries of Ireland.

Ireland Sends Its Best

Gercke needed priests to serve the growing array of parishes. For help he turned to his friend, Bishop John B. MacGinley, the retired bishop of Monterey-Fresno, who was residing in his native Ireland. MacGinley generously assisted Gercke in finding priests in the Emerald Isle who might wish to go to Arizona.

» *Monsignor Neil McHugh (on left) and Reverend Paul P. Smith (on right), pastor of Ss. Simon and Jude Parish, greet Most Reverend Patrick Lennon (center), Bishop of Kildare, Ireland, during the bishop's visit to Arizona in 1969.*
Credit: Archives of the Diocese of Phoenix

One of the first to come after World War II, Father (later Monsignor) Neil McHugh, arrived in 1946 and founded Most Holy Trinity Parish in 1951. Following McHugh the next year were five young Irish priests. Three of the five—all graduates of St. Patrick College in Carlow—went on to serve in the Phoenix diocese: Eugene Maguire, Daniel McCready and Cornelius Moynihan. Maguire came from County Leitrim, McCready from County Donegal and Moynihan from County Cork. All had been ordained the same day, June 1, 1947. Other priests would hail from the famous All Hallows Seminary—an important supplier of priests for the American Church. One of the priests MacGinley invited was Father Eugene M. O'Carroll who recalled, "My father had just died and my mother talked to him [MacGinley] and said I was interested in the seminary, but with my father dead, money was going to be a problem." The young O'Carroll, then 17 years old, went to see MacGinley who asked if he wanted to go to Tucson. O'Carroll said yes, and so he went.

Father (later Monsignor) John McMahon came to the United States in 1948. A native of County Cavan, he later reminisced that he had originally wanted to become a veterinarian, but also had an interest in the seminary. He wrote letters to both a veterinary college and the seminary—and only an acceptance from the seminary had come back. (He later discovered that his mother had torn up the acceptance to the veterinary school.) He too was urged to join the Tucson diocese and took the long trip across the ocean and three days by train to Arizona. Adjustment to the aridity of the desert was hard for a man who had known only the greenery of Ireland, but later he came to love the Arizona environment and served the Church with exceptional skill and sagacity. In 1953 Bishop Gercke assigned him to travel back to Ireland and recruit priests for Arizona. Father (later Monsignor) Thomas Hever recalled McMahon had spoken at his high school and encouraged his desire to serve in Arizona. Various incentives were offered to the young men considering missionary life in America, and sometimes the harshness of the climate or environment was downplayed. McMahon, one recalled, "didn't show us too many pictures of the desert. I think he showed

us northern Arizona." The prospect of quickly becoming a pastor in Arizona—an office that could take a typical priest in Ireland 40 years to attain—enticed several of the young men. McMahon recruited 15 men.

» *These Loreto Sisters from Ireland served Ss. Simon and Jude Cathedral School.*
Credit: Archives of the Diocese of Phoenix

A total of 60 men came from Ireland, joining the Diocese of Tucson, and a significant number of them remained in ministry in Phoenix. They arrived amidst the hustle and explosive growth of postwar Phoenix, coped with the searing heat of the summer months, and adjusted to the ebb and flow of vacationers, who crammed into their churches during the winter "snow bird" season. Father (later Monsignor) Daniel McCready was characteristic. Arriving in Tempe in 1955 and assigned to Our Lady of Mount Carmel, "He moved in," one of his friends recalled, "when there was nothing much here." Of the other Irish priests like McCready, he commented, "These guys got assigned to parishes young...but there was not much to work with. They really had to struggle."

Ireland not only gave up its sons to Arizona, but also its daughters. In 1954 a group of Loreto Sisters (Institute of the Blessed Virgin Mary) began a ministry at the school founded by Ss. Simon and Jude Parish (later the cathedral). Warmly embraced and loved by the parishioners of the one-day cathedral church, the sisters continue to minister there to this day. The Loreto Sisters also serve in Prescott and Flagstaff.

Catholic Grade Schools and High Schools During the Bishop Gercke Era

As noted earlier, St. Mary Church created separate high schools for boys and girls. For a time these were the only Catholic high schools in the city. Later Jesuit-run Brophy College Preparatory siphoned off a number of the male students.

The Brophy family, Irish immigrants intricately tied up with the history of the Southwest, gave lavishly to the local Church. Memorializing her husband, William Henry Brophy, Mrs. Ellen Brophy helped found Brophy College Preparatory in 1928. Located five miles from the then center of Phoenix, its beautiful buildings were described by one local newspaper as "The Taj Mahal of the Desert." The school chapel, richly decorated with exquisite stained glass and a beautiful reredos, also doubled as the church for St. Francis Xavier Parish. Open only to boys, Brophy turned out only seven graduating classes before it closed in 1935 due to the Great Depression.

In 1943 St. Francis Xavier Parish, under the leadership of the Jesuits, invited the Sisters of Charity of the Blessed Virgin Mary to phase in a four-year high school curriculum for young women on the "unused" Brophy campus, thus beginning Xavier College Preparatory for girls. The sisters had arrived in Phoenix from their motherhouse in Dubuque, Iowa, to start up St. Francis Xavier Elementary School in September 1936. More sisters arrived, and 17 girls enrolled in the first class of Xavier College Preparatory; and an additional year of study was added each year until they achieved a full high school curriculum. The first graduates received their diplomas in 1947. Brophy College Preparatory re-opened in 1952, and high schoolers of both genders taxed

» *Brophy College Preparatory.* *Credit: Archives of the Diocese of Phoenix*

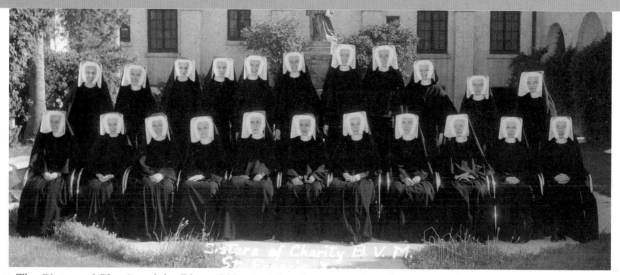

» *The Sisters of Charity of the Blessed Virgin Mary began serving the people of Phoenix in the late 1930's.*
Credit: Archives of the Sisters of Charity of the Blessed Virgin Mary, Dubuque, Iowa

» *Xavier College Preparatory (1952-1953).*
Credit: Archives of the Sisters of Charity of the Blessed Virgin Mary, Dubuque, Iowa

the building's limits. In April 1956 a new building for Xavier College Preparatory was constructed on property just east of Brophy. Xavier remained a parish high school until 1968, when it became a diocesan school.

Other parts of the city also wanted schools. In 1940 the Sisters of Charity of the Blessed Virgin Mary had opened an elementary school at the recently created St. Agnes Parish. In 1943 they began work at St. Matthew's, teaching out of motel rooms until an elementary school building was ready. In 1945 they began ministering to school children at Our Lady of Mount Carmel in Tempe.

In the suburb of Chandler, Father Joseph N. Patterson, pastor of St. Mary's in Chandler, founded Seton Catholic Elementary School in 1952 to serve primarily the Hispanic immigrant population in the expanding areas of Chandler, Mesa and Tempe. The school later expanded to include a high school, Seton Catholic High School. Father Patterson donated some of the property for both schools, and the faculty included Sisters of Charity of Seton Hill, who also served parochial schools in the diocese.

Ministry to the Poor

Catholic Charities has served people of all ages and faiths for more than 75 years. In 2008 they offered approximately 50 programs at more than 100 sites, serving more than 200,000 people in central and northern Arizona. They established their first office in Phoenix in 1933 to advocate for children and help people suffering through the Great Depression. Over the years, they have expanded, adding two additional service centers in the Phoenix area and two others in Prescott and Flagstaff to serve Yavapai, Coconino, Mohave, Navajo and Apache counties.

As Phoenix grew, it sorted itself out in terms of race and class; well-off citizens moved north of the central business district. South Phoenix developed

» *People in south Phoenix sometimes lived in very difficult circumstances.*
Credit: Archives of the Diocese of Phoenix

» *Confirmation by Bishop Daniel Gercke at St. Monica Church, Phoenix.*
Credit: Archives of the Diocese of Phoenix

almost as a separate world—impoverished, dirty and filled with various neighborhoods peopled by poor Mexicans and African Americans. South Phoenix was desolate, but in 1937 began to receive systematic attention from Franciscan Father Emmett McLoughlin. McLoughlin founded St. Monica's Mission in 1936 in one of the poorest areas of Phoenix. Located near 7th Avenue and Buckeye in a former A & P grocery store, between the railroad tracks and the Salt River, the church soon became a hub for the poor. McLoughlin provided clothing and meals to the needy. Due to the heartbreaking infant mortality rate in the area, St. Monica's opened a clinic where poor women could give birth. That eventually grew into St. Monica Hospital, today Phoenix Memorial Hospital. McLoughlin built affordable housing for the impoverished inhabitants of the area.

When he had conflicts with his Franciscan and diocesan superiors, McLoughlin departed from the priesthood, married and wrote books highly critical of the Church he once served. Whatever judgment may be made of his battles with the Church and his departure from the priesthood, his work in this difficult and poverty-stricken part of Phoenix left a lasting imprint. St. Monica's languished a bit after McLoughlin left, but a new pastor assigned in 1956, Father Terence Sheridan, revived it and Bishop Gercke renamed it St. Pius X Parish.

McLoughlin's Franciscan confrere, Father Albert Braun, O.F.M., was equally flinty and determined. Shortly after his ordination in 1915, Father Braun had become an Army chaplain and served in Europe during World War I. When he returned, he was assigned to the Mescalero Apaches in south central New Mexico. Working in this difficult and challenging assignment, Braun distinguished himself as a capable, tough-minded and highly respected missionary. In the 1930s he was chaplain to the New Deal era Civilian Conservation Corps (CCC)—a military-like operation that recruited unemployed young men for extensive environmental work around the United States. His CCC appointment flipped over to another Army chaplaincy commission when World War II began, and he was dispatched to the Philippines. In 1942 the Japanese captured Father Braun, and he found himself part of the Bataan Death March. He kept himself and others alive by stealing food rations.

» *Reverend Albert Braun, O.F.M.*
Credit: Archives of the Roman Catholic Diocese of Tucson

» *Sister Mary Luca Junk, a Sister of the Precious Blood, legendary for her work with the poor in Phoenix.*
Credit: Archives of the Diocese of Phoenix

After his liberation, Father Braun returned to civilian status and went to Phoenix where he taught at St. Mary High School. Like McLoughlin, Braun began to walk the streets of south Phoenix where he helped build Sacred Heart Parish in the Golden Gate barrio. "Bring me a brick," he said to his parishioners, "and I will build you a church." The small church, which still stands, is a tribute to the faith of this doughty friar and the spirit of the people with whom he worked. In 1973 the church building was closed when Sky Harbor Airport expanded in its direction and wiped out nearby neighborhoods. Due to the efforts of local activists, the church, however, was spared and sits isolated and alone surrounded by a wire fence—a visible reminder of the durability of the man who built it.

Bishop Francis Green (1960-1969)

Bishop Gercke was succeeded by his co-worker, Bishop Francis Green. Francis Joseph Green was also a transplanted easterner. Born in Corning, New York, on June 7, 1906, he was raised by his mother (his father had died when he was five). In 1921, when he was 15, Green and his mother moved to Prescott. Already interested in the priesthood, he petitioned to be a seminarian for Tucson just as Bishop Granjon was dying. Receiving an indifferent reply from the local chancellor, Green applied on his own to St. Joseph Preparatory Seminary in Mountain View, California, in 1922. Eventually

Gercke heard of him and accepted him as a student for the diocese. Green completed his studies at St. Patrick Seminary in Menlo Park, California, and was ordained in May 1932. The previous Christmas, while he was at home in Prescott serving as deacon at the midnight Mass, his mother collapsed and died. After ordination to the priesthood, he was appointed chancellor and served two years in diocesan administration. In 1934 he was assigned to Our Lady of Mount Carmel Parish in Tempe where he helped to develop the Newman Club at Arizona State University. In 1937 Bishop Gercke assigned him to Ss. Peter and Paul Parish in Tucson where he remained for 15 years. During that time Gercke developed more and more confidence in Green and appointed him Vicar General. In 1953 he was named auxiliary bishop of Tucson. In 1960 he became coadjutor to Gercke and succeeded him as diocesan bishop that same year.

» *A youthful picture of Bishop Francis Green.*
Credit: Archives of the Roman Catholic
Diocese of Tucson

The population of the Tucson diocese rose steadily from 1960 to 1968. It was during this period that the U.S. population shifted dramatically from the East and Midwest to the South and West of the country—an area that came to be called the Sunbelt. The tremendous spike in population in the affected states created demands for new housing, schools and other services—among them new churches to serve their needs. Many of the newcomers brought with them the long habits of faithful Catholic practice, and parochial expansion took place at a rapid rate.

Catholic Grade Schools and High Schools During the Bishop Green Era

» *Gerard High School.*
Credit: Archives of the Diocese of Phoenix

With each parish a new Catholic grade school was built and teaching sisters came to tend the young charges. In the period 1945 to 1969, 15 new elementary schools and three high schools opened. Serving these schools were 17 congregations of women religious.

Already noted was the re-opening of Brophy College Preparatory as a high school in 1952. As well, two new Catholic high schools were established during the postwar years. In 1962 Gerard Catholic High School opened its doors. Named for Monsignor Edward Gerard, a French missionary who began his work in Arizona in 1870, it served Catholic teens on the east side of Phoenix. On the west side, Bourgade High School, named for Bishop Peter Bourgade, also opened in 1962. Placed under the administration of the Marist Community, its first leader was Father John Hillmann. In the early 1970s the Marists transferred control of Bourgade to the priests and brothers of the Congregation of the Holy Cross. A medley of religious sisters–the Sisters of Charity, Sisters of the Precious Blood, the Humility of Mary Sisters and the Dominican Sisters of Adrian–and priests of the Diocese of Phoenix assisted them. Both schools shared an architecturally similar design, a cost-saving measure to help the diocese economize.

The Impact of Vatican II

Bishop Green was one of more than 2,000 bishops who attended Vatican Council II in Rome between 1962-1965. This ecumenical council implemented a series of far reaching reforms in a number of areas of Church life. Important calls for renewal of the liturgy, religious life and the training and ministry of priests came out of the council. Guidance was given for ecumenical engagement, the role of the laity, missionary activity, Christian education and religious liberty as part of the general "aggiornamento" envisioned by Blessed John XXIII and continued by his successor Pope Paul VI. Bishop Green carefully implemented the reforms of the council, creating a committee to put in place the liturgical changes in the Mass (e.g., transition to the vernacular, turning the altar toward the people or *versus populi*, etc.). He also created a consultative body of priests to advise him on matters pertinent to Church life. The pace of Vatican II inspired renewal and appeared to go well, with most people appreciating the change. Some resisted certain aspects of the liturgical restructuring, while others seemed to take them too far. The latter was the case at the Newman Center in Tempe.

» *Bourgade High School.*
Credit: Archives of the Diocese of Phoenix

» *Bust of Blessed John XXIII.*
Credit: Heritage Collection,
Archives of the Diocese of Phoenix

Ministry to Higher Education

Bishop Green and his predecessors had assigned a high priority to ministry on the increasing number of college campuses in Arizona. The expanding state university system had campuses in Tempe, Tucson and Flagstaff. The Tucson campus recruited Dominican priests from its Midwestern province to minister to its students, and Maricopa's fast-growing Tempe campus had a Newman Center run by diocesan priests.

Originally chartered in 1932, the All Saints Newman Center at Tempe had as its first chaplain Father James Peter Davis (later Archbishop of San Juan de Puerto Rico and then of Santa Fe). The center went through a series of chaplains–including Green who came in 1934–but parish priests held the primary responsibility for tending to the students, which they did as best they could in conjunction with their other duties. In 1957

the center was able to purchase two parcels of land next to Our Lady of Mount Carmel Church for their center. A separate Newman foundation formed in 1959, and Father William Lynch, who had been ministering there since 1956, became the first full-time chaplain. In 1963 the last of the diocesan priests, Father Thomas Walsh, arrived. By then a new chapel had been built to accommodate the growing numbers.

» *Father Walsh, All Saints Newman Center.*
Credit: Archives of the Diocese of Phoenix

» *The Tempe Newman Center was an important meeting place for the Catholic community at Arizona State University.*
Credit: Archives of the Diocese of Phoenix

» *Auxiliary Bishop Francis Green blessing the bell of*
St. Agnes Church (1953).
Credit: Archives of the Diocese of Phoenix

The All Saints Newman Center under Walsh was a seedbed for the protest politics of the 1960s as the director took firm stands against the Vietnam War and supported the reform movements that flourished in this period, e.g., Civil Rights and equality for women. Father Walsh eagerly introduced the liturgical changes of Vatican II, and in 1965 held one of the first Folk Masses in the state. He also introduced women as ushers, asked lay people, male and female, to preach the homilies once a month and added a popular outdoor "Mass on the Grass."

Bishop Green was soon besieged with complaints about Walsh, and he himself was not amused by the liberties Walsh took with liturgical matters. Eventually, Walsh was transferred, and

negotiations opened with Father Paul Scanlon, O.P., provincial of the Western Province of the Dominicans. In June 1969 the Dominicans from Oakland, California, arrived. Father Gerald Buckley was the first director, and worked through some of the bad feelings remaining over the dismissal of the popular Father Walsh. Father Thomas DeMan succeeded Buckley, and he also managed to bring peace and stability to the center. The intellectual Dominicans brought trained scholars, theologians and others who provided ongoing education on Scripture, bioethics and social issues.

Local priests served other campuses in Arizona. Phoenix College had its own chaplain, for a time Father Doug Nohava, who ran the New Covenant Newman Center–a "friendly house" across the street from the campus. A Newman Club had formed in 1930 at what was then Northern Arizona State Teacher's College, later Northern Arizona University. This group initially met under the direction of nearby Our Lady of Guadalupe Church. Between 1964 and 1966, an advisory board of members organized, acquired property and built Holy Trinity Newman Center. In December 1965 Father Richard Toerner became Holy Trinity's first full-time director.

Toward a New Diocese

Unlike the "ancient" Diocese of Tucson, which had to be carved out of a harsh environment, limited human and financial resources, and uneven social and economic growth, the Diocese of Phoenix was born with a solid infrastructure of parishes, schools, social welfare institutions and a responsible and dedicated corps of clergy, religious and laity. The burgeoning growth of Maricopa County and its insistent demands for sustained attention, planning and cohesion were now too much to ignore.

CHAPTER 2

The McCarthy Years
(1969-1976)

"I am an Arizonan, I am a Phoenician, I am one of you"

» *Bishop Green was often asked to turn over a ceremonial spade of dirt to formally inaugurate new construction in the growing Tucson diocese. He is depicted here at the groundbreaking of Gerard High School in Phoenix. Arizona Catholic leaders worked hard to meet the demands of a rapidly growing Catholic population.*
Credit: Archives of the Diocese of Phoenix

The rumors of a new Diocese of Phoenix had ebbed and flowed throughout the 1960s. Although only 125 miles away, Tucson, with its slower pattern of growth and its attachment to its Hispanic past, seemed culturally remote from the sprawling areas in Maricopa County. Bishop Francis Green visited occasionally, staying at St. Gregory Parish, but the requirements of administration kept him tethered to Tucson. Some resented sending money to Tucson when it was needed in Phoenix. Paradoxically, some priests may have expressed public frustration with the distance–physical and cultural–but also liked the relative autonomy they enjoyed running their parishes without the direct oversight of the local bishop or chancery.

In fact, however, the sheer growth of metropolitan Phoenix moved the long-standing question of a new diocese to the front burner.

Indeed, during the 1960s, the number of people living in Maricopa County, the largest in Arizona, grew from 663,510 to 967,522, and the population of Phoenix rose from 439,170 to 581,562. The problem of managing the parochial development was becoming increasingly complex and required a more systematic and hands-on approach. Land had to be purchased, and new church buildings had to be erected. Older structures needed expansion, and clergy and religious had to be found to provide basic services.

Given the growth, why was the creation of the new diocese delayed until 1969? One plausible reason was that the international Catholic Church was in the midst of Vatican Council II. Many things appeared to be put on hold as conciliar liturgical reform and changes in other critical areas of Church life took precedence.

Another reason was that Bishop Green was not enthusiastic about the prospect of losing the revenue from some of the parishes in Maricopa County. All diocesan bishops in the West worried about finances, and Green publicly admitted his financial concerns about a new diocese in 1968: "We know," Green told the *Arizona Republic*, "that almost half those [400,000 Arizona] Catholics are among minority groups who are the object of poverty." He continued, "There is no question that the area [Arizona] is big enough to divide and the population, if it were a productive population, is big enough to support two dioceses. But our growth has come only in the last 20 years, so everything we have is on borrowed money. And still we try to give our people the same services they had in their parishes back East." Green might also have observed that developing regions such as Arizona had a large number of young Catholic families who, while generous to the Church, also faced mortgages, taxes and the costs of child rearing. What was left for the Church often was not enough to help build and maintain the church buildings and schools Catholics wanted for their communities. Financial concerns notwithstanding, population growth and the demands of managing expansion required a new diocese.

» *At Blessed Sacrament Parish in Tolleson, Masses were held under Arizona's clear skies even before the new church was under roof.*
Credit: Archives of the Diocese of Phoenix

The Long and Winding Road (1966-1969)

Once Vatican II formally ended in December 1965, rumors of a Diocese of Phoenix grew stronger throughout 1966. In July 1967 an article in the *Arizona Republic*, headlined "Phoenix May Get Catholic Bishop and Diocese," pointed out that Phoenix's population, more than 500,000, exceeded cities like El Paso, Gallup and even Tucson, which had all been created as dioceses. It also speculated on boundaries, the site of the new cathedral and the appointment of a bishop.

Acknowledging the increased tempo of the rumors, Monsignor Robert Fuller, chancellor of the Diocese of Tucson, noted, discussions "have been rife for at least a year." He predicted, "There is no doubt that the day will come when the City of Phoenix will be the seat of a diocese of its own." But the chancellor poured cold water on any imminent appointment, commenting that Apostolic Delegate Egidio Vagnozzi had only recently been replaced by Archbishop Luigi Raimondi, who was not slated to take up his post until September 1967. The new delegate would need time to assess conditions in the United States.

In early 1968 the 15 member Priest Senate of the Diocese of Tucson drafted a letter asking for a new diocese. Signed by senate president Father James McFadden of St. Louis the King Parish in Glendale, the request was sent to Apostolic Delegate Raimondi as well as to Cardinals John Dearden of Detroit (president of the National Council of Catholic Bishops) and Francis McIntyre of Los Angeles and Archbishop James P. Davis of Santa Fe, New Mexico. In October 1968 Apostolic Delegate Raimondi traveled to Tucson for the dedication of the restored St. Augustine Cathedral. This offered him a chance to confer with Bishop Green in person. Then Raimondi traveled to Phoenix for a luncheon with the priests–a most unusual gesture, interpreted correctly as an opportunity for face-to-face consultation about a new diocese.

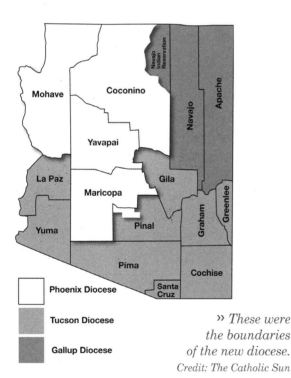

» These were the boundaries of the new diocese.
Credit: The Catholic Sun

In late August 1969, Bishop Green learned that the division would soon take place. The formal announcement came on September 3, 1969. The new diocese had been carefully drawn, consisting of Coconino, Mohave and Yavapai counties, which were being detached from Gallup, and from Tucson all of Maricopa County plus the Pinal County portion of the Gila River Indian Reservation. The entire Navajo, Apache and Hopi Indian reservations remained in Gallup. The Diocese of Phoenix would inherit nearly 200,000

Catholics served by 58 parishes, 26 missions, 197 priests, 265 religious sisters and 12 religious brothers. Also coming under the auspices of the new diocese were 28 elementary schools, six high schools and one general hospital.

Green met a small press conference in front of the Tucson cathedral to laud Pope Paul VI's decision and express his hope that "the close ties which have bound me to the priests, religious and laity of the Phoenix area will never be severed." But he once again observed the financial difficulties ahead for both growing areas. Both Tucson and Phoenix dioceses "will have to tighten our belts a little financially."

At the same time, the name of the first bishop, Edward A. McCarthy, was released. Bishop McCarthy's press statement welcomed the assignment, paid tribute to Bishop Green and stated he was looking forward to serving in Phoenix: "We have the unique opportunity of fashioning by our united effort, a new family of God's people in the genuine spirit of the Second Vatican Council." Catholics in the pew applauded the change. Connie Levesque, an early employee of the fledgling diocese recalled her feelings in a 20-year retrospective of the diocese, "We felt like we were part of it. With Tucson, we felt like we were removed; we were 100 miles away."

» A group of nearly two thousand turned out at Sky Harbor Airport to welcome Bishop Edward McCarthy in December 1969.
Credit: Archives of the Diocese of Phoenix

Bishop Edward A. McCarthy

» *Bishop McCarthy entered into his new ministry in Arizona with great enthusiasm.*
Credit: Archives of the Diocese of Phoenix

The 51-year-old McCarthy greeted 2,000 well wishers who welcomed him on December 1, 1969, at Phoenix's Sky Harbor Airport. Sword carrying Knights of Colombus, Indian dancers from St. John the Baptist and mariachis were among the crowd. As he swept down the movable stairway of the airliner that had transported him from his native Cincinnati to Phoenix he announced, "As of this moment, I can say proudly–I am an Arizonan, I am a Phoenician, I am one of you." Governor Jack Williams assured him, "You come among friends, Bishop." For the next six and a half years, the Midwestern McCarthy would learn the varied topography and constituencies of his nearly 44,000 square mile diocese.

» *Governor Jack Williams (right) was among the civic dignitaries who welcomed Bishop McCarthy.*
Credit: Archives of the Diocese of Phoenix

Bishop McCarthy hailed from the Midwest, and his installation trip was only his second to the state–the earlier one a private visit to confer with Bishop Green and to inspect potential sites for his cathedral church. He had risen to prominence in the Church through the traditional pattern of faithful service in the chancery and canon law circles from which bishops were selected. The confidence reposed in him by his ecclesiastical superiors, Archbishops Timothy McNicholas, O.P., and Karl J. Alter, recommended him for the challenges of the new diocese.

» *Bishop Edward McCarthy, seated in the cathedra of Ss. Simon and Jude Cathedral, receives the crosier from Apostolic Delegate Luigi Raimondi.*
Credit: Archives of the Diocese of Phoenix

Edward Anthony McCarthy was born April 10, 1918, in Cincinnati, Ohio, one of five children of Edward E. and Catherine A. McCarthy. Four of the McCarthy children had entered the priesthood or religious life. Two of McCarthy's brothers, Norbert and Donald became priests of the Archdiocese of Cincinnati and his sister Catherine (known as Sister Grace Miriam in religion) became a Sister of Charity. His other sister Grace married a contractor,

Robert Beischel, and resided in Cincinnati. Young McCarthy attended St. Boniface parochial school and Roger Bacon High School. He entered St. Gregory Preparatory Seminary and later Mount St. Mary of the West major seminary in Cincinnati. Archbishop John Timothy McNicholas, O.P., ordained him to the priesthood on May 29, 1943. In 1944 McNicholas appointed the young priest his secretary and then sent him to study at The Catholic University of America where he finished a doctorate in canon law in 1948. The next year McCarthy was sent to the Apollinaire, the school of canon law at Rome's Lateran University, and while at the Lateran also secured a doctorate in Sacred Theology from the Angelicum. He returned to Cincinnati where he served in the archdiocesan tribunal, and worked as secretary and master of ceremonies to Archbishop McNicholas. When McNicholas died in April 1950, Archbishop Karl J. Alter retained McCarthy. Alter had him appointed an auxiliary bishop in June 1965 and made him Vicar General in 1966. McCarthy also chaired the Commission on Liturgy and Sacred Music and took an interest in the social issues of racism and poverty that were engaging the Church and secular society in the late 1960s.

Adapting to the American West

Clearly, McCarthy was administratively and theologically prepared to handle a new diocese. But first, he had to adjust to his new environment—one very different from the established Catholic culture of his native Cincinnati. Father (later Bishop) Thomas O'Brien recalled being one of the first persons to speak to McCarthy after the diocese was established. In that conversation, McCarthy revealed a typical Midwesterner's image of the "wild West" and wondered how many Indians there were in the diocese. (O'Brien didn't know.)

It was apparent McCarthy knew little of the spatial and cultural realities of the American Southwest. During an airplane trip to attend the installation of Monsignor Jerome Hastrich as bishop of Gallup, he learned a great deal. Bad weather made it impossible to land in Gallup,

and as the plane circled Phoenix, McCarthy gazed out the window and marveled at the size of the metropolitan area—a region he had thought was mostly empty desert. "All of these big cities I was seeing [from the airplane] were all Phoenix—from different angles."

» *Bishop McCarthy, a Midwesterner, took time to learn about the geography and people of his new diocese.*
Credit: Archives of the Diocese of Phoenix

Adapting to the weather and the variegated geography of Arizona was challenge enough, but McCarthy also had to adjust to the new demography—one quite different from the Catholic world in which he had grown up and begun his priestly ministry. The Archdiocese of Cincinnati (indeed the entire Midwest) was an area known for its sharply etched ethnic neighborhoods, its venerable and architecturally imposing parish churches and its dense network of Catholic institutions: schools, hospitals and orphanages. Phoenix was quite a change from the stable, well-established neighborhoods where steepled churches loomed large over communities, and Catholic schools and other institutions were part of the local landscape. The fast growing Valley of the Sun consisted of suburban neighborhoods with winding streets, air conditioned homes, schools and shopping centers. Here modernistic or functional church buildings, surrounded by huge parking lots, were common. In northern

Arizona, McCarthy saw many of the tourist sites that brought thousands flocking to the region every year. Many of the Catholics he met on Confirmation or church dedication visits or at social events had come from the Midwest or the East and were somewhat rootless. With the exception of many Mexican people, who had lived here for generations, extended families were not the rule here nor were there long generations of Catholics whose family names were synonymous with churches. The oldest church in Phoenix, St. Mary's, was founded in 1881–by which time Cincinnati already had 45 churches. Likewise, he arrived just as more and more Americans were either permanently relocating to Phoenix or coming during the cold winters of the East, Midwest, Canada and the Pacific Northwest. "Snow birds" swelled parish populations during the winter and deflated them in the hot summer months. Entrepreneurs like Del Webb built retirement communities such as Sun City (1960). St. Clement of Rome Parish, founded in 1970, was a community set up for this constituency. Finally, there was the "West of the imagination," which McCarthy like many Americans knew only from movies, television and novels–a land of Indians, cowboys, cactus, mining towns, desert and tumbleweed.

» *Bishop McCarthy enters into the good fun of whacking a piñata. Youngsters are waiting to scramble for the candy and other goodies that will soon spill out.*
Credit: Archives of the Diocese of Phoenix

McCarthy came to consider Phoenix his home and did not envision leaving. He was a gregarious, hardworking and intelligent man, blessed with organizational skills and a knack for picking the right people to help him. Although initially he may have viewed his native clergy as somewhat "backward," bringing in some outsiders to help with

key tasks, he soon realized the priests, religious and laity of Phoenix were every bit as sophisticated and competent as outside "experts."

Taking Charge

Among Bishop McCarthy's first decisions was the selection of the site of the cathedral. Several capacious Phoenix churches vied for the spot, including St. Agnes', St. Gregory's and even historic St. Mary's. But Bishop McCarthy chose Ss. Simon and Jude Church. Founded in 1953 in a growing residential area, the parish had built a huge 1,000-seat church in 1966, specifically designed with the newly revised liturgy in mind. Its 75-foot bell tower allowed it to reign over the area. Father Paul Smith, the church's Irish-born founding pastor was "routed out of bed early...to receive the news that his church had been chosen as the diocesan cathedral.... It is a very great honor." McCarthy's installation on December 2, 1969, at Ss. Simon and Jude was a solemn but historic event, launching the new diocese on the first phase of its development.

» *Bishop McCarthy chose Ss. Simon and Jude Church as the cathedral of the new diocese.*
Ss. Simon and Jude was founded in 1953 and had built a successful school, staffed by the Loreto Sisters.
Credit: Archives of the Diocese of Phoenix

At Monsignor Bernard Gordon's urging, McCarthy appointed 34-year-old Father Thomas J. O'Brien as his secretary and master of ceremonies. McCarthy briefly lived in a suite at St. Joseph Hospital. A temporary administrative center was carved out of a section of a Catholic Charities building on West Northern Avenue, but McCarthy wanted something more permanent and centrally located as the headquarters of the diocese.

The Diocesan Center

As Father O'Brien drove him around the streets of Phoenix, McCarthy noticed the large St. Mary Convent on East Monroe Street, the residence of the Sisters of the Precious Blood. The site was directly across from the city's newly planned Civic Plaza, a center point of urban renewal. In January 1970 McCarthy was a dinner guest of the Precious Blood Sisters. "After the evening meal," one of the sisters wrote in the community chronicle, "the bishop toured the convent and expressed his intention that it would one day become his chancery." With the consent of the sisters, McCarthy sent aides, architects, electricians and plumbers to examine the convent and draw up blueprints for its renovation. Plans to relocate the sisters had to be altered when Casa Linda, a residence for unwed mothers where the sisters had planned to live temporarily, had an unexpected influx of new clients leaving no room. As a result, the sisters remained for a time in the renovated west wing of the convent.

With a deadline of mid-August, workers began renovating the east wing. Sisters who taught in the school all day sometimes came home to find the sinks and walls of their rooms torn out. Gradually spaces were carved out for new offices as well as for suites to house Bishop McCarthy, Father Thomas O'Brien and Carmelite Father William O'Brien, a professor of canon law whom McCarthy had enticed to come to Phoenix.

In August McCarthy announced the completion of the project, making it clear he intended the move to be part of "the Church's interest in identifying with the dynamic renewal of the downtown area." He hoped its central location would make it accessible to people in the metropolitan area and, by locating it next to St. Mary Church, link the diocese with its historic past. The center opened. In addition to the residential facilities, it also included a chapel and offices for the education department, the business administrator and the marriage tribunal, and various conference rooms, including one with a round table. The table and the center itself reflected the spirit of collegiality and active listening that McCarthy brought to his post-Vatican II diocese. Meanwhile, the decision to remain in the downtown won kudos from local leaders like Phoenix mayor John D. Driggs who commented, "I am most pleased to learn that the entire Catholic Diocesan Center is being removed to the downtown Phoenix area across from our new Civic Plaza."

» *Bishop McCarthy renovated the convent of the Sisters of the Precious Blood for the first Pastoral Center. Today's Diocesan Pastoral Center has replaced this structure.*
Credit: Archives of the Diocese of Phoenix

» *This skyline of the city of Phoenix (c. 1970)– note the location of the Diocesan Pastoral Center.*
Credit: Archives of the Diocese of Phoenix

A Start

» Bishop McCarthy encouraged the formation of lay groups that would advance the work of the Church in the Diocese of Phoenix. Here he is pictured at the first board meeting of the Diocesan Council of Catholic Women in October 1970.
Credit: Archives of the Diocese of Phoenix

The first year of the diocese was a whirlwind. In January McCarthy went to Immaculate Heart of Mary Parish to hold his first ordination—for Claretian John Anthony Moreno. In May he held the first diocesan priestly ordinations in the newly-designated cathedral, imposing hands on William Parenteau and Robert Skagen.

Taking a cue from Bishop Green and other bishops around the country, he began to build up diocesan reserves by launching the Charity and Development Appeal (CDA). Father (later Monsignor) John J. McMahon headed the first of these annual collections, which has had a history of exceeding their goals. During the first full year of the diocese, more than $845,000 was collected, and by 1971 the collection brought in more than $1 million. 1972 was a banner year—the CDA bumped over its $1,050,000 goal to $1,108,919—reflecting the growing number of Catholics in the Phoenix diocese, now surpassing the 200,000 mark, or 19 percent of the population in the four counties under its jurisdiction. By 2005 the diocese collected $10 million through this well-planned appeal.

Reaching Out to South Phoenix: The Work of the St. Vincent de Paul Society

Mindful of the groundwork men like Fathers Braun and McLoughlin had laid, Bishop McCarthy wanted to maintain an active Church presence on Phoenix's poor south side. Ambitious plans to have a social center in the midst of the barrios were announced with great fanfare, but never panned out.

However, one of the bulwarks of the area was the St. Vincent de Paul Charity Dining Room, located at a former restaurant on West Washington Street, which had been in operation since November 20, 1952, and had fed literally millions of hungry Phoenicians. By 1972 it had served more than seven million free meals—about a 1,000 per day and sometimes as high as 3,500 in peak seasons. This popular charitable group had begun in the Phoenix area in April 1946 when Tommy Johnstone, a New Yorker familiar with the society, recruited four other men to help Father Louis Shoen, O.F.M., of St. Mary Church form the first parish group. By 1949 the St. Vincent de Paul Conference—consisting of parishioners from St. Agnes, St. Francis Xavier and St. Mary churches—united to form the Particular Council of Maricopa County. From this small beginning, five priests and 25 members, the programs of the St. Vincent de Paul Society expanded considerably in every part of the diocese.

» St. Vincent de Paul Charity Dining Room.
Credit: Archives of the Diocese of Phoenix

» *The work of the St. Vincent de Paul Society has been a mainstay of Catholic outreach to the poor for many years in the Diocese of Phoenix.*
Credit: Archives of the Diocese of Phoenix

Church. Groundbreaking for the church, designed by Scottsdale architect Francis Schulz, took place at Easter 1971 and by the next Easter the growing congregation was in its new facilities. Resurrection was a modern church, with flexible space within that could be used as a small chapel or multipurpose room. In July 1970 the formation of St. Augustine's in west Phoenix had been announced, headed by Father William Reid. Before he departed in the summer of 1976, McCarthy would found 19 new parishes (see chart) and approve millions of dollars of new construction.

» *Resurrection Church in Tempe was the first parish founded by Bishop McCarthy.*
Credit: Archives of the Diocese of Phoenix

The contributions of the generous lay Vincentians and their efforts to offer person-to-person service to those who are needy and suffering grew and expanded as the population of Arizona grew. By 2008 this group was sponsoring five dining rooms, 17 thrift shops and various programs providing medical and dental care, assisting those with substance abuse problems, ministering to those in jail and caring for the homeless. A transitional homeless shelter, Ozanam Manor opened on East Monroe Street in Phoenix to help people shift from a life on the streets to stable homes and lives.

Parochial Growth

McCarthy's first new parish, in the fast-growing Mesa-Tempe area, was created in the spring of 1970, and was appropriately named Resurrection. Founding pastor Father Philip J. Poirier helped launch the community, initially holding the opening Masses at Mesa Community College and confessions at a nearby Lutheran

The pace of parish activity increased, and Mass attendance grew as the diocese introduced the practice of Saturday anticipated Mass in 1970. The expansion of the McCarthy era differed from the previous burst under Bishops Gercke and Green, which mandated school construction before the construction of a new church. Newer parishes built the church structure first with centers for parish meetings and weekly catechetical instruction following. Not every parish had a parochial school.

Parish Development During the McCarthy Years

Year established	Parish	City	County
1970	Resurrection	Tempe	Maricopa
1970	Our Lady of Guadalupe	Guadalupe	Maricopa
1970	St. Clement of Rome	Sun City	Maricopa
1970	St. Augustine	Phoenix	Maricopa
1972	Our Lady of Joy	Carefree	Maricopa
1972	All Saints	Mesa	Maricopa
1972	St. Margaret	Tempe	Maricopa
1973	St. William	Cashion	Maricopa
1973	Our Lady of the Valley	Phoenix	Maricopa
1973	St. Martin de Porres	Phoenix	Maricopa
1973	Holy Spirit	Tempe	Maricopa
1974	St. Helen	Glendale	Maricopa
1974	St. Raphael	Glendale	Maricopa
1974	Blessed Sacrament	Scottsdale	Maricopa
1975	St. Thomas Aquinas	Avondale	Maricopa
1976	Ascension	Fountain Hills	Maricopa
1976	St. Edward the Confessor	Phoenix	Maricopa
1976	St. Paul	Phoenix	Maricopa
1976	St. Elizabeth Seton	Sun City	Maricopa

The astute Father John McMahon was charged with acquiring the property for the new parishes, going about the border of Phoenix purchasing parcels in the growing metropolitan area and also in other areas of the diocese, such as Bullhead City. Although these purchases required some outlay of diocesan funds, they made some tidy profits for the diocese down the line. Father McMahon and his colleagues, Fathers Eugene Maguire and Richard Moyer, sometimes snatched up parcels in the line of development, never spending beyond $5,000 an acre. They purchased 40 acres around Scottsdale for $120,000 and added strategic portions to it by land trades. Later they sold it for $4.5 million–of which 3.5 acres were needed by the local airport for a runway extension. McMahon and his collaborators became adept at these kinds of deals, and sometimes through land swaps were able to trade parcels for land where parishes could be planted. Nonetheless, land acquisition along with the increasing demand for diocesan services taxed the fund-raising and parish assessment systems.

» *Father (later Monsignor) Richard Moyer (pictured here at right) directed Catholic Charities under Bishop McCarthy. His technological and financial expertise were effectively used to build up the young diocese.*

Credit: Archives of the Diocese of Phoenix

Included in the land purchases were 60 acres of Ponderosa pines in the middle of the Prescott National Forest, bought in 1973. McCarthy considered the area ideal for a campground for the youth of Phoenix. Set in the midst of the forest, six miles from the city of Prescott, the property was at an elevation of 6,700 feet–cool, tranquil and undeveloped. McCarthy called it "Camp Tepeyac" in honor of the hill in Mexico where the Blessed Virgin Mary had appeared to Juan Diego. Over the course of time, parishes contributed resources and labor to build a series of lodges there. The camp opened in 1978 and was used for retreats, days of recollection and workshops. In 2004 the Life Teen, Inc., program purchased the property.

Monsignor Donohoe: A New Role

» *Monsignor Robert Donohoe (center), founding pastor of St. Agnes Parish, was for many years one of the leading Catholic clergy in the city of Phoenix. He was widely admired by many in the civic and ecumenical communities, and is pictured here with Mayor Milton Graham (left) and lawyer William Rielly (right).*
Credit: Archives of the Diocese of Phoenix

Phoenix's most visible churchman, Monsignor Robert Donohoe, spearheaded Bishop McCarthy's outreach to the wider Phoenix and Arizona communities. Donohoe had requested a new assignment when McCarthy came on board, insisting "32 years as pastor is unfair to both pastor and the people." He admitted, "It's hard to take a stand like this but I felt they needed new blood." In July 1972 McCarthy turned over Donohoe's

beloved St. Agnes' to the Carmelites. McCarthy then began to utilize Donohoe's extensive contacts with the "movers and shakers" in the area, appointing him director of community relations. McCarthy's successor, Bishop James Rausch, put Donohoe in charge of diocesan ecumenical affairs. Until his death in 1999, Donohoe was a respected and well-received figure not only among Phoenicians of various faith traditions, but in the wider circles of Arizona society and government.

Monsignor Donohoe was also a state delegate to a 1971 White House Conference on Aging. Arizona had its share of retirees and a large health-care industry. Taking care of the aged and infirm was an important part of the ministerial demands of the diocese. In 1972 the diocese helped establish the Foundation for Senior Living, which received a grant from the Campaign for Human Development to start a day-care center for the elderly. In October 1974 it solidified its organization, consisting of 17 affiliated corporations, under the umbrella of a not-for-profit corporation. Its services encompassed adult health and foster care, assisted living, community action programs, affordable housing and senior nutrition centers. It also oversaw behavior group homes and ten senior apartment sites with 372 units, including an apartment complex in Williams.

Adult Faith Formation: The Kino Institute

Vatican II brought with it a demand for theological updating for clergy, religious and laity. A cascade of new material in critical areas of Church life–scripture, dogma, liturgy, moral theology and Church history–sent many priests, sisters and religious educators back to the classroom. Unlike his native Cincinnati, Phoenix had no institution of Catholic higher education from which Bishop McCarthy could draw upon to help sponsor educational programs. Neither were there public schools offering a religious orientation on the college level. Beginning such an enterprise was far beyond the capabilities of the diocese, so McCarthy provided a helpful alternative, which addressed the need for ongoing education.

» *Early Kino Institute staff on Northern Avenue.* Credit: Archives of the Diocese of Phoenix

Shortly after the Carmelites took over St. Agnes Parish in 1972, the parish became the center for the Kino Institute–the diocesan religious education center, named for Jesuit missionary to the Southwest, Eusebio Kino. The institute generated concern and enthusiasm for continuing adult theological education by offering an array of courses and public lectures at various locations around the diocese. It also supported diocesan efforts in research and study. The institute was to have an ecumenical arm to engage whenever possible other church communities. The institute formally opened on September 6, 1972, with an address by Father Roland E. Murphy, O. Carm., professor of the Old Testament at Duke University. The following day the institute hosted a clergy conference, featuring Father (later Cardinal) Avery Dulles, S.J., professor of systematic theology at Woodstock College in New York. Heading up the institute was Father Leo McCarthy, O.Carm., and W. Richard Regan, a permanent deacon. Its first ecumenical dialogue was held in December 1973 and included an extended discussion on the role of Mary.

The institute offerings consisted of eight-week term courses at 26 different locations around the diocese, including Prescott, Kingman and Flagstaff. By 1974 more than 2,000 students had taken Kino-sponsored courses. In 1979 a collaborative program with the University of San Francisco allowed the institute to offer a master's degree in religious education and pastoral ministries through classes taken at the Phoenix campus. Among the real assets of the institute was its 10,000 volume library, one of the finest collections of books and periodicals pertaining to theology, spirituality, morality, religious education, pastoral ministry and canon law in the Southwest. Housed at first in an institute center on Northern Avenue and later moved to the Diocesan Pastoral Center, the library was processed by Carmelite Father George Hosko. Sisters Bibiane Roy, O.P., and Darcy Peletich, O.S.F., who served as librarians, helped keep the collection current and well preserved. By 2006 this collection had grown to 25,000 volumes. It also included nearly 1,000 Spanish-language resources. The University of San Francisco contributed more than $100,000 to the maintenance of the library over the years.

A guiding intellectual light behind Kino was Carmelite Father Ernest Larkin, whom Bishop McCarthy enticed to be "theologian in residence." Larkin, a native of Chicago, was ordained in 1946 and did graduate work in English at The Catholic University of America and also studied at the Angelicum in Rome where he received a doctorate in theology. He taught dogmatic and spiritual theology at Whitefriars Hall, the Carmelite Seminary in Washington, D.C., and in 1960 was appointed an associate professor of spiritual theology at Catholic University. Until his return to Chicago in 1981, Larkin helped steer the institute's programs in a solid direction and meet a critical need of the growing Church in the Southwest.

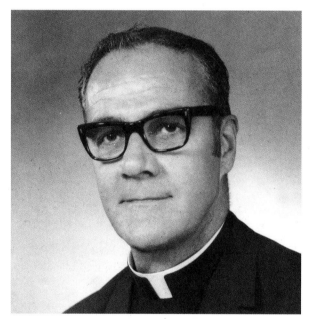

» *Carmelite Father Ernest Larkin was a guiding intellectual force at the Kino Institute during its early years.*
Credit: Archives of the Diocese of Phoenix

The Franciscan Renewal Center (The Casa de Paz y Bien)

Area Catholics also found help from the Franciscan Renewal Center in Scottsdale. The Franciscan friars opened this retreat center in 1951 at the request of Bishop Gercke. Father Owen da Silva, O.F.M., a leader in the Franciscan retreat movement, visited Phoenix to look for an appropriate site. Da Silva, a renowned expert on

the music of the California missions, had already established retreat houses in San Juan Bautista and Santa Cruz, California. Searching around Paradise Valley, he walked into the Kachina Lodge, a local resort owned by John Mills, who also owned Phoenix's famous Westward Ho Hotel. "This is the place," da Silva exclaimed when he visited the site for a luncheon. Mills graciously sold the property, and it was quickly transformed into a friary and retreat center and renamed Casa de Paz y Bien (House of Peace and Good). Its name was simplified in 1970 to The Franciscan Renewal Center, but it is still known by its Spanish name. The center specialized in traditional retreats given by Franciscan retreat masters. It also offered the innovation of retreats for married couples–something as yet uncommon in the 1950s. It was at the Casa that Phoenix liturgical history was made, when in October 1964 Bishop Green (then at Vatican II) gave permission for the Mass to be celebrated in English during a priests retreat. Father Theodore Radtke celebrated the Mass, facing the congregation; Father Daniel McCready was the lector and commentator, and Father Cornelius Moynihan the server.

» *Early photograph of The Franciscan Renewal Center.*
Credit: Archives of the Diocese of Phoenix.

In 1973 Phoenix native Franciscan Father Barry Brunsmann was assigned to the center and brought his interest in linking spiritual and psychological growth. Working with local superior Father Michael Weishaar, Brunsmann offered counseling services to Phoenix Catholics, and the grounds and facilities were steadily improved with swimming pool, spa and gardens. During

» The Franciscan Friars of the Santa Barbara Province began their retreat house in the 1950s.
Credit: Archives of the Diocese of Phoenix

the 1970s the retreat house chapel hosted five Sunday Masses–most of them filled with eager worshipers–including special masses for children who loved the friendly friars.

The Casa programs of the 1970s also contributed substantially to the intellectual life of the new-born Phoenix diocese. The friars imported an impressive array of speakers for the "Dimension Seventies" series and also sponsored courses in scripture, world religion and social problems.

Diocesan Administration

Bishop McCarthy relied on good advice from a variety of people. In 1970 he established a Priest Senate. These 17 priests met regularly with the bishop who consulted with them on major issues. In 1972 he created a Diocesan Pastoral Council, consisting of lay, religious and clerical representatives.

McCarthy replaced the deanery system he inherited from Tucson, which divided up the diocese into territorial entities looked after by a dean. He replaced it with a series of vicariates to oversee critical areas of Church life: social welfare, education and ethnic ministries. He had no chancellor, but had his secretary, Father Thomas O'Brien, doing the same work without the title. McCarthy also expanded the central offices staff to meet the needs of the growing diocese. He hired Jerry Burns, the former director of the

National Council of Catholic Men, as director of the Office of Communications, and appointed Monsignor Bernard Gordon as Vicar General and Father (later Monsignor) Richard W. Moyer as director of Catholic Charities. Moyer was a native of Ohio, had been in the Navy and had come to Arizona in 1964 after finishing studies at St. Meinrad Seminary (where Thomas O'Brien had been a few years ahead of him). He had served as associate director of Catholic Charities in Phoenix when it was part of Tucson. From his offices on West Northern, Moyer oversaw a host of important diocesan programs: the Tri-City Catholic Social Service, the Foundation for Senior Living, Sacred Heart Day Care Living, Casa Linda Lodge and oversight of social justice and life issues for the diocese. In the allocation of funds from the annual drive, Charities always received a very large share–$139,000 in 1971.

» Father Richard Moyer celebrating a teen Mass.
Credit: Archives of the Diocese of Phoenix

Catholic education, a special interest for McCarthy when he was in Cincinnati, became a major priority in Phoenix. His first efforts to recruit a professional superintendent of schools were not successful. In 1974 McCarthy appointed Father John Hillman, formerly a Marist priest who had incardinated into the Phoenix diocese in 1969. Hillman brought a wealth of experience and stability to the job, having been a seminary rector in Georgia, the founding principal of Bourgade High School in 1962, and from 1970 to 1974 the

religious order priests who wished to minister in the growing diocese.

McCarthy also hoped at some point to be able to use the gifts and talents of a number of former priests who resided in his diocese. In a move later condemned by some, the Priest Senate and Bishop McCarthy arranged a social get-together with the many former priests at the Franciscan Renewal Center. "I am convinced," McCarthy told the *Arizona Republic*, "that some of these men are still anxious to serve the Church." When the gathering became the source of scandal and controversy, McCarthy explained compassionately, "Most of these men have moved here from other parts of the country. Many are bearing grave human suffering either mentally or physically–some say they are treated like lepers–some are jobless.... As their bishop, I think I need to be concerned." He and the Priest Senate hoped the former priests' years in teaching or social service could be utilized.

» *Bishop McCarthy worked hard to forge close bonds with the priests of the diocese.*
Credit: Archives of the Diocese of Phoenix

Permanent Diaconate

Bishop McCarthy ordained ten to the permanent diaconate on May 29, 1972, in Ss. Simon and Jude Cathedral. The permanent diaconate had been re-instituted to its full integrity as a distinct order by the letter Sacrorum Diaconatus Ordinem of Pope Paul VI in June 1967. This restored order envisioned a three-fold scope of service shared with bishops and priests: charity, word and liturgy. The Catholic Church in America warmly embraced this "new" form of ministry (though the diaconate was an ancient institution).

Father (later Monsignor) Eugene Maguire, pastor of Our Lady of Perpetual Help in Scottsdale, and his parish musician (and former seminarian) Irving Fleming were among the early advocates of this ministry in Phoenix. Both Fleming and Maguire had read articles about the restoration of the diaconate and wrote to McCarthy shortly after the prelate's installation about the possibilities of instituting the program. Others interested and knowledgeable about the restored order were Thomas Phelan, religious education coordinator at Our Lady of Perpetual Help, and Richard Regan of neighboring St. Daniel the Prophet Parish. Regan had recently completed a one-year course of theological studies at the University of San Francisco. Three months after his arrival, McCarthy convened a meeting of interested men whom Fleming and the local Cursillo Movement had surfaced. That first meeting, held at St. Joseph Hospital, gave the men an opportunity to speak about their interests and call to ministry. Finally, McCarthy stopped the banter and asked, "Why would I want to ordain you?" Each man responded, one by one. From that first meeting, McCarthy launched one of the first permanent diaconate programs in the United States, placing it under the direction of Carmelite Father William O'Brien. In September 1970 ten men began the program. They ranged in age from 37 to 54. Fernando Vega of Tempe, an educator, was the first Mexican American to become a Catholic deacon in the United States.

These first deacons hit an uneven reception in the diocese. Some pastors embraced them wholeheartedly, putting them to work in a variety of ministries. Other deacons did not fare so well– as pastors and others did not understand their function nor welcome their special gifts. As time went on, however, formation and educational programs in Phoenix and around the country were expanded and improved. The number of deacons–ordained for Phoenix and those who moved into the diocese from other areas–soon began to increase their ranks.

» *On May 29, 1972, Bishop McCarthy ordained the first men to the permanent diaconate. This program grew steadily over the years.*
Credit: Archives of the Diocese of Phoenix

Spiritual Life

Catholic spiritual life experienced a season of growth and transformation in the period after Vatican II (this included movements that predated the council like Cursillo). The traditional Catholic devotions, e.g., Marian piety, novenas and Eucharistic adoration and Benediction, continued to inspire and fortify the faith. But other popular religious movements made their appearance and deepened the faith life of thousands.

The Cursillo Movement attained widespread popularity in Phoenix beginning in 1959 with the leadership of the Santa Cruz family at Immaculate Heart of Mary Church. The couple had been immersed in the Cursillo Movement in Texas and brought it home to Phoenix. These small courses in Christianity consisted of an intense, weekend-long experience. Begun in 1949 by a group of laymen who met at the San Honorato Monastery on the island of Majorca, this program of spiritual exercises and shared community provided an

important contrast to the regular devotional and liturgical life of Catholics. These courses became very popular in the American West, especially where there were growing Latino communities. The Cursillo experience included songs, lively worship services and post-cursillo meetings called ultreyas, which perpetuated Cursillo ideas and energized people to live what they had experienced. Phoenix's Claretian community became the sponsors for these events, with the initial Cursillo weekends taking place in the gym and kitchen of Immaculate Heart of Mary Parish.

In 1963 the Claretians moved the program to the former La Fonda Fiesta Guest Ranch located in northeast Phoenix at the base of Camelback Mountain. They renamed the ranch Mount Claret Cursillo Center, and in 1969 built a new chapel. From their humble beginnings in the church gym in 1959 until the 1990s, the Phoenix movement hosted 580 Cursillo weekends in Spanish and English with an average of 40 men or women each weekend. Father Marcel Salinas, C.M.F., became an important leader in this work. In 1987 the Claretians decided to sell the property. Through the leadership of Monsignor John McMahon, a group of loyal Cursillistas and other dedicated Phoenicians helped raise the money to purchase it. In July 1988 the property was transferred to the Diocese of Phoenix, which initially renamed it the Diocesan Renewal Center, but later it went back to the more familiar Mount Claret Retreat Center.

» *Mount Claret Retreat Center.*
Credit: Archives of the Diocese of Phoenix

The Charismatic Renewal Takes Root

In the post-conciliar era, some devotional life was downplayed in favor of an enhanced focus on the Mass and the Holy Scriptures. Yet, the hunger for individual prayer and a more intense personal spirituality still existed and found an outlet in the Catholic Charismatic Renewal. Pentecostalism swept through mainline Churches in the 1950s and came to the door of the Catholic Church through a stirring at Pittsburgh's Duquesne University in 1969 when two men who prayed regularly to the Holy Spirit began to experience charismatic gifts.

Catholics throughout the Diocese of Phoenix caught this fire, too–some of it came from migrations to the Arizona capital. Small prayer meetings were held at Loyola Hall of Brophy College Preparatory, Ss. Simon and Jude Cathedral and St. Mark Parish in Phoenix as well as in Prescott, Mesa and at the All Saints Newman Center in Tempe. By 1972 there were approximately 300 charismatics in the Phoenix diocese. The number of prayer meetings increased over the years, and occasionally Phoenix would host a major conference bringing in headline speakers. In 1973 Bishop McCarthy appointed Father Ernest Larkin as the diocesan liaison to the growing movement, which increased to an estimated 3,000 to 4,000 charismatics and about 45 prayer groups by 1982. Charismatic groups set up their own association called Catholic Renewal Ministries in the early 1980s. In 2002 it was brought under the auspices of the diocese. A charismatic covenant community called People of Joy also began in the Phoenix diocese in the early 1970s. This group built a community center in Tempe in 1978 and amalgamated with three other similar communities in California. Known today as the City of the Lord, the community brings together 300 adults for prayer and instruction.

Spiritual Life Institute

Even before Pope Paul VI established the Diocese of Phoenix, opportunities for more mystical and contemplative experiences were available at the Spiritual Life Institute near Sedona. Discalced Carmelite, Father William McNamara, O.C.D., had received approval from

his religious superiors for an ecumenical form of contemplative life. McNamara settled in Sedona where he founded the Spiritual Life Institute and administered Holy Cross Chapel. The institute provided opportunities for prayer and spiritual enrichment. Various scholars such as Rabbi Abraham Heschel, Norman Cousins and Father Andrew Greeley came to speak at retreat-seminars.

» *The Chapel of the Holy Cross near Sedona, Arizona.*
Credit: Archives of the Diocese of Phoenix

In 1983 the institute purchased property in the pristine solitude of the Sangre de Cristo Mountains of Crestone, Colorado. The care of the chapel then reverted to the Diocese of Phoenix.

Public Issues: Abortion and Workers' Rights

McCarthy's position as bishop in the state capital put him in some of the swirling currents of Arizona's politics. McCarthy himself did not seem overtly interested in being a power broker, having more than enough to do managing the affairs of his rapidly growing diocese. But some public issues could not be ignored.

Like all American bishops, McCarthy decried the January 22, 1973, Roe v. Wade decision of the United States Supreme Court. "I am appalled," McCarthy thundered, "that the Supreme Court would so interpret our Constitution as to open the door for wholesale slaughter of the innocents." Annually, Phoenix Catholics organize a march on the state capitol to lament the tragic court decision. Active Catholic lobbying sought legislation to curtail and even end the practice of abortion in Arizona.

The treatment of farm workers also pulled McCarthy into the political fray. The efforts of California-based César Chávez to organize the workers had been a remote issue to the Midwestern McCarthy. Since 1962 Chávez had been active among the workers in California's Central Valley, hoping unionization would be a step to more humane working conditions and better wages. Landowners bridled against this interference and pushed back. Conflict over the unionization issue rocked California, and Chávez staged a dramatic march from Delano to Sacramento in 1966, accentuating his Catholic faith and his commitment to non-violent change. Many Catholic priests and even some bishops strongly supported him. Events in California brought a response from the national Bishops' Conference, which fervently backed the rights of the workers to organize and bargain collectively.

McCarthy became personally acquainted with this issue when he visited the migrant labor camps northwest of Phoenix in 1971. At that time he took a highly publicized tour of five of them, inspecting housing and workers' conditions first hand. In some camps he saw small shacks without heat, water or toilet facilities—in one of which lived a mother, father and ten children. As most American bishops in the West, McCarthy publicly supported Chávez's organization. However, strong opposition from growers, who had warm encouragement from Arizona's traditionally union-hostile environment, resulted in the passage of a tough anti-strike farm bill. Matters grew more

contentious when farm workers and some of their clerical advocates attempted to recall conservative Governor Jack Williams and used the bishop's name in support. McCarthy openly renounced the move and ordered that no Catholic parish take a public stand in the recall effort.

» *Father (later Monsignor) Edward Ryle was a strong voice for social justice in Arizona. Well-known in clergy and political circles, Ryle's strong advocacy of Catholic positions on public policy, like the abolition of the death penalty, won him respect and admiration from many.*
Credit: Archives of the Diocese of Phoenix

The plight of the farm workers and the fate of legislation pertaining to them highlighted the need for a serious lobbying arm for the bishops in Arizona's state capital. In 1973 the bishops of Phoenix, Tucson and Gallup created an advocacy group—the Arizona Catholic Conference. This body, headed for 19 years by Tucson priest (later Monsignor) Edward J. Ryle, who had extensive experience working with Catholic Charities for the Tucson and Phoenix dioceses, and later for the National Conference of Catholic Charities, provided steady leadership and guidance for

Catholic issues. Known as "God's lobbyist," Monsignor Ryle was a tireless advocate for the poor and oppressed until his retirement in 2003.

McCarthy and Hispanics

McCarthy's tenure in Phoenix took place during a rising tide of ethnic pride and even militance among the hundreds of thousands of Hispanics in the West. Fueled in part by some of the protest movements of the 1960s and inspired in no small measure by men like César Chávez, Hispanics began to make their voices heard in places where they had previously been powerless.

» *Bishop McCarthy worked hard to enter into the lives and culture of Hispanic Catholics.*
Credit: Archives of the Diocese of Phoenix

» *In 1971 Bishop McCarthy dedicated the Diocese of Phoenix to the patronage of Our Lady of Guadalupe.*
Credit: Archives of the Diocese of Phoenix

Hispanic Catholics in Phoenix and Flagstaff had long held the bitterness of their treatment at the hands of Anglo Catholics. Feelings still ran quite high in Phoenix, but the creation of Immaculate Heart of Mary Parish, run by the Claretians, had provided them with a gathering place and locus for their ethnic expressions of faith. Immaculate Heart became a magnet for Maricopa County Hispanic families who traveled from Glendale and Tolleson to attend Mass at the venerable church.

Even before McCarthy arrived, however, the Claretians had been planning to leave Immaculate Heart Parish. McCarthy knew this, but had kept silent until the details could be worked out. Nonetheless, news of the transfer was leaked to the secular press who erroneously suggested the Claretians were being "removed" from the parish rather than departing due to needs elsewhere. When the diocese let it be known that it might not be able to replace the popular Claretians with Mexican-American priests, the Hispanic community erupted. Some wanted to know why the people had not been consulted. Others wanted to know if this meant Immaculate Heart Parish would be anglicized. McCarthy tried to reassure a delegation who came to meet with him that he wanted the Mexican-American character of the parish to remain. On November 5, 1970, the Claretians said farewell, and McCarthy sent a team, consisting of Tucson's Father Jose Hurtado as pastor, and Fathers Andre Boulanger and Charles O'Hern as assistants. Hurtado picked up on the spirit of the community and led with vigor until his untimely death in a car accident in 1981.

Bishop McCarthy eased tensions somewhat when in December 1971 at a huge open-air Mass attended by 7,000, he dedicated the new diocese to the patronage of Our Lady of Guadalupe—a gesture that many Hispanics of the diocese found deeply moving. In 1974 McCarthy appointed a vicar for the Spanish-speaking and attempted to develop the then popular Communidades de Base, a local organizational technique for Hispanic Catholics.

Farewell

· · · · · · · · · ·

Toward the end of 1975 Bishop McCarthy hosted one more huge diocesan event—the Festival of Faith. Designed to commemorate the end of the 1975 Holy Year, the sixth anniversary of the diocese and the beginning of the bicentennial year of the United States, the Mass drew more than 12,000 Diocese of Phoenix Catholics to the Veterans Memorial Coliseum on the evening of December 3rd. Apostolic Delegate Jean Jadot presided, and the preacher was the silver-tongued Archbishop Fulton J. Sheen—known and loved by generation of Catholics. The 80-year-old Sheen's preaching still had the fine-tuned eloquence he had perfected on radio and television. In the end, he urged his listeners to make the daily Holy Hour to sustain their faith. "Faith gives us security, joy," he exclaimed. "When we believe the incredible, we can do the impossible."

Perhaps Sheen's words were echoing in McCarthy's ears when he received a call from Jadot asking him to become the coadjutor to Colman Carroll, the aging archbishop of Miami, Florida. With dutiful obedience and a heavy heart, he bade farewell to the diocese in the summer of 1976. At his successor's installation in March 1977, he offered a closing prayer, suggesting what he had learned and what he would miss as he transferred to the tropical climes of Florida: "In the days ahead," he prayed, "may there be a new birth of faith, prayer and love in this Church of Phoenix. From Bullhead City to Wickieup, from Kingman to Flagstaff, to Prescott to Gila Bend to Phoenix, may the enlivening Spirit call forth the flower of holiness like the cool irrigation waters turning the desert to color and splendor." Graciously then he stepped aside and a newer, younger man, 48-year-old James S. Rausch came forward to take the reins of the Phoenix Church.

» The Festival of Faith was a diocesan celebration of the American bicentennial and featured the dynamic preaching of Archbishop Fulton J. Sheen. Apostolic Delegate Jean Jadot presided at the Eucharist.
Credit: Archives of the Diocese of Phoenix

» Bishop McCarthy bid Arizona farewell with a heavy heart. He built on the foundation of Catholic life left by his predecessors and helped launch the new Diocese of Phoenix on a solid path.
Credit: Archives of the Diocese of Phoenix

CHAPTER 3

The Rausch Years
(1977-1981)

"Si se puede"

» *The formal installation of Bishop James Steven Rausch as the second bishop of Phoenix, March 22, 1977.*
Credit: Archives of the Diocese of Phoenix

The bells of St. Mary Church (later Basilica) began pealing at 4:45 p.m. on the afternoon of March 22, 1977. Four cardinals, 50 bishops and close to 400 priests and deacons processed into Symphony Hall led by 30 children representing the diverse ethnic groups of the Phoenix diocese. Inside, more than 2,000 Catholics waited to meet their new bishop. At the end of the procession, Bishop James S. Rausch appeared, and immediately the hall filled with cheers and spontaneous applause. With him were Apostolic Delegate, Archbishop Jean Jadot who had selected him for the position, and Archbishop Robert Sanchez of Santa Fe, metropolitan bishop of the province.

After Archbishop Sanchez ceremonially installed him as Bishop of Phoenix, Rausch acknowledged the solemnity of the moment and paid tribute to his predecessor, pledging to continue "what Archbishop McCarthy began so well among you and with you." McCarthy viewed the warm welcome that enveloped his successor and later at the formal banquet quipped, "I now know a little how a man feels when his first wife remarries."

The installation was the capstone of a series of events welcoming Rausch to Phoenix. The day before at Ss. Simon and Jude Cathedral, in the presence of the diocesan consultors and the rest of the priests of the diocese, the papal documents announcing his appointment had been proclaimed. The priests, hoping to make their new bishop feel welcome, presented him with a miter embedded with Arizona-mined malachite stones and a ring set in Kingman turquoise. Rausch received the congratulations of his presbyteral collaborators and assured some continuity with the former administration by reappointing Monsignor Bernard Gordon as Vicar General and Fathers Thomas O'Brien and William O'Brien as staff members. On the day after the installation, Rausch met with the deacons and sisters of the diocese, "They are the ones who make the ministry work," he said.

Rausch endeavored to keep pace with Phoenix's phenomenal growth. He would also labor to keep the local Church abreast of important national issues. "Ebullient, generous and kind," one fellow bishop described him. Rausch was also hard-charging, demanding and sometimes impatient ("a Type A personality" in the words of a cleric who revered him). His secretary, Heloise Blommel, remembered him in a later retrospective noting, "He was a fair person. He was hard on some people—the ones that needed it—but he was never unfair." Those years were, in the memory of some of the priests and laity, best summed up by the oft quoted Dickens' cliché, "the best of times and the worst of times."

Rausch: The Early Years

» Bishop Rausch as a young man.
Credit: Archives of the Diocese of Phoenix

James Steven Rausch was born September 4, 1928, in Albany, Minnesota, Stearns County, a small town in the central part of Minnesota and in the Diocese of St. Cloud. Rausch was one of six children (he had one sister, two halfbrothers and two halfsisters) of James and Anna Ohmann Rausch. The elder Rausch ran a country store in the rural community of Farming, Minnesota, and young James attended the local Seven Dolors Catholic elementary school and for a time Albany High School. Discerning a call to the priesthood, he entered a minor seminary run by the Crosier Fathers at Onamia in 1946. In 1952 he decided to become a diocesan priest, and Bishop Peter Bartholome sent him to St. John University in Collegeville. Bartholome ordained him on June 2, 1956, in St. Cloud's St. Mary Cathedral. Appointed first to the cathedral, he served his first year as an assistant pastor. He was then assigned to teach at Cathedral High from 1957 to 1967. While teaching high school religion and economics, he finished a master's degree in education at St. Thomas College (University) in St. Paul and did graduate work in economics at the University of Minnesota.

» Bishop Rausch spent his early years in the priesthood as a high school instructor.
Credit: Archives of the Diocese of Phoenix

Rausch looked back fondly on his teaching years; his constant contact with young people gave him a feel for the idealism and fears of those growing up in the 1950s and 1960s. He recalled later that his encounters with youth who were deeply conflicted about serving in Vietnam gave him some sympathy for President Jimmy Carter's pardon of draft evaders in the mid-1970s. A new coadjutor bishop, George Spelz, arrived in

St. Cloud in 1966 and identified Rausch as a bright star and urged Bishop Bartholome to send him to Rome for studies at the Gregorian University. Rausch dipped into the field of "pastoral sociology," specializing in the economics of development with a 1969 dissertation titled "The Case of Congress Against U.S. Foreign Assistance, 1964-1968." In 1970 he was invited to join the staff of the newly reorganized National Conference of Catholic Bishops and United States Catholic Conference (NCCB/USCC). Here he served as assistant to the general secretary, Bishop Joseph Bernardin.

The newly re-organized conference, formerly the National Catholic Welfare Conference (NCWC), consisted of two entities–the NCCB and the USCC. The former was the official organization of the American bishops and had 25 committees of changing membership (bishops and staffers) working on pastoral issues of the American Church, e.g., priestly vocations. The latter was a policy arm devoted to external concerns of the Church, e.g., education, labor, peace and justice. The USCC was the main channel of communication between the bishops and the American government and professionals in various fields, e.g., education, health care, etc. The general secretary who had a 150 member staff coordinated the work of both of these entities. Rausch's expertise in development and his deep concern for social justice were a natural fit for the direction of the USCC. In 1972 he succeeded Bernardin as general secretary and held the post until his transfer to Phoenix. Working in his office at the old NCWC building in Washington, D.C., Rausch produced reams of position papers, organized meetings of the bishops, oversaw the affairs of the growing conference and maintained links with key political figures whose support was necessary for the Church in America.

Rausch lobbied effectively for the initiatives and priorities established by the conference and worked well with several high ranking figures in the hierarchy, including Cardinal John Krol of Philadelphia. In 1973 Krol consecrated him an auxiliary bishop of St. Cloud. The elevation to episcopal orders was not intended for pastoral purposes–he did not confirm, ordain or perform other episcopal duties–but as a protocol wedge providing leverage in dealing with other bishops and people of rank in public life.

Rausch oversaw a number of projects during his years in Washington–including the coordination of the Call to Action Conference in Detroit in 1975. He also cultivated his interest in economic development, especially in Latin America, and worked closely with officials in developing nations such as Colombia, Ecuador, Venezuela and Peru. At his urging in the 1976 presidential election, the leading bishops of the conference held meetings with both candidates Jimmy Carter and Gerald Ford to discuss the issues of concern to American Catholics–a first for the episcopal conference. Rausch's personal political sympathies were no doubt for the Democrats since his friend Walter Mondale was on the Democratic ticket. In 1978 he was awarded the Pax Christi Award at his alma mater, St. John University in Collegeville.

The Bishops' Conference: A Source of U.S. Bishops

The conference was Rausch's work and passion. It was also his ticket to advancement in the hierarchy. Bishop McCarthy had advanced through the old network of chancery and canon law connections and patronage. By the time Rausch came on the scene, the process of determining new bishops had changed–in part as a result of Vatican II's emphasis on collegiality. Lay persons and priests were consulted about the skills required for vacant dioceses. A new apostolic delegate, Archbishop Jean Jadot, was determined to select men of proven intellectual and spiritual repute, but who also were aware of the demands of pastoral life. To assist in making selections, Jadot relied not only on the networks of bishops and "kingmakers" in the American hierarchy, but also upon the episcopal conference, which he believed had a good sense of the type of men American dioceses needed. As a result, many who worked in higher level jobs in the conference were selected to head dioceses of their own. This was most notably true of Bishop Joseph Bernardin who left the conference to lead the Archdiocese of Cincinnati and then of Chicago. It also happened to Bishop Thomas Kelly, O.P., who went to Louisville to become archbishop and to Monsignor Robert Lynch who became bishop of St. Petersburg. Rausch's years of service, his engagement with key issues of great concern during the 1970s, his cultivation of the patronage of men like Cardinal Krol all worked to his advantage. On January 25, 1977, Apostolic Delegate Jean Jadot announced Rausch's appointment to Phoenix.

Those who responded to the survey insisted on a man of vigor and good health–a holy, humble, prayerful administrator who spoke or who would learn Spanish and who would have a thirst for social justice and a love for the poor. Some respondents emphasized the unique conditions of the Diocese of Phoenix: the high number of elderly and retirees, the dramatic growth of the Spanish-speaking, and the rootlessness of many who were detached from family ties. Rausch came to Phoenix with the same initiative and enthusiasm he had brought to the conference, but he had a steep learning curve.

» Bishop Rausch, pictured here with Apostolic Delegate Jean Jadot and Vice President Walter F. Mondale. Mondale and Rausch, both Minnesotans, enjoyed a friendly relationship.

» Bishop Rausch was an energetic and forward-looking leader. His intelligence and capacity for hard work allowed him to move forward in the hierarchy.
Credit: Archives of the Diocese of Phoenix

"Prepare the Way"

When he was ordained a bishop in 1973, Rausch chose as his episcopal motto the heraldic words of John the Baptist, "Prepare the Way." Before Rausch arrived in the Valley of the Sun, local Catholics also tried to prepare the way by surveying 55 parishes. Parishioners were asked: What sort of diocese is this? What special problems will face the new bishop? What sort of man should he be?

Lacking extensive parish experience, he did not display the well-honed pastoral skills of priests who had spent years "in the trenches." Likewise, his somewhat forceful decision making– sometimes without consultation–rubbed some the wrong way, including priests who were more accustomed to the gentlemanly McCarthy who tried to hear a number of voices on subjects of concern. On the day of Rausch's installation, one of his episcopal friends cautioned Father Thomas O'Brien that Rausch's style might require some adjustment on the part of staff, priests and laity. O'Brien did indeed note this as he loyally served Rausch–and befriended him.

Rausch had trouble with some of his priests, who did not respond well to his ways of doing things. Some priests, however, loved Rausch, and he in turn relied on them for support and backing. Few people were neutral about him, and even those with differences respected him and his office.

» *Bishop Rausch's relationship with his priests had its bumpy spots, but most of the clergy respected and admired him.*
Credit: Archives of the Diocese of Phoenix

Taking Charge
....

Rausch arrived in Phoenix just as the Lenten season was in full swing. Although he still tended to affairs in Washington, D.C. (his replacement did not come on board until the summer), he did what he could to meet and greet various groups. Good Friday 1977 found him on the road. In the morning he visited developmentally disabled children, prisoners in the county jail, an alcoholic rehabilitation center and the Sacred Heart Home for the Aged. In the afternoon he presided at the liturgical service of the Passion of the Lord at Ss. Simon and Jude Cathedral. On that same day he issued a statement urging an end to capital punishment, "to extend the fullest possible protection to every human life," and arguing what would become known as the "seamless garment" approach to life issues. This outlook, advanced by

Cardinal Joseph Bernardin, was also a motif of his preaching on life issues. Speaking to a pro-life group one year, gathered for a Mass on the Feast of the Annunciation, he insisted that life at all stages of development from conception through old age and death had value and dignity. "If you exclude one bit of this, you are really not a pro-life person. We must be concerned about the total range of human rights if we are going to be human and totally pro-life."

Rausch was everywhere that first year. On his first Easter in Phoenix, he celebrated a sunrise Mass in the courtyard of St. Agnes Church for the diocesan sponsored New Day program for 60 divorced and separated Catholics. He appeared at all of the high school graduations. At one gathering of 700 youth, he reminisced about his days as a high school teacher. He no doubt made priests very happy by approving the first salary increase in seven years ($145 to $200 a month plus a raise in the auto allowance). Religious sisters also saw a boost in pay. As time went on he appointed his secretary, Thomas O'Brien, as a second Vicar General to the aging Monsignor Bernard Gordon. Gordon welcomed the appointment of the younger man, "The tremendous growth of the Church in Arizona makes it imperative for the bishop to enlarge his staff." Once Father Bernard Ronan took over as episcopal secretary, O'Brien moved to the pastorate of St. Catherine of Siena Parish in Phoenix. In February 1981 Rausch asked the pope to make O'Brien a monsignor—the very first one created in the Diocese of Phoenix.

A mini-controversy stirred in early 1978 when Rausch bought a home for himself in a residential neighborhood. The large ranch-style house had ample room for entertaining, a chapel and dining areas for guests. The move brought out picketers who protested the purchase—claiming the chancery building where McCarthy had lived should have been good enough for Bishop Rausch. McCarthy came to Rausch's defense, telling *ALIVE* and others he had intended to buy a home himself, but "they called me to Miami before I got around to it." He insisted his chancery quarters were only temporary and that in fact he had begun setting funds aside for a house.

1978: The Year of the Three Popes

» *Bishop Rausch greeting Pope John Paul II at the Vatican.*

» *Bishop Rausch with Pope Paul VI.*

The year 1978 was a transitional one for the Catholic Church–although many did not know what lay ahead. The diocese appropriately mourned the death of Paul VI on August 6, 1978, and many believed the election of his successor, Cardinal Albino Luciani, who took the name Pope John Paul I, was exactly what Father Andrew Greeley (a sometime Arizona resident) had called for, "a holy hopeful man who smiles." The "September Pope," John Paul I, foreswore the triple tiara his predecessors had worn and charmed the world with his brief papacy, which ended on September 28th when he was found dead in his bed. Another conclave brought the election of Cardinal Karol Wojtyla of Krakow, Poland, to the papacy. Taking the name John Paul II, he began a 26-year reign that transformed the papacy and the Church. Bishop Rausch was one of a number of American bishops who had actually met the future pontiff prior to his election when Rausch traveled to Poland in May 1976. The new pontificate would touch the lives of Arizona Catholics in many ways. As Pope John Paul II stood on the balcony of St. Peter's on that soft autumn night

of his election in October 1978, no one in Phoenix could have imagined that a mere nine years later he would be standing on the balcony of their own St. Mary Church with another bishop of Phoenix waving to thousands of the faithful.

Parochial Growth and Expansion in the Rausch Years

Arizona was growing rapidly between 1970 and 1980. The general state population surged by 53 percent, jumping from 1,775,399 to 2,718,215. Phoenix alone soared from 581,562 to 789,704 raising its rank from the 20th largest city in the United States to the ninth largest. Maricopa County, which held the largest portion of Arizona's population, broke the million mark, surging from 967,522 to 1.5 million. Mohave County more than doubled in size from 25,857 to 55,865 and Coconino went from 48,326 to 75,008 while Yavapai grew from 36,733 to 68,145. Each of these counties had their own dynamic and history. Their local economies represented the array of opportunities available in Arizona–manufacturing, tourism, water sports, gambling and even some farming and mining.

Since a number of the newcomers were Catholics—especially the growing number of Hispanics who came to Arizona for work and to reunite with families—parish growth and expansion were inevitable. Typical was St. John Vianney Parish founded in 1965 in Sedona. The parish straddled both Yavapai and Coconino counties. Sedona had become a tourist attraction and soon the church was hemmed in by commercial development. Purchasing a new site for a future church, with enough room for classrooms and meeting facilities, was a key priority for the parish's pastor, Father Eugene J. McCarthy. The demands of growth were great, and in his brief term Rausch gave approval for five parishes.

» Credit: Heritage Collection, Archives of the Diocese of Phoenix

Parish Development During the Rausch Years

Year established	Parish	City	County
1978	Holy Cross	Mesa	Maricopa
1978	St. Timothy	Mesa	Maricopa
1979	St. Joan of Arc	Phoenix	Maricopa
1979	Our Lady of Lourdes (Prince of Peace Church 1999)	Sun City West	Maricopa
1980	St. Patrick	Scottsdale	Maricopa

Raising Funds

Money for diocesan projects—including land acquisition and church building—continued to come from the annual Charity and Development Appeal. Key to the appeal's success were the generous lay people who contributed time, talent and treasure to it. Since 1971 the appeal had relied on the work of the popular cartoonist from Paradise Valley, Bil Keane, who drew the syndicated panel "Family Circus," which appeared in more than 1,000 American newspapers. Each year Keane would create a new panel to advertise the drive—sometimes portraying the local bishop knocking at the door of the cartoon family. Every year a prominent Arizonan was selected to lend his or her name to promote the drive. In 1982 Bil Keane headed up the appeal. In 1977 newspaper

» Cartoonist Bil Keane created this visual, picturing Bishop Rausch, for the Catholic Diocesan Appeal.
Credit: Archives of the Diocese of Phoenix

columnist and humorist Erma Bombeck chaired the appeal, which brought in more than $1.4 million.

Culiacán: "It's not Christian for certain unjust situations to continue. It is not just, it is not human."

Rausch as Agent of Social Justice

Rausch's work on the Bishops' Conference and his own academic study made him especially aware of the pressing social issues of the day. As he stepped into the Southwest, he found himself immersed in the farm-labor issue. Like most American bishops, he strongly supported the efforts of César Chávez and the United Farm Workers, which lobbied for coverage under the Fair Labor Standards Act. Many priests and religious supported and marched with Chávez during his contest with the growers in California's Central Valley.

Bishop Rausch's friendship with Chávez and his support for the movement became crystal clear in an August 1977 address to the convention of the United Farm Workers in Fresno, California. Filling in for Bishop Joseph Donnelly, the auxiliary bishop of Hartford and a staunch supporter of the United Farm Workers, Rausch addressed "my good friend...César Chávez" and thanked him for the honor of speaking to the group, declaring that although he was fairly new to the region and the issues at hand, it was his intention to be an advocate for the farm workers whom he believed were being denied their right to organize and bargain collectively. "This right is so basic and so fundamental from the point of view of Catholic social teaching that Church leaders are bound in conscience to stand side by side, through thick and thin with those who are being denied an opportunity to exercise this right.... César Chávez was correct. Si se puede. It can be done."

Rausch no doubt received the same complaints McCarthy had when he too had advocated for better conditions for workers. However, here Rausch's tough-minded personality steeled him. He quoted the words of Pope John Paul II who on his first trip as pope to nearby Mexico had spoken of the plight of landless peasants and workers in

Phoenix: Ongoing Liturgical Renewal

One of Bishop Rausch's first tasks was to set up an Office of Worship under the direction of Sister Anthony Poerio. The Chicago Heights native was a sister of the American branch of the Institute of the Blessed Virgin Mary and had come to Phoenix in 1971. (Another group of Irish I.B.V.M. sisters was at the cathedral, however, the two groups have amalgamated in recent years.) The new office was intended to work with others to coordinate liturgical life through educational programs, workshops and major diocesan liturgical celebrations.

» *Sister Anthony Poerio, pictured here with Blessed Teresa, was director of the diocesan Office of Worship.*
Credit: *Archives of the Diocese of Phoenix*

Other factors came together to make Phoenix an important liturgical center for the American Southwest. In 1972 North American Liturgy Resources (NALR), a major liturgical music house, located in Phoenix–increasing the region's popularity as a hub for aspiring musicians. NALR recorded and promoted the works of the St. Louis Jesuits and the monks of Weston Priory.

The popular hymn book, *Glory and Praise* was put out by NALR. Until the Oregon Catholic Press purchased it in 1994, NALR was a major force in Church music in the United States.

Recently-ordained Father (later Monsignor) Dale Fushek joined Sister Poerio in 1981 and began to take the demanding summer sessions in liturgy offered at the University of Notre Dame. Workshops and liturgical meetings, especially in the cold winter months, found Phoenix welcoming young musicians like the St. Louis Jesuits and famed international liturgical composers such as Father Lucien Deiss, C.S.Sp. Phoenix composer Rory Cooney found local choirs to help highlight his music, while the youthful looking Dameans–Gary Ault, Darryl Ducote, Buddy Ceasar and Mike Balhoff–performed at a Youth Liturgy Day in early 1981. Sister Poerio even caught up with an early composer, Ray Repp, the voice behind older liturgical favorites like *Allelu, I Am the Resurrection* and *Here We Are*, who lamented the state of Church music in 1980, "Ten years ago, there seemed to be more life and vibrancy."

» *Bishop Rausch encouraged an active liturgical life for diocesan Catholics.*
Credit: Archives of the Diocese of Phoenix

The Rite of Christian Initiation of Adults

Among the key liturgical and catechetical changes to occur during the Rausch years was the restoration of the Catechumenate and the revised Rite of Christian Initiation for Adults (RCIA). Sister Poerio worked closely with Deacon John Meyer, director of catechetics, to introduce the RCIA to Phoenix. The leading expert in the field, Dr. Christiane Brusselmans, held a "Beginnings and Beyond" workshop and assured Phoenix Catholics, "It was the way the early Church initiated newcomers, deepened their faith and took them on the spiritual journey to the sacraments of initiation." Laying out the stages from initial inquiry to the Catechumenate through Election and Initiation, and concluding with Mystagogia, Brusselmans accurately predicted that the widespread implementation of this ancient practice would bring about the renewal of parishes. Rausch strongly backed the RCIA. Poerio recalled that repeat RCIA workshops always filled to overflowing. The numbers showing up for the annual Rite of Election at Ss. Simon and Jude Cathedral were small at first, but the program continued to grow even after Rausch's death. By 2003 more than 2,000 catechumens and candidates were entering into full membership at Easter.

Ordained Ministry in Phoenix

Increasing the number of seminarians had been an early priority for Bishop Rausch with many of the young men coming from outside of Arizona. Rausch appointed Father John Cunningham as vocation director of the diocese in 1977. In 1980 the diocese had 37 seminarians–15 in college and 22 in theology. Twelve of them had families out of state and their ages ranged from 19 to 58. Some came with extensive educations, two were converts and one pair was a father and son. Phoenix seminarians continued to attend seminaries around the country: St. Meinrad Seminary in Indiana, St. John Seminary in Camarillo, St. Thomas Seminary in Denver and the

Theological College of The Catholic University of America.

Religious order priests continued to provide pastoral service to the people of the Phoenix diocese. Representative groups included the Franciscans, Dominicans, Jesuits, Claretians and Carmelites, but also Holy Cross Fathers, the Crosiers, the Salvatorians and the Vincentians. In 1980, eleven years after the founding of the diocese, religious orders of men operated 19 of the 79 parishes in the diocese. They also served as hospital chaplains and high school instructors.

» *Bishop Rausch with priests and transitional deacons serving in the Diocese of Phoenix.*
Credit: Archives of the Diocese of Phoenix

Rausch also received a new priest from an unexpected source–the Episcopal Church. When the Vatican allowed the welcoming of former Episcopal clergy into the Church and granted them ordination even though they were married, Bishop Rausch accepted Father Douglas Lorig of St. Andrew's Episcopal Church in Nogales. Lorig was married with four children. On July 31, 1980, in the Diocesan Center's Cenacle Chapel, Rausch ordained Lorig to the transitional diaconate. Later that same year Bishop Rausch ordained Lorig to the priesthood.

The Permanent Diaconate

The growth of the permanent diaconate continued apace, but changes in its leadership took place as well. Father William O'Brien stepped down as head of the formation program, and for a time Father Bernard Ronan directed it. When Ronan departed the post, the deacons were given charge of their formation. Rausch ordained groups of permanent deacons each year of his episcopate–19 in all.

As noted earlier, the uneven reception of the deacons by the clergy required some adjustments on all sides, and better instruction and training programs. Bishop Rausch himself wanted time to study the program. He temporarily suspended it with an eye to fashioning a better and strong ministry.

Study Leading to Action: Marriage and Youth Ministry

Although he could at times be "overly" decisive, Bishop Rausch came to see the value of studying and consulting with a wide range of people. In a technique that would be used by his successor, Rausch formed task forces and ad hoc committees to analyze problems and make recommendations. Marriage policy, youth programs and the possible formation of a new northern diocese were among the issues he approached in this way.

Worldwide Marriage Encounter, a marriage enrichment program founded in Spain, was warmly received in the diocese. In early 1978 a national meeting was held at St. Agnes Parish, hosted by the Carmelites and attracting more than 200 representatives, including 25 priests from the western states. The Marriage Encounter program worked well with essentially stable and happy couples, but marital breakups were a fact of life among Phoenix Catholics. Much could be done to counsel troubled marriages through Catholic Charities and the Franciscan Renewal Center, but the key was helping young couples understand the sacrament. Bishop Rausch formed a Marriage Task Force composed of priests and lay people to examine the reasons for divorce and what could be done to improve long-term prospects for stable marriages. The result was the formulation of a uniform diocesan marriage policy, mandating a six-month preparation period for serious reflection and an opportunity for in-depth sacramental preparation. It also included some one-on-one counseling and direction from the priest or deacon presiding at the wedding. Couples were to take a helpful pre-marital inventory, indicating maturity and levels of communication about critical areas such as children, finances, personal interests, sexuality and religion. Written up in a small brochure entitled "A Wedding is A Day: A Marriage is for All the Days of Your Life" and handed out through the parishes, the norms went into effect July 1, 1979. It was one of the first such policies in the United States Catholic Church.

» *Marriage Encounter, a program based in Spain, was popular in the Diocese of Phoenix and encouraged stronger Catholic marriages.*
Credit: Archives of the Diocese of Phoenix

The policy hit some pockets of resistance, but—with refinements—it became an accepted and even welcomed part of the pastoral practices of the diocese. One year after its implementation, *ALIVE* conducted a survey of a number of people who worked with the policy and some couples who experienced it. Most were positive in their assessment—and some, like Franciscan friar Anthony Garibaldi who worked with many married couples at St. Mary's, advised that the waiting period be as long as a year. "Marriage is a lifelong sacrament," he remarked, "and requires a lot of preparation."

Likewise Rausch directed a study of youth issues with a group of young priests, urging diocesan assistance in setting up parish youth programs. Youth-oriented ministries flourished, and the diocese was a national leader in Youth Ministry for a number of years.

In the 1970s the Franciscan Renewal Center began to host a series of teen and young adult Masses, replete with lively music, energetic and engaged preaching, and even multimedia presentations with films from the Paulists and others. Franciscan friar Barry Brunsman, who helped plan the events with other staff, recalled they were consistently packed with young people.

A Northern Arizona Diocese?

An ongoing challenge was the integration of the northern counties of the diocese into a greater sense of belonging to the Church of Phoenix. Rausch at one point resurrected a plan to create a northern diocese with Flagstaff as its headquarters. Encouragement to study this had come from Archbishop Jadot who pressed the question with the two Arizona bishops, Rausch and Green, and Bishop Jerome Hastrich of Gallup. Rausch presented the idea first to his consultors and the priests of the area—and then formed an ad hoc committee to discuss the question. This issue was not resolved before he died.

The cumulative effect of these consultative efforts was perhaps the clearest sign that James Rausch was truly settling into his position, hearing and understanding his priests better and seeing the uniqueness of Catholicism in the Southwest. His personality would never change, but his ability to lead and inspire seemed to be on the rise.

» Blessed Teresa of Calcutta.

The Curtain Falls

. . . .

The years had been full of action—preaching, writing, serving on committees of the Bishops' Conference and overseeing the ongoing growth of a dynamic Southwestern diocese. Some of Rausch's days focused on dealing with clergy personnel issues. There were nettlesome issues, but to some of his advisors, like Monsignor Thomas O'Brien, it appeared Rausch was finally hitting his stride as a diocesan bishop.

In mid-1981 Rausch decided to have a quiet remembrance of his 25th anniversary of priestly ordination. The jubilee would not be a big celebration, he informed his staff, but he invited retired Milwaukee Archbishop William E. Cousins to give a day of recollection for priests at Ss. Simon and Jude Cathedral on May 12. At that event, the priests gave their bishop a new set of vestments. On May 17 Rausch handed out 94 catechist and youth minister certifications.

The next day, May 18 he and Dominican priest and physician John Flannery had agreed to go for a drive to Sedona, have lunch and walk around Tlaquepaque, a popular tourist attraction. Rausch had complained earlier in the day of pains, which he attributed to indigestion. Stopping for a moment at Smitty's pharmacy near Bell Road and the Black Canyon Freeway, Rausch ran into the store to purchase antacid pills and collapsed on to the floor. An off-duty firefighter gave Rausch mouth-to-mouth and cardiopulmonary resuscitation for about 20 minutes until an ambulance arrived. Forty-six minutes later, Phoenix's second bishop was declared dead at the age of 52, just a couple of weeks short of his actual ordination anniversary.

The diocesan consultors quickly met and elected Monsignor Thomas O'Brien to temporarily head the See as plans were made for the first episcopal funeral Phoenix would have. Rausch's old friend, Archbishop John Roach of Minneapolis-St. Paul preached to the packed crowd in the cathedral, and Bishop Rausch was laid to rest in St. Francis Cemetery. A marker of African granite over his resting place reads: "Eternal Father, bless our Bishop James, loyal servant of your Church who dedicated himself to prepare the way." He had prepared the way for Thomas O'Brien.

» Bishop Rausch's years in Phoenix were brief, but he made a strong impression on all who met and worked with him.
Credit: Archives of the Diocese of Phoenix

CHAPTER 4

The O'Brien Years (1981-2003)

"We belong to one another in a way with the Spirit as its origin"

» *Retired Bishop William Gomes is pictured here turning over a ceremonial spade of earth for St. Joan of Arc Parish.*
Credit: Archives of the Diocese of Phoenix

The care of the vacant diocese was entrusted to the steady hand of Monsignor Thomas O'Brien. O'Brien kept busy—enlisting the services of Santa Fe Archbishop Robert Sanchez who performed ordinations and confirmations during the interregnum. He was helped by two retired bishops, Ernest Primeau of New Hampshire and William G. Gomes of Poona, India, who made Arizona their home. Primeau, a priest of the Archdiocese of Chicago, had worked in Rome for many years as the head of Chicago House, a students residence for priests and seminarians from his archdiocese. A well-beloved Roman insider, Primeau was appointed Bishop of Manchester, New Hampshire, in 1959 and retired in 1974. Gomes, a priest of the Archdiocese of Bombay, had been consecrated a bishop by Pope John XXIII and served in the Diocese of Poona from 1967-1976. He assisted the Indian Bishops' Conference in the area of ecumenical affairs. In 1977 he came to the United States and worked in Manchester until his retirement in 1981. He then took up residence with a family in Scottsdale. A third retired prelate also lived in the Diocese of Phoenix, Archbishop Paul C. Marcinkus, who had served many years in the Vatican and in 1990 returned to the United States and eventually came to Arizona where he performed pastoral services.

» *A youthful Father Thomas O'Brien (c. 1963).*
Credit: Archives of the Diocese of Phoenix

O'Brien went forward with the hiring of a Diocesan Superintendent of Elementary Education, Dominican Brother Frederick Narberes. He also presided at a Catholic-Episcopalian dialogue gathered around the Diocesan Center's famous round table, calling it "the most important meeting ever held in this room since the Diocesan Center opened." But even as he kept a steady hand on the tiller, speculation and hopes for Bishop Rausch's successor began to surface. O'Brien advised that the waiting time be used for healing: "We need this time as a kind of mourning period, just to allow the diocese time for human response to its loss."

Just before Thanksgiving on November 25, 1981, Pope John Paul II selected the 46-year-old Thomas Joseph O'Brien to be Phoenix's third bishop. Monsignor Thomas O'Brien appeared to be the perfect choice—young, a capable administrator and attuned to the needs of the local Church. No one would have to break in the long-serving cleric. He understood the distinct culture of the Southwest and how to most effectively proclaim the Gospel in this part of the Vineyard of the Lord.

» *Bishop Thomas J. O'Brien,*
third bishop of Phoenix.
Credit: Archives of the Diocese of Phoenix

Bishop O'Brien was born in Indianapolis on November 29, 1935, to Frank and Mary Ellen (O'Donnell) O'Brien. He attended St. Catherine of Siena grade school in Indianapolis. Of his decision to become a priest, made by the time he was in fifth grade, he declared, "That's all I ever wanted to be. There wasn't another alternative." His parents were active in the Church, and his father sang for 42 years in the Schola Cantorum of the cathedral. Priests frequented the O'Brien home for meals and sing-a-longs with the musical family. Young Thomas inherited this love of music and was a good soloist. In 1949 he entered

St. Meinrad Seminary, a Benedictine monastery in southern Indiana that included a high school, college and major seminary. O'Brien mingled with students from a number of Midwestern dioceses and candidates for the monastic priesthood of the abbey. His family moved to Scottsdale, and young Thomas affiliated with the Diocese of Tucson. His father never lived to see him ordained a priest, but watched as his son assisted as deacon at a Christmas Mass in 1960.

Archbishop Paul C. Schulte ordained O'Brien at St. Meinrad Seminary on May 7, 1961. He celebrated his first Mass at Our Lady of Perpetual Help in Scottsdale. Monsignor Robert Donohoe, the Dean of Maricopa County preached at his first Mass. Bishop Green assigned him to Immaculate Conception Parish in Douglas. The handsome and personable young priest was so moved by the Hispanic parishioners there that he resolved to teach himself Spanish. The friendships and memories of Douglas remained with him throughout his life, and his command of Spanish served him well. Later he was assigned to St. Theresa's and St. Gregory's in Phoenix. At the latter, he frequently met Bishop Green who stayed at the rectory on his trips to Phoenix. The call from Bishop McCarthy to serve as his secretary and de-facto chancellor cut short O'Brien's time as an assistant pastor. Rausch, too, kept him close and as noted earlier appointed him Vicar General. O'Brien was kindhearted, totally devoted to the Church, discreet and optimistic but not naive. Priests liked and trusted him. He had good leadership instincts, and those who later surrounded him were deeply devoted and loyal to him.

When the Apostolic Delegate, Archbishop Pio Laghi, phoned him with the news of his appointment as bishop, O'Brien replied, "Oh no. No, I don't think so." The delegate gently chided, "I think you should say, yes." Whatever his private misgivings, O'Brien's public reaction to the appointment elicited words of humble gratitude, "I am very grateful for the confidence the Church has placed in me in allowing me to serve as shepherd of this beloved Diocese of Phoenix and I respond with all my heart."

Father John Doran, the editor of *ALIVE*, spoke to the stability O'Brien's appointment promised, "Our diocese is welcoming its third bishop in 12 short years. The time which Archbishop McCarthy and Bishop Rausch spent among us was all too short. May the time Bishop Thomas O'Brien spends be much longer. His youth and vigor promise this."

He chose as his episcopal motto "To Build Up the Body of Christ"–a motif he put into action during his years of service. The very day he received news of his appointment, he traveled to Immaculate Heart Parish to preside at the funeral of its pastor, Father Jose Hurtado–a much loved and outspoken proponent of social justice who advocated strongly for the Hispanic people. Keeping the growing Hispanic community connected to the larger Church and integrating their gifts of culture and faith into the Catholic mix was an important priority for O'Brien.

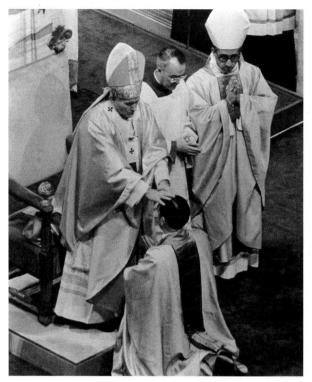

» *Pope John Paul II imposes hands on Bishop O'Brien (January 6, 1982).*
Credit: Archives of the Diocese of Phoenix

Ordination in Rome

To his great surprise, O'Brien learned that Pope John Paul II wished to personally confer episcopal orders on him on the Feast of the Epiphany, January 6, 1982, at St. Peter Basilica in Rome. Pope John Paul II had chosen the day to ordain 30 bishops from around the world as a sign of the universality of the faith, symbolized by the Three Magi. More than 200 Arizona Catholics, clergy and even Archbishop McCarthy, joined him in the Eternal City for the historic event.

The new bishop returned to Phoenix for his formal installation on January 18, 1982, by Apostolic Delegate Pio Laghi. He was officially welcomed at a huge celebration of more than 14,000 people at the Arizona State University Activity Center. Receiving the crozier from Santa Fe Archbishop Robert Sanchez, O'Brien spoke to the people he was now to shepherd: "Tonight, you and I take on a special relationship. We belong to one another in a way with the Spirit as its origin.... What a privilege is mine now to serve you as your bishop."

Creating a New Team

O'Brien moved to fill important staff positions. He appointed Father James E. McFadden as chancellor. McFadden, the founding pastor of St. Louis the King in Glendale, was a native of Douglas, Arizona, and ordained in 1940. Respected by priests and laity, McFadden was created a monsignor in 1987. He died in 1990, and from 1989 to 1992 Father Timothy Davern was chancellor. Ms. Marge Injasoulian then briefly held the position (1992-1993) until Sister of Charity Mary Ann Winters was appointed (1993-2004).

Bishop O'Brien drew into his inner circle Father (later Monsignor) Richard Moyer. Moyer had been ordained in 1964, and between 1969 and 1971 attended The Catholic University where he was sent for advanced studies in social work. As noted earlier, Moyer won the trust of Bishop McCarthy who appointed him to head Catholic Charities in Phoenix. In 1975 Moyer became pastor of St. Jerome Parish in Phoenix; in 1982 O'Brien appointed him as a second Vicar General, and in 1984 vicar for northern Arizona. In 1988 Moyer served briefly as pastor of the cathedral, and in 1990 O'Brien appointed him chief financial officer. O'Brien appointed Father Dale Fushek as second Vicar General in 2000. In December 2001 Fushek was elevated, at O'Brien's request, to the rank of monsignor. Father Timothy Davern, a native of Arizona, served as O'Brien's vice chancellor, chancellor and judicial vicar. Davern had entered St. Meinrad Seminary after graduating from the University of Notre Dame. In 1983 Father Davern was sent to The Catholic University and studied canon law.

Primavera and Vision 2000

Planning processes and activities were a top priority in many dioceses in the 1980s. Bishop McCarthy had attempted to establish development goals in the 1970s, but Bishop Rausch did not have procedures in place at the time of his death to keep things going. In consultation with his advisors, the Priest Senate and others, O'Brien sought the input of at least 5,000 people in the diocese through a program given the hopeful name of Primavera (Springtime). Set to stretch from early 1985 to May 1986, its goal was simple: "to help this young diocese to understand where it has been, where it is now, and where it is going."

The process of consultation, O'Brien recalled, was "tedious" and time consuming. A steering committee, chaired by Carmelite Father Fred Tillotson, organized groups and began the process. Area meetings were organized and opportunities were given to voice concerns and propose programs that fit into the categories of the ministries of word, worship and service. Small groups assigned priorities to the top six programs, and the larger assembly of those gathered voted on them. A computer at the Kino Institute analyzed the ballots, and a questionnaire was formulated to be sent to 19,000 members of the diocese. A strategic planning committee reviewed the major areas of concern and the results of the questionnaire. The bishop and his staff forged the final recommendations. At a Pentecost Sunday convocation, May 18, 1986, Bishop

O'Brien announced eight priorities: community worship, Church leadership, unity of the Church, evangelization and faith development, social justice, special needs of the Hispanic people, care for the aged and communications. Specific strategies were laid out to make sure these priorities were implemented, including the appointment of Father Tillotson as executive assistant for Pastoral Policy and Planning.

» *Father Fred Tillotson, O.Carm., helped facilitate the Primavera sessions and was responsible for its implementation.*
Credit: Archives of the Diocese of Phoenix

In 1994 Bishop O'Brien undertook another consultation to establish an updated set of goals, propelling the diocese to 2000. Vision 2000 created five long-range objectives: cultural diversity, leadership development, equitable distribution of resources, the Church as an active force in society, and strengthening and nurturing the family. It also hammered out an impressive mission statement. O'Brien used these as guidelines to direct diocesan priorities for the remainder of his tenure as bishop.

» *This printed card text of the diocesan mission statement (1994) was intended to be carried by people.*
Credit: Archives of the Diocese of Phoenix

Mission Statement of the Diocese of Phoenix as We Build, Bless and Become the Body of Christ

Because of our Baptism, the Holy Spirit calls us, the people of The Roman Catholic Church of Phoenix, to conversion as we come together to be nourished in the Eucharist, proclaim the Good News of Jesus Christ, and serve the needs of all God's people.

To be faithful to our baptismal call and our tradition, we accept the challenge to:
• build a prayerful community which welcomes and celebrates our cultural diversity;
• reach out actively and invite all, without prejudice, to experience the love and forgiveness of Jesus Christ;
• and distribute justly our resources with the poor and share with each other the gifts God has given to us.
December 2, 1994

Financial Affairs

Bishop Rausch had created a diocesan finance council. Bishop O'Brien added new members– including the trusted Moyer–and relied on them heavily. One of the more unsettling moments early in his tenure was when Bishop O'Brien learned the diocese was deeply (but not insurmountably) in debt. The diocese had loaned large sums of money to parishes to build churches. These funds had been borrowed from banks at extremely high rates of interest, some loans as high as 21 percent. Church building and expansion were essential to meet the needs of the growing number of Catholics, especially in Maricopa County, so the debt, though serious, was understandable.

With help from Church sources, O'Brien refinanced the debt. Generous grants to rural and outlying areas of the diocese by the Catholic Church Extension Society, the American Board of Catholic Missions, and the Commission for Catholic Work Among the Colored People and Indians (today known as the Black and Indian Mission Office) also eased the burden. These benefactions alone, O'Brien reported in 1987, came in at nearly $1.5 million. Fortunately, the increasing cash flow from the CDA helped with day-to-day operations–the collection had grown steadily from its original $845,231 in 1970 to more than $9.6 million in 2002. With good planning and the help of low-interest loans, the bishop was able to pay off the debt by 1987. In 1992 the diocese was again compelled to do a bit of belt-tightening. Sixteen Diocesan Center employees were laid off, and there was a modest increase in parish assessments to curtail a projected $1.9 million deficit. Parishes with money in the diocesan central account were asked to donate the interest on their savings to help the diocese through the financial crunch.

» *Bil Keane produced this cartoon for the Catholic Diocesan Appeal, picturing Bishop O'Brien and former Notre Dame and Green Bay Packers' coach Dan Devine.*
Credit: Archives of the Diocese of Phoenix

When Monsignor Moyer became Chief Financial Officer in 1990, he changed the formula for lending money for church construction. At a meeting at St. Mary's in early 1991, the details were finalized: henceforth, parishes would be required to have 35 percent of the total needed for construction in the bank and 35 percent in three-year pledges. The diocese would then loan the remaining 30 percent. One of the strengths of this plan was that it usually took three years to draw up plans and complete construction, so the resulting mortgage was generally only 30 percent of the total cost.

Bishop O'Brien created an endowment fund, the Catholic Community Foundation, in 1983 with James D. Bruner, a local bank executive, as its first chairman of the board. Bruner oversaw the fund and encouraged estate donations for it. Mary Anne McKone helped Bishop O'Brien establish a black tie affair, the Crozier Dinner, which raised funds and publicized the foundation and its goals. By 1990 the fund had $2 million and was handing out grants to schools, radio and television programs, and for religious and adult education programs.

A New Catholic Newspaper

The declining fortunes of *ALIVE* were an issue the new bishop felt the need to address. The publication had been sustained by subsidies and advertisements. Its circulation of fewer than 6,000 in a diocese of nearly 275,000 registered Catholics suggested it was no longer a viable medium of communication for the diocese. When its editor, Father John Doran, retired in November 1982, Bishop O'Brien asked Monsignor Donohoe to find a new communications director. The bishop also sought advice on a better means of communication for the diocese. The communications committee recommended discontinuing *ALIVE* in favor of a bi-monthly newspaper.

A meeting of the priests on October 14, 1983, at St. Theresa Parish hall provided the opportunity to discuss the proposal to start the bi-monthly paper. The priests agreed with the mission of the new journal and were willing to have parishes and advertising cover its budget. The final issue of *ALIVE* appeared in January 1984 and carried an article by recently-hired communications director Marge Injasoulian announcing a more comprehensive and developed approach–a diocesan tabloid, "which would be mailed free, twice a month to every registered Catholic household in the diocese." A naming contest was held, and Connie Hansen of Ss. Simon and Jude Cathedral submitted the winning entry: *The Catholic Sun*.

» *Chris Gunty was the first editor of The Catholic Sun.*
Credit: Archives of the Diocese of Phoenix

Sixty people applied for the position of managing editor, and a committee picked Christopher Gunty a veteran of *The Chicago Catholic*, the official paper of the Archdiocese of Chicago. Gunty began his tenure on January 21, 1985, and started hiring staff and coordinating the release of the first edition, which arrived in Phoenix homes in early April 1985.

Parish Expansion

Financial constraints notwithstanding, O'Brien had to establish new parishes. Population statistics tell it all. The city of Phoenix grew from 789,704 in 1980 to 983,403 in 1990. These numbers continued to swell, eventually making Phoenix the sixth most populous city in America. Between 1980 and 1990, the growth of the counties of the diocese was simply phenomenal. Maricopa County soared from 1.5 million to 2.1 million. Coconino grew from 75,008 to 96,591, Mohave from 55,865 to 93,497 and Yavapai from 68,145 to 107,714. By 2000 there were more than 3 million people in Maricopa County.

» *Marge Injasoulian took charge of upgrading and improving Catholic communications during Bishop O'Brien's years.*
Credit: Archives of the Diocese of Phoenix

A development committee under Father (later Monsignor) John McMahon made recommendations for property purchases and tentative parish boundaries. Parish and school growth continued at a rapid clip. In 1985 alone five new parishes were created. At the same time, the vocation shortage began to hit–and the prospect of fewer and fewer priests had an impact on the nature of church building. The trend in Phoenix as in other dioceses was to build larger churches, thereby reducing the need to hold as many Masses.

» Msgr. John J. McMahon celebrating his fortieth anniversary of ordination. Bishop O'Brien on his right.
Credit: Archives of the Diocese of Phoenix

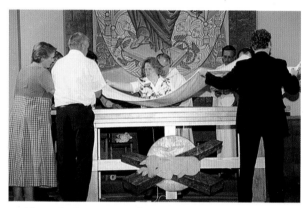

» Altar dedication at St. Anne Parish in Gilbert.
Credit: Archives of the Diocese of Phoenix

Parish Development During the O'Brien Years

Year established	Parish	City	County
1982	St. James	Glendale	Maricopa
1984	St. Germaine	Prescott Valley	Yavapai
1985	St. Andrew the Apostle	Chandler	Maricopa
1985	St. Bridget	Mesa	Maricopa
1985	Corpus Christi	Phoenix	Maricopa
1985	St. Benedict	Phoenix	Maricopa
1985	St. Luke	Phoenix	Maricopa
1988	St. Steven	Sun Lakes	Maricopa
1994	St. Bernard of Clairvaux	Scottsdale	Maricopa
1995	St. Bernadette	Scottsdale	Maricopa
1997	San Francisco de Asís*	Flagstaff	Coconino
1997	St. Thomas More	Glendale	Maricopa
2000	St. Clare of Assisi	Surprise	Maricopa
2002	St. Gabriel the Archangel	Cave Creek	Maricopa
2002	St. Mary Magdalene	Gilbert	Maricopa

* San Francisco de Asís Parish was formed as the result of the parish consolidation in Flagstaff (i.e., Nativity of the Blessed Virgin Mary, Our Lady of Guadalupe, St. Pius X and the Holy Trinity Catholic Newman Center).

Care for the Poor and Marginalized: André House and Maggie's Place

Concerns for the homeless and working poor of the valley led to the foundation of André House by two Congregation of the Holy Cross priests, Fathers Michael Baxter and John Fitzgerald, in 1984. Co-founder Father John Fitzgerald remembers leaving the University of Notre Dame and heading west to "do something radical." Traveling through the country and visiting various Catholic social service programs in the spring of 1984, his eyes opened to the rapidly growing number of homeless. Combining elements of the Catholic Worker Movement with the Congregation of the Holy Cross charism, the organization daily feeds and provides other basic services, e.g., hot showers and clothing, for those living on the streets, in shelters and in low-cost housing. Located in the heart of Phoenix's Capital Mall District, André House was providing nearly 600 hot meals a day by 2004.

» *The André House, an apostolate of the Holy Cross Community, serves the needs of the poor.*
Credit: Archives of the Diocese of Phoenix

Five young women, all sharing a common interest in social justice and a desire to establish a "house of hospitality" in the Catholic Worker tradition, founded Maggie's Place in 2000. This home for pregnant women and young mothers began in a 1926 bungalow in downtown Phoenix that volunteers spent nine months gutting and restoring. Maggie's Place, later called The Magdalene House, welcomed its first mothers on Mother's Day, May 13, 2000, with an outdoor Mass and block party. The program's success led to the building of a backyard cottage–providing space for a classroom/recreational room, chapel and storage–named Mahkenzie Hall, in remembrance of the second child of Maggie's Place to die in early infancy. In June 2001 Maggie's Place purchased the apartment complex next door and began renovations for La Casa de la Madre, which opened in 2002 as "step-two" housing. In January 2005 Maggie's Place opened a home in Tempe, The Elizabeth House, and the following January renovation began on a building in Glendale for The Michael House. In April 2006 the nonprofit organization purchased another building near their original site, which they named The Fiat House, to accommodate their administrative needs and for outreach to alumnae. Maggie's Place has become a model program and now includes its first out-of-state community, The Mary House, located in northern Idaho.

Cultivating Diversity in the Diocese

Primavera's priority of evangelization and faith development moved forward under Bishop O'Brien. African-American Catholics in Phoenix were a small group, but had early on been the concern of church workers like Father Emmett McLoughlin in south Phoenix. In 1989 Bishop O'Brien appointed the Committee of Black Catholic Concerns, chaired by Octavia Kennedy, to advise him on African-American needs. One important committee member was Constance "Connie" Beachem who moved to Phoenix in 1946. A daily communicant at Resurrection Parish, she was active in Catholic Social Services. The committee became the Office of Black Catholic Ministry in 1992 and organized a Unity Mass in 1995, which was held every third Sunday at St. Pius X Mission. Using Gospel-style music, the Mass was intended to gather black Catholics who lived in various parts of the city to raise awareness of their heritage and promote Catholicism. In 2000 Bishop O'Brien appointed Marie Chavis Ausberry as the first full-time director of Black Catholic ministry. She was followed by Jacquelin Rideau. A diocesan census revealed there were 3,400 African-American Catholic families registered in the diocese. In January 2005 Isaiah "Kit" Marshall took over as head of this diocesan office.

» *The Unity Mass at St. Pius X highlightes African-American music and liturgical style.*

Among the areas of expansion in the 1990s was a modest increase in the number of ethnic parishes. In 1992 Bishop O'Brien reported to the Vatican "a large in-migration of Asians," which had grown to almost 45,000. Arrivals from Vietnam in the 1970s, many of them Catholic, began the process of creating a Vietnamese Catholic parish. Like the Hispanics, the Vietnamese Catholic community first came together in the basement of St. Mary Basilica, ministered to by a Canadian priest who had spent many years in Vietnam. As the community grew, so did the need for more space, and it began a period of migration from one parish to another—moving from St. Mary's to St. Matthew's where they remained until 1985, and then on to St. Gregory's and Sacred Heart. A seven member pastoral community, elected by the Vietnamese community in 1992, worked with diocesan and parish officials and decided to move to Most Holy Trinity Parish. On February 6, 1994, they celebrated their first Mass there.

In 2007 the community broke ground for the elegant Vietnamese Martyrs Church on the corner of Northern and 29th Avenue in Phoenix.

» *The Vietnamese Community is an active and vibrant Catholic presence in the Diocese of Phoenix (2008).*
Credit: John Glover

Korean Catholics made their home at St. Daniel Parish in Scottsdale, where Father Jin Soo Shin celebrated Mass in Korean every Sunday. Later they moved to Queen of Peace Parish. Large numbers of Filipino Catholics also made their presence felt in local parishes and communities. In April 1995 Bishop O'Brien established a Polish Apostolate. Salvatorian Father Edward Wanat had begun celebrating Mass in Polish at Brophy Chapel once a month in September 1986. The Polish Catholic community later celebrated Mass at St. Theresa in Phoenix until they were able to purchase property for Our Lady of Czestochowa Church.

» *Offertory procession at the annual cultural diversity mass.*
Credit: Archives of the Diocese of Phoenix

Eastern Rite Catholic Churches

Eastern Rite Catholics grew with the population as well. Byzantine Catholics of two different nationalities were among the first to bring their distinctive worship to the Arizona capital. Ukrainian Catholics opened a mission in Phoenix in 1957 with visiting priests coming in for Divine Liturgy. They found a permanent site in 1961. Members of the Ruthenian Byzantine Rite had begun making their presence felt as early as the mid-1960s. By 1968 they had purchased an old Orthodox church, naming it St. Stephen Byzantine Ruthenian Church. They remained under the Byzantine Catholic Eparchy of Van Nuys, California. In 1994 after California's Northridge earthquake, eparchial and administrative offices were relocated to St. Stephen's, which became the pro-cathedral of the relocated eparchate. In 1992 St. Thomas the Apostle (not to be confused with the Latin rite parish of the same name) was established as a mission of St. Stephen's.

Maronite Catholics celebrated their sacred liturgies in St. Joseph Church, which was founded in 1991. A Syro-Malabar Mission would later be established in 2008. Melkite Catholics used St. Stephen's to launch their new congregation in December 1983. The group moved eventually to St. Joan of Arc Church in 1985, and then temporarily to St. Thomas until they purchased property in 1986 for St. John of the Desert. In 1995 Mar-Auraha Chaldean Catholic Church opened to serve the 100 Chaldean families who attended at the time.

The Spanish-Speaking

As noted earlier, O'Brien's first assignment in Douglas had brought him in contact with Hispanics–whom he had barely known from his life and schooling in Indiana. While in Douglas, he developed a strong empathy with Hispanic people, and after he became bishop established a Hispanic Pastoral Council and made sure that other diocesan boards had Spanish-speaking representation. In 1982 he appointed Father (later Monsignor) Antonio Sotelo as vicar for Hispanics. Sotelo had entered the Franciscan Seminary in Santa Barbara, California, at a young age. Ordained as a Franciscan in 1958, he soon linked up with the growing Cursillo Movement and became one of its early supporters. He eventually became a priest of the Diocese of Phoenix and was made a monsignor in 2009.

» *St. Stephen Byzantine Pro-Cathedral.*
Credit: John Glover

» *Father (later Monsignor) Antonio Sotelo played an important role in the development of Hispanic ministry.*
Credit: Archives of the Diocese of Phoenix

In 1997 O'Brien selected layman Jose Robles, Jr., as the new farm-worker outreach coordinator in the Office of Hispanic Ministry and later as head of the office. Robles had known O'Brien since 1961, having served Mass for him at Immaculate Conception Church in Douglas. As a young boy, Robles had broken his leg, spending 93 days in the hospital; O'Brien had visited him nearly every day.

» *Jose Robles, Director of Hispanic Ministry, a close friend of Bishop O'Brien.*
Credit: Archives of the Diocese of Phoenix

In 1987 O'Brien wrote to Rome, "One of the priorities established in Primavera was to emphasize the unique role Hispanic people play in the diocese.... In the last century, the Hispanic population has been augmented by increased emigration and natural growth." The bishop noted this dynamic again in his 1992 report, "Twenty percent of the general population are Hispanic." In the 1990s Arizona became one of the major entry points for Mexican and Central American migrants. Political unrest in El Salvador and the rise of a leftist government in Nicaragua sent many fleeing north.

Given this growth, Immaculate Heart could no longer be the only site offering Spanish Masses.

Other places began to accommodate Spanish-speaking parishioners. Typical was St. Daniel the Prophet Parish in Scottsdale, which began offering a Mass in Spanish, first monthly, then weekly–eventually drawing parishioners from nearby Tempe. By 2002 there were 18 parishes in Phoenix holding Spanish Masses. St. Catherine of Siena had the largest Hispanic population, followed by St. Vincent de Paul, St. Agnes and Ss. Simon and Jude Cathedral. Twenty-two parishes outside the city limits offered Mass in Spanish–many of them in the Phoenix metropolitan area. Outside of Phoenix, St. Mary's in Chandler, St. Anne's in Gilbert and St. John Vianney's in Goodyear registered the highest number of Hispanics. The Cathedral of Ss. Simon and Jude sponsored Santa Rosa Chapel for its Hispanic parishioners as Our Lady of Perpetual Help in Glendale also had a chapel for the Spanish-speaking. Bishop O'Brien admitted later the diocese was not ready for the flood of Spanish-speaking and did not have enough priests to deal with the increase in numbers. In 1986 he mandated Phoenix seminarians learn Spanish as part of their preparation for ministry.

The spread of Hispanic parish life became evident in December 2001 when *The Catholic Sun* recorded the various Guadalupe celebrations around the diocese. One thousand gathered for the final prayers of a novena and Mass to Our Lady at St. Catherine of Siena. The celebration had included a 5 a.m. *las mañanitas* and a 6 p.m. procession attended by 2,000. Similar festivities took place at Most Holy Trinity. At St. Margaret Mary in Bullhead City, parishioners attended a midnight Mass and on the day of the feast processed through the streets for 45 minutes with a float depicting the miracle of the roses. In Sedona hundreds gathered for the rosary, novena and a fiesta while singing favorite hymns like, O *Maria, Madre Mia.*

Catholic Schools and Religious Education

School expansion accompanied parochial growth. Dominican Sister Elizabeth Meegan had been the school superintendent since August

1988. When she moved to a new job in Pittsburgh, associate superintendent MaryBeth Mueller was appointed head of the office on October 16, 1992. Mueller was the first lay person to hold the position. It would be her task to oversee a rebirth of interest and development in Catholic schools. The building of Catholic schools had pretty much stopped for 30 years–the last full elementary school complex being erected at St. Jerome's in 1966–three years before the creation of the diocese. The diocese's demographic shift outward to newer suburbs had resulted in the closure of two Phoenix schools, Gerard High School in 1989 and the venerable St. Mary Elementary School in 1994. In 1992 Holy Cross Father Joseph Corpora, pastor of St. John Vianney in Goodyear, began a preschool, adding a grade each year through the fourth grade. A gifted fund-raiser and able to rely on his connections with the Holy Cross Congregation, Corpora found the means to serve the 200 students who began to press for more space–for art and music, a library and computer labs–and to parents who wanted more grades. Bishop O'Brien dedicated a new school facility to handle grades five through eight on December 7, 1997. In 1997 there were 28 Catholic elementary and secondary schools in the diocese, enrolling 11,500 students.

A Future Schools Task Force, created by Bishop O'Brien, released findings in May 1996, recommending a $40 million fund-raising drive. O'Brien took this to his advisory councils who recommended scaling back the targeted amount. The fund drive, called "Today's Children–Tomorrow's Leaders," began in the fall of 1997 and exceeded the $25 million goal set by its planners, finishing up with a total of $35,494,690, of which $7.5 million was to be used to build two inter-parish schools–Pope John XXIII (1999) in Scottsdale and St. John Bosco (2000) in Phoenix–while $13.3 million went for renovating and repairing existing schools, some of them dating back to the 1950s. More than $4 million was to be used for tuition assistance. Pre-schools opened at Our Lady of Joy, Resurrection, St. Vincent de Paul and Our Lady of the Lake–all parishes without prior pre-school programs. St. Timothy Academy opened in Mesa in 2001. In September 2002 a $27 million Notre Dame Preparatory in north Scottsdale greeted incoming freshmen and sophomores for the first time.

» *Pope John XXIII School.*
Credit: *John Glover*

» *St. John Bosco School.*
Credit: *John Glover*

» *MaryBeth Mueller,*
Diocesan Superintendent of Schools.
Credit: *Archives of the Diocese of Phoenix*

Men continued to be attracted to this vital ministry. Some, like Deacon Albert Gonzalez who for many years served the poor in the Phoenix area, embraced wholeheartedly the special task of deacons to care for the poor. O'Brien also assigned deacons as "parish life coordinators." Such was the case of long-serving Deacon Thomas Phelan who temporarily left his engineering career after his 1972 ordination to teach religion at St. Mary High School. He returned to engineering in 1980 and retired in 1999, becoming the administrator of St. Francis of Assisi Parish in Bagdad, a mining town 60 miles west of Wickenburg. Spanish-speaking deacons, like Deacon Tony Chavez of Blessed Sacrament in Tolleson, became respected and much beloved figures in their parish communities. As time went on acceptance of deacons improved. Pastors like St. Helen's Father Robert Voss had four permanent deacons who maintained "high profiles" at the Glendale church. The number of deacons grew steadily. In 1982 the Phoenix diocese had 73 permanent deacons; in 1986 there were 89, and by 1993 there were 134.

Women Religious

Women religious have always been an important force in education, mentoring generations of young Catholics and instilling in them not only a strong Catholic identity, but also a sense of self-worth and confidence. Sister Marian Grace Brandt, S.C., a native of Pennsylvania had begun teaching when she was 17. She was eventually assigned as principal of Our Lady of Perpetual Help School in Scottsdale, and proudly noted of her work, "We have third generation families in this school.... A parent bringing their child here can expect that we're going to emphasize Catholicism." Sister Joan Fitzgerald, B.V.M., arrived at Xavier College Preparatory in 1962 and eventually became principal. Of the graduates of the school, she expressed, "I hope they realize they are really gifted people when they leave." Other women religious were active in social welfare enterprises and other kinds of pastoral ministry. Sister of St. Joseph, Adele O'Sullivan, a medical doctor, is the medical director of health care for the homeless at a Maricopa County-sponsored clinic on West Madison Street in Phoenix. Her desire to help the homeless with some of the necessities of life led to the formation of a non-profit organization known as Circle the City, sponsored by the Sisters of St. Joseph. These efforts to provide health care, housing and vision services for the uninsured earned her the title "Best Good Samaritan" from *Reader's Digest* in 2006.

» *Sister Joan Fitzgerald*
of Xavier College Preparatory.
Credit: Archives of the Diocese of Phoenix

The Sisters of Mercy expanded the scope of St. Joseph Hospital. Although the number of sisters working in the hospital declined, the sisters remained prominent health-care advocates in Arizona. In 2006 they opened Mercy Gilbert Medical Center. Other communities of women who ministered to the needs of the poor included the Missionaries of Charity who established a house to care for the poor in south Phoenix. Sisters also held important diocesan posts. Sister Anthony Poerio, I.B.V.M., as noted earlier directed the Office of Worship while Sister of Charity Mary Ann Winters served as diocesan chancellor and Sisters Bridget Ann Henderson, B.V.M., and Elizabeth Meegan, O.P., served as administrators in the diocesan school department.

Yet the numbers of sisters were shrinking. In early 1986 the Sisters of Our Lady of Charity of the Good Shepherd announced they were leaving Phoenix after more than 50 years of ministry. They had come to Phoenix during the 1930s to minister to troubled women and young girls. They began in a small cottage, then eventually operated the Patterdell School for Girls, which once had enrolled between 150 and 200 girls. They had a convent at 19th Avenue and Northern.

» *Mercy Sister Mary Assumpta Murray is pictured here with Bishop Rausch and T. Abner Huff beginning an addition to St. Joseph Hospital.*
Credit: Archives of the Diocese of Phoenix

In August 1985 the Sacred Heart Home for the Aged, run by the Little Sisters of the Poor since 1960, announced it too would be closing its doors in 1986, a decision forced in part by the construction of the nearby Papago/Interstate 10 Freeway, the financial demands of the aging facility and the lack of vocations to the sisterhood. One by one, as well, beloved educators with long careers in Phoenix began to retire and return to their motherhouses.

Despite declining numbers of religious sisters, local Catholics celebrated the sisters' work and ministries. In 2001 the Sisters of Notre Dame de Namur celebrated 50 years of service to the Church in Arizona. Five sisters from Cincinnati had stepped off the train in Phoenix in August 1950 to begin a school at Our Lady of Perpetual Help

in Glendale. The sisters recalled the temperature was 120 in the shade, the hottest day on record in 50 years. Dressed head to toe in heavy black habits, they must have wondered what they had gotten themselves into. Few of their first students spoke any English, and none of the sisters spoke Spanish. Their ministry included teaching catechism in the smaller farming communities in the west valley to the children of migrant workers and also on the reservation. In 2001 there were still 17 Sisters of Notre Dame de Namur serving in Arizona.

» *Religious orders of women have worked in a variety of ministries from teaching to ministering directly to the poor.*
Credit: Archives of the Diocese of Phoenix

» *Sacred Heart Home for the Aged, run by the Little Sisters of the Poor since 1960, closed in 1986.*
Credit: Archives of the Diocese of Phoenix

The Papal Visit

Phoenix was soon to become an important center of Catholic life with an array of very skilled, faithful and highly competent men and women, lay and clerical–all of whom provided the diocese with the resources to host a papal visit. The papal visit required a year and a half of preparation.

Sometime in 1985 the National Conference of Catholic Bishops let it be known that Pope John Paul II intended to visit cities of the western and southern states. When Bishop O'Brien learned of this, he spoke with some of his confidants who urged him to volunteer the city of Phoenix as a site. At a meeting of the regional bishops in Colorado, O'Brien made known to Monsignor Robert Lynch, an associate general secretary of the Bishops' Conference, that he wanted to place Phoenix on the list. A formal letter of invitation to the Pope was drafted and sent via the Bishops' Conference. To his great pleasure, in November 1986 O'Brien received a phone call from Bishop Thomas Kelly, O.P., the general secretary, informing him Phoenix had been selected. As part of an eight-day tour, taking the pope from Miami to San Francisco, the pontiff planned a 24-hour stop in Phoenix on September 14, 1987. Arrangements would include a Mass at Sun Devil Stadium in Tempe, a greeting from the balcony of St. Mary Church (raised to the status of basilica in 1985) and a prayer service at Ss. Simon and Jude Cathedral. The pope also intended to address Catholic health-care workers and Native Americans, both meeting in conventions in Phoenix.

A local executive committee was impaneled to take charge of the various aspects of the visit. Chaired by Father John McMahon, pastor of St. Theresa in Phoenix, the committee included physician Mary Jo French and Judy Wischer, president of American Continental Corporation. McMahon commented, "I was quietly in my office, and the bishop popped in and said, 'The pope is coming. Would you coordinate things?'" Endless meetings ensued, contacts with the national Bishops' Conference, Vatican emissaries and the Secret Service. Twenty-two committees formed to cover the major aspects of the visit. McMahon's strong right hand in organizing the affairs was Harvey Newquist.

» *The Planning Committee for the Papal Visit.*
Credit: Archives of the Diocese of Phoenix

Newquist was by this time a well known figure in Catholic circles in Phoenix. A native of Wisconsin, he semi-retired to Arizona in 1973 and devoted himself more fully to his wife and eight children, and also shared his considerable organizational talents with the Church and community. Newquist's organizational skills and broad community contacts were pivotal in coordinating the myriad of details surrounding the one-day papal visit. He was able to raise money

IN THE WORK OF SERVICE
U·N·I·T·Y
FIRST PASTORAL VISIT TO ARIZONA, SEPTEMBER 14, 1987
ARIZONA STATE UNIVERSITY, SUN DEVIL STADIUM, TEMPE, AZ

» *Pope John Paul II Visit to Arizona on September 14, 1987.*
Credit: Archives of the Diocese of Phoenix

and recruit volunteers (10,000 in all) who made it a success. Seventy-five billboards promoting the "Time to Re-Member" took advantage of the moment to invite lapsed Catholics back into the fold. Even non-Catholic Arizonans participated with 12 people of various religious beliefs commissioning a life-sized sculpture of Pope John Paul II to sit in front of the Diocesan Center. The 800-pound statue featured the pope with arms outstretched in welcome.

>> *Harvey Newquist, local businessman, played an important role in coordinating the papal events.*
Credit: Archives of the Diocese of Phoenix

Providing hospitality to visiting bishops and clergy fell to Father Richard Moyer whose mastery of computer and electronic technology made this task easier. Liturgical planning was the province of Sister Anthony Poerio and Father Dale Fushek, who worked tirelessly, organizing choirs and the liturgical environments of various papal events, especially of Sun Devil Stadium. In a 2008 interview, Poerio recalled the various stages of planning and the need to run every detail through the Bishops' Conference and planners in Rome. The result was a spectacular display of faith, love of the Pope, pride in the diocese, fine music and devout prayer that was a credit to the diocese and the Catholic Church in the United States.

A Day to Remember

The pontiff's airplane Shepherd I touched down at Sky Harbor Airport on September 14, 1987. After welcoming comments, he was taken to St. Joseph Hospital where he visited patients, staff, board members and others associated with the ministry of healing. He was also serenaded in Polish by the staff who surprised him by singing the popular Polish song *Stolat* in his honor.

>> *Pope John Paul II arriving in Phoenix.*
Credit: Archives of the Diocese of Phoenix

» *The pontiff kisses a child while visiting St. Joseph Hospital.*
Credit: Archives of the Diocese of Phoenix

» *On the balcony of St. Mary's Basilica, the pope greets the thousands who turned out to welcome him.*
Credit: The Arizona Republic

As the pope rode along Central Avenue, a proud Bishop O'Brien at his side, more than 150,000 people from all parts of the Southwest and Mexico lined the motorcade route. Cheers, banners and songs greeted the smiling and gesturing pontiff as he made his way to St. Mary Basilica. There, in front of the refurbished and spruced up "mother church" of Phoenix, about 100,000 people gathered on the Civic Plaza deck to greet the pontiff to the singing of the diocesan Hispanic choir.

» *Pope John Paul II and Bishop O'Brien receive a tremendous welcome as they motorcade through Phoenix.*
Credit: Archives of the Diocese of Phoenix

Next came a meeting with the National Catholic Health Association—one of the main reasons for the pope's Phoenix stop. More than 2,500 representatives from Catholic hospitals, care centers and nursing homes and a variety of other facilities were on hand to hear the pontiff decry abortion and euthanasia, but also to hear him offer his first formal public statement on AIDS. The spread of this deadly virus created a "crisis of immense proportions," and the pope called on the Catholic community to rise to the need and live out the parable of the Good Samaritan. He next visited with priests, deacons, religious and ecumenical leaders at Ss. Simon and Jude Cathedral and then had lunch with regional bishops and briefly rested at Bishop O'Brien's home. Next, John Paul II had a powerful meeting with Native Americans gathered for the Tekakwitha Conference, held by a national Catholic Indian organization. Fourteen thousand Indians from various tribes met with the pope at the Veterans Memorial Coliseum. Pope John Paul II praised their faith and spirituality, and he heard from Alfretta M. Antone, vice-president of the Salt River Pima-Maricopa Community, who spoke of past injustices to native peoples and urged the pontiff to support their hopes for a restored place in American life: "We ask you to intervene with all people of good will to preserve our homelands for our families, our children and the generation to follow us.... We want to live in harmony with all people and all of creation. We choose to keep alive for all generations the ways of living carved in the stone and bones of our ancestors. We are open to share and receive whatever is good for the life of the human family with all people of good will. Our traditions, our languages, our cultures with their rich teachings and values, our songs and dances, our stories and paintings, our art and ways of living celebrate who we are as a people of many tribes." At the end of the busy and draining day, the energetic pontiff celebrated Mass at Sun Devil Stadium. A huge crowd of nearly 80,000 jammed the stadium to celebrate the liturgical feast of the Triumph of the Holy Cross.

» *The pope meets women religious at Ss. Simon and Jude Cathedral.*
Credit: Archives of the Diocese of Phoenix

» *Accompanied by Monsignor Robert Donohoe, the pope greets interfaith leaders.*
Credit: Archives of the Diocese of Phoenix

» *Pope John Paul II at the Tekakwitha Conference where he meets Native Americans.*
Credit: Archives of the Diocese of Phoenix

» *A liturgy on the Feast of the Exaltation of the Holy Cross is the climax of the Holy Father's visit.*
Credit: Archives of the Diocese of Phoenix

The following morning the pontiff left in a jubilant glow. Before he said farewell he created Fathers McFadden, McMahon and Moyer monsignori on the spot. As the papal plane lifted off, Bishop O'Brien gave his communications director Marge Injasoulian a grateful thumbs up. The hard work and planning by everyone had come off splendidly. Plaques commemorate Pope John Paul II's visit wherever he had been and various photos of the charismatic pope appeared everywhere. People knew something special had happened. It was a defining moment for the Diocese of Phoenix and is cherished to this day.

The Visit of Mother Teresa

» *In 1989 Blessed Teresa of Calcutta opened a convent of the Missionaries of Charity in Phoenix. Mother Teresa with Bishop O'Brien.*
Credit: Archives of the Diocese of Phoenix

A new Religious congregation came to minister in Phoenix, thus providing another important moment–the visit of (Blessed) Mother Teresa of Calcutta. The Nobel laureate and founder of the Missionaries of Charity had sent an advanced contingent of sisters who, with help from Father Dale Fushek, found a place on West Taylor Avenue from which to launch their ministry to the poor. Mother Teresa arrived on February 1, 1989, for a 42-hour whirlwind tour to open the mission and look for a site for a homeless shelter. Bishop O'Brien welcomed her at the airport, and crowds turned out to meet her. She greeted them and Mayor Terry Goddard warmly, then she began her visit to settings where the poor were tended–including the St. Vincent de Paul Charity Dining Room. She expressed concern that the West Taylor Avenue locale was not centrally located enough for the poor. "We must be available to them," she told Father Fushek. "If they cannot get to us it is no use because they are the only reason we came." She greeted 500 priests, deacons and consecrated religious Catholics at a prayer service at Ss. Simon and Jude Cathedral, and on February 2 more than 15,000 people packed the Veterans Memorial Coliseum to hear the world-renowned missionary tell uplifting stories of her ministry, lament the scourge of abortion and urge Eucharistic adoration, praying the rosary and simple acts of love.

Mother Teresa left Phoenix with a pledge of $5,000 from Governor Rose Mofford to purchase a shelter for the homeless. Other funds poured in, collected by the chancery. Eight days later, she was back to inspect a new residence for her sisters and a potential site for the needed homeless shelter. Walking around the impoverished south side neighborhoods, the sisters had found an even larger vacant convent at Our Lady of Fatima Mission near Seventeenth Avenue and Buckeye Road–and the diocese owned the property next to it. Mother Teresa had gathered together $33,000, which she handed to Father Fushek. This money and other generous donations were used to build "The Gift of Mary House."

» *Mother Teresa at prayer rally.*
Credit: Archives of the Diocese of Phoenix

Large-Scale Liturgical Celebrations

One of the highlights of the papal visit was the celebration of spectacularly staged diocesan liturgy, which inspired, rallied and gave visibility to the rapidly growing diocese. Large-scale celebrations had begun under Bishop McCarthy– the Guadalupe celebration, the ARISE liturgies on Holy Thursday in 1971 and 1972, and the 1975 Festival of Faith Mass, featuring Archbishop Fulton J. Sheen. Planning and executing these prayerful events became a special priority for Bishop O'Brien and his advisors.

» *Ash Wednesday Rite of Election, February 1997.*
Credit: Archives of the Diocese of Phoenix

» *Large-scale liturgies helped form bonds of diocesan unity.*
The Twenty-fifth anniversary of the Diocese of Phoenix, December 1994.
Credit: Archives of the Diocese of Phoenix

The papal liturgy set a benchmark. Building off the 1987 experience, O'Brien and his staff laid plans for a celebration of the silver anniversary of the diocese with a festive Eucharist in the America West Arena. On December 5, 1994, more than 12,000 people came to the arena despite a driving rain. Fifteen bishops, including Archbishop McCarthy, joined Bishop O'Brien for the event. To music provided by a 250-voice choir and 50-member orchestra from St. Timothy Parish, the emotional liturgy brought many to tears during the Our Father. The mere mention of the visits of Pope John Paul II and Mother Teresa caused people to burst into applause.

Pope John Paul II's call to celebrate the year 2000 as a year of jubilee set in motion another chain of colorful and memorable liturgies. The pontiff asked that each year leading up to the millennium be devoted to an extended meditation on the Persons of the Holy Trinity. Hence there was a year of the Father, and the Holy Spirit and the Son. Overseen by Father Fushek and Sister Poerio, a mammoth Rite of Election and Ash Wednesday ceremony took place at the Blockbuster Desert Sky Pavilion in February 1997. The bishop welcomed more than 1,400 catechumens and candidates from 70 parishes, and all were marked with the ritual sign of Lenten repentance.

A second millennium-oriented event took place on May 30, 1998, at Bank One Ballpark. Here Bishop O'Brien, assisted by the clergy, celebrated the Sacrament of Confirmation for 3,000 teens in the presence of a crowd of 28,000. A Eucharistic Congress was held in 2000 at Wells Fargo Arena.

» *Confirmation, Bank One Ballpark, May 1998.*
Credit: Archives of the Diocese of Phoenix

» *Eucharistic Congress, Wells Fargo Arena, 2000.*
Credit: Archives of the Diocese of Phoenix

Flagstaff

One of the by-products of re-thinking the assignment and allocation of priests were the needs of the Church in Flagstaff. Bishop Rausch's investigations regarding a new diocese in northern Arizona had come to a halt with his death, and Bishop O'Brien did not revive them, financial feasibility being the primary stumbling block. The three parishes of the community (Nativity of the Blessed Virgin Mary, Our Lady of Guadalupe and St. Pius X) and Holy Trinity Catholic Newman Center at Northern Arizona University, where services were also held, each had a priest. The allocation of four priests to such a relatively small number of parishioners (2,000), when some Phoenix parishes had as many or more congregants, led to a recommendation to study consolidating the Flagstaff parishes.

In early December 1996 Bishop O'Brien traveled to Flagstaff to listen to the concerns of parishioners about the proposed consolidation. The commission, organized to study the issue, had recommended to O'Brien that there be just one parish in Flagstaff with multiple facilities. O'Brien outlined the new plan and hoped a

larger church—to seat 800-1,200 people—could be built on a suitable location. At the same time he promised that Nativity of the Blessed Virgin Mary and Our Lady of Guadalupe would continue to be used for special occasions. These efforts stirred considerable opposition, particularly from Hispanic parishioners who worried that their beloved Our Lady of Guadalupe Church would be sold. Consolidation resulted in the formation of a new parish, San Francisco de Asís, created in 1997. In March 1997 O'Brien appointed Father Douglas J. Nohava as pastor of the newly merged parishes. Nohava began his work of consolidation on July 1 but died on the job. The process continues to this day.

Working with Youth

Bishop Rausch had begun a task force to study Catholic services to youth and youth ministry programs. One member of the youth task force, Father Dale Fushek, made his own distinctive contribution to teens and young adults with the popular Life Teen Program.

» *Bishop O'Brien assigned a high priority to working with youth.*
Credit: Archives of the Diocese of Phoenix

Fushek was born in 1952 in Cleveland, and as a child he and his family relocated to Arizona where he attended Our Lady of Perpetual Help Elementary School in Scottsdale and Central High in Phoenix. Fushek was ordained in 1978. He noted his interest in teen ministry began when he was in the seminary at St. John's in Camarillo. Assigned to Holy Spirit Parish in 1977 as a deacon, Fushek started a teen group called "Young Spirits." In his first assignment at St. Jerome's in 1978, he started a group called ACT (Active Christian Teens). Called to work full time in the Office of Worship under Bishop O'Brien, Father Fushek continued to work with youth on a part-time basis at St. Louis the King in a program called "Insight." In 1985 he was assigned as pastor to St. Timothy Parish in Mesa and there started Life Teen for the teens in his parish. The enthusiastic teen liturgies, with contemporary Christian music, reflected Fushek's belief in the Mass as "the center of our parish life." "Liturgy is evangelization," he observed in an interview. "Every single person who comes to Mass is an active evangelizer by just singing God's praises, by proclaiming God's faith. By proclaiming their faith in God, they're evangelizing other people in the Church." The Life Teen Mass sought to build a sense of inclusion, "to provide them an opportunity to belong and have some sense that they belong to something bigger than themselves." Life nights, where religious topics were geared to win the attention of teens, followed these dynamic liturgies. St. Timothy's became a showplace for youth ministry, and Life Teen spread throughout the Southwest and into California and other places in the nation and foreign countries.

» *The Life Teen program, begun in Phoenix, soon spread across the U.S. and into a number of foreign countries.*
Credit: Archives of the Diocese of Phoenix

Life Teen still represents one of Phoenix's major contributions to the wider Church, and it helped to energize the sometimes challenging task of educating high school age youth. On May 26, 1987, Life Teen became a separate corporation. By 2008 the program was used in more than 1,200 parishes nationwide and in 20 countries around the world. Life Teen camps in Georgia and Arizona introduced youth to Catholic teaching and liturgy. Many good things have come from this program: ardent Catholic lay men and women, enthusiasm for liturgy, vocations to the priesthood and religious life–and above all a personal and powerful love for the Lord Jesus and his mother Mary. "Catholicism rocks!" one young participant said of the experience of Life Teen in his parish. Love for the Eucharist, Adoration of the Blessed Sacrament, regular confession and a hunger for religious instruction made these young people and their parishes stronger.

» *Youth retreats at Camp Tepeyac were an important training ground for young Catholic leaders.*
Credit: Archives of the Diocese of Phoenix

congregations and paying out settlements. In June 2002 the American bishops met in Dallas and there agreed to a zero tolerance policy and drew up a compendium of policies–"The Charter for the Protection of Children and Young People." In June of 2002 Bishop O'Brien sent a pastoral letter to the diocese offering a heartfelt apology for the suffering caused by the priests, admitting he had failed in some situations. The diocese put forth its efforts to seek out and assist anyone sexually abused by a priest (diocesan or religious) and to offer counseling and financial settlements.

O'Brien went ahead with plans for a diocesan synod. "Nurturing Our Hope" was the theme of the gathering, which opened on December 12, 2002, with a Mass at Ss. Simon and Jude Cathedral. But the shadow of the sex abuse scandal dogged him even there. In his opening sermon, he mentioned it: "During the last year the Catholic Church in this country and in our diocese has been besieged by the horror of sexual abuse and the manner [in which] it has been handled. Both situations in our society and diocese remind us of our human frailties and limitations." The synod began its deliberations, but ended when Bishop O'Brien resigned.

The New Diocesan Pastoral Center

Running in tandem with these developments was the construction of the new Pastoral Center, which provided Bishop O'Brien some distraction from his mounting problems. O'Brien was determined–as had been Bishop McCarthy–to make sure the Catholic Church had a visible presence in downtown Phoenix. This became all the more important as the initial Diocesan Center began to show its age. Architectural plans were drawn, and a plan was devised to tear it and St. Mary School down and acquire enough property to build a much improved Diocesan Pastoral Center. That the center remain in the heart of downtown was exactly what Bishop O'Brien felt was important. Its proximity to St. Mary Basilica visibly connected it with the historic roots of Catholic life in Phoenix.

» *The Diocesan center under construction.*
Credit: Archives of the Diocese of Phoenix

In anticipation of one day further developing the Diocesan Pastoral Center, O'Brien had already purchased parcels of land next to the former convent. Originally built for 45 sisters, the center was now 50 years old and held 100 employees and 34 offices. There was a need for a structure to handle the growing demand for services and to house a Catholic newspaper. Monsignor Dale Fushek, project coordinator, noted to tech-savvy Catholics: "The building was never intended to handle the phone lines, the computer network and the technological advances that are now needed to run an office." Generous contributions from parishes and the Virginia G. Piper Trust in part underwrote the cost of the new 65,000 square foot structure.

In May 2001 the diocesan staff temporarily relocated to the Catholic Healthcare West offices on North Third Avenue. By the time of the groundbreaking on the Feast of Our Lady of Guadalupe that year, a huge canyon of earth had been removed from the site. What remained was the old St. Mary School. Closed in 1994, some still hoped the old building could be re-opened or at least re-used. However, when this was shown to be impractical, a portion of one of its entrances was left as a memorial to those who had attended or worked at the school.

In June 2002 the old St. Mary School came down. Fourth Street between Monroe and Van Buren was permanently closed, allowing the diocese to build a plaza–both it and the center's chapel were named after Virginia G. Piper. Designed by VOA Associates and constructed by Opus Southwest, the new center included underground parking, spacious rooms and offices, a chapel decorated with the memorabilia of the papal visit and an elegant copper dome. By May 2003 the structure was complete, and O'Brien and the diocesan staff moved in. The life-sized statue of Pope John Paul II, donated at the time of his visit, symbolically welcomed visitors coming to the main entrance. Before the Diocesan Pastoral Center could be formally dedicated, however, one more sad moment gripped the diocese and engulfed the man who had helped plan the center.

» *Circle of Peace, Virginia G. Piper Plaza.*
Credit: Archives of the Diocese of Phoenix

» *The new Diocesan center was completed in 2003.*
Credit: Archives of the Diocese of Phoenix

On February 17, 2004, the 68-year-old O'Brien was found guilty and given community service time. On March 26, he was sentenced to four years of supervised probation and 1,000 hours of community service. Reactions were mixed. Monsignor Fushek expressed the feelings of many: "I think people understand that a split-second decision does not define a whole life."

Bishop O'Brien's Departure

In June 2003 life took a tragic turn for Bishop O'Brien and brought a premature end to his tenure as Phoenix's bishop. On the evening of June 14, Bishop O'Brien struck 43-year-old James L. Reed with his car. O'Brien later recalled he was unaware he had hit anybody and when the thud hit his car, he feared someone had thrown a rock at his passing car or was trying to kidnap him. Witnesses identified O'Brien's car, and on June 16, 2003, Bishop O'Brien was charged with leaving the scene of a fatal accident. What followed in the ensuing months was a time of highly public agony for Bishop O'Brien, the Reed family and the entire Church of Phoenix.

Archbishop Michael Sheehan's Interregnum

On June 17, 2003, Bishop O'Brien resigned. Vicar General Richard Moyer phoned the papal nuncio and the metropolitan archbishop of the region, Michael Sheehan of Santa Fe, with the news of O'Brien's accident and resignation. Archbishop Sheehan was appointed temporary apostolic administrator. The Santa Fe prelate brought considerable experience to the situation having administered the Archdiocese of Santa Fe for a brief period while he was Bishop of Lubbock, Texas.

Charged with keeping the diocese afloat, Archbishop Sheehan tried to bring a sense of joy and hope to diocesan staff and the Catholics of the region. "When I arrived, their [sic] seemed to be a great sadness and a lack of hope on the part of many of the people I met," he stated in an interview with *The Catholic Sun*. On his first day on the job, Sheehan met with media in an effort to reassure the diocese that all would be well. Archbishop Sheehan worked closely with Monsignor Moyer to hold the diocese together until a successor could be appointed. Moyer later recalled how helpful Sheehan had been and paid tribute to his efforts to help the diocese along at a painful time.

Archbishop Sheehan served the Diocese of Phoenix until December. In the months between June and December 2003, he shuttled back and forth, twice weekly, between Albuquerque and Phoenix. "Sometimes I have to pray on the plane," he quipped to a reporter. In August he speculated Phoenix could have a new bishop by Christmas 2003. When he was in Phoenix, he celebrated a series of healing Masses around the diocese and

» *Archbishop Michael Sheehan of Santa Fe became Apostolic Administrator of the Diocese of Phoenix. He sought to reassure the shaken diocese that all would be well.*
Credit: The Catholic Sun

tried to boost sagging spirits among the clergy, religious and laity.

Archbishop Sheehan also made a point of reaching out to Hispanic and Native American communities during his brief term. He described a November visit to St. Peter's Native American mission school as a "powerful personal experience." Another highlight of his time in the Phoenix diocese came when a team of independent auditors revealed that the diocese had successfully implemented the U.S. bishops' "Charter for the Protection of Children and Young People." He stated, "That was a legacy I wanted to leave with the diocese." Many believed the archbishop had done more than keep the diocese afloat. He had returned the local Church to solid footing.

Archbishop Sheehan kept in touch with Bishop O'Brien who had been his friend. In September 2003 a brief moment of sunlight penetrated the gloom as the new Pastoral Center was formally dedicated. O'Brien was given a prominent role in the ceremonies and had the occasion to hear words of appreciation and praise for his leadership. This ceremony offered the Catholics of the diocese an opportunity to thank Bishop O'Brien for his years of service.

By the end of November, Archbishop Sheehan's prediction had come true—a new bishop would be in place by Christmas. In December 2003 O'Brien's successor, Thomas Olmsted, bishop of Wichita, came quietly into the diocese.

» *Papal Mass program (detail).*
Credit: Archives of the Diocese of Phoenix

The Olmsted Era
(2003-   )

"Let us keep our eyes fixed on Jesus"

» *Bishop Thomas Olmsted making opening remarks as he is welcomed as the fourth bishop of Phoenix.*
Credit: The Catholic Sun

On November 25, 2003, 56-year-old Bishop Thomas James Olmsted arrived at the newly built Diocesan Pastoral Center, prayed in the chapel and then met the waiting press. Tall, lanky and bespectacled, Olmsted spoke of his surprise at hearing of his appointment, but he noted with assurance, "I have no doubt this is God's will...and I accept in the spirit of ready obedience and gratitude." On December 20, he entered Ss. Simon and Jude Cathedral and became the fourth bishop to take his seat on the cathedra.

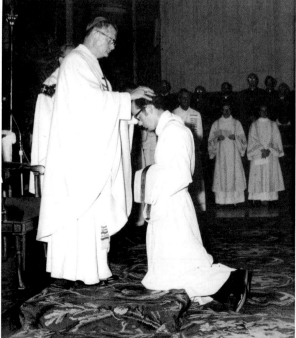

» *Father Thomas Olmsted's priestly ordination by Bishop (later Cardinal) James Hickey.*
Credit: Catholic Advance, Diocese of Wichita

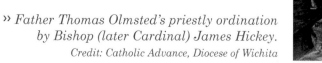

» *Young Father Olmsted.*
Credit: Catholic Advance, Diocese of Wichita

Bishop Thomas James Olmsted was born January 21, 1947, in Maryville, Kansas, one of six children of Pat and Helen Hughes Olmsted. He grew up in a two-story, three-bedroom home on the Kansas-Nebraska border and attended a single-room grade school near Oketo, Kansas, and a small rural high school in Summerfield, Kansas. Discerning a call to the priesthood, he affiliated with the Diocese of Lincoln, Nebraska, and entered St. Thomas Seminary in Denver, finishing the college program in 1969. As a seminarian he had worked in Baja, California, and developed a love for the poor–and learned to speak Spanish. He completed his studies in Rome and was ordained in St. Peter's Basilica in Rome on July 2, 1973. He was appointed an assistant pastor at the Cathedral of the Risen Christ in Lincoln for three years. In his first year of priesthood, he joined Jesus Caritas, a fraternity of priests influenced by the life and teachings of Blessed Charles de Foucauld. The call for priestly fraternity, a commitment to an hour a day of Eucharistic prayer, and a conscious effort to remain close to those who make up his chapter of the group are still today defining features of his life. Quoting the epistle to the Hebrews, he summed up the core of his priestly ministry, "Let us keep our eyes fixed on Jesus who inspires and perfects our faith."

Serious, reserved and studious–and an avid baseball fan–Father Olmsted was sent to Rome's Gregorian University from 1976 to 1979 to study canon law. While there, he was on hand for the election of Pope John Paul II and was appointed to the Secretariat of State where he assisted the Holy Father in matters dealing with the English-speaking Church. He also provided spiritual direction to the seminarians at the Pontifical North American College in Rome and became a monsignor (chaplain of honor) in 1984 and a prelate of honor in 1988. He returned to Lincoln in 1988 and in 1989 was appointed pastor of St. Vincent de Paul Church in Seward and worked in the Lincoln diocesan marriage tribunal. In 1993 he was selected to join the faculty of the Pontifical College Josephinum in Columbus, Ohio, serving first as dean of formation, and in 1997 president and rector of this sole pontifical seminary outside of Italy. On April 20, 1999, Bishop Eugene Gerber of the Diocese of Wichita, assisted by Archbishop James P. Keleher of Kansas City and Bishop Fabian Bruskewitz of Lincoln, consecrated him coadjutor bishop of Wichita. On October 4, 2001, the feast of St. Francis, he succeeded Gerber as the head of the diocese. The small Wichita diocese (20,021 square miles) counted 115,537 Catholics, and Bishop Olmsted led it with a steady hand. He placed deep emphasis on personal prayer and conversion, urged respect for life, and was a militant foe of abortion and a strong advocate for natural family planning. He loved and admired Pope John Paul II and the pontiff's call for evangelization, and when he came to Phoenix these would be some of his priorities.

» *Episcopal ordination of Bishop Olmsted in Wichita (1999).* Credit: Catholic Advance, Diocese of Wichita

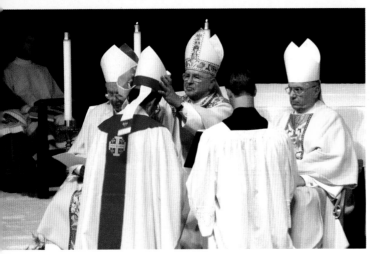

» *Bishop Thomas Olmsted's episcopal ordination with Bishop Eugene Gerber as principal consecrator and Archbishop James Keleher and Bishop Fabian Bruskiewitz as co-consecrators.*
Credit: Catholic Advance, Diocese of Wichita

Coming to Phoenix

When he entered Phoenix, he came into a diocese more than twice the geographic size of his Kansas post—and with more than 550,000 registered Catholics. In his installation homily, he called the diocese to prayer, "When we pray, we open the door to Christ. We accept in faith the invitation of Jesus recorded in the last book of the Bible, where he says, 'Behold I stand at the door and knock. If any one hears my voice and opens the door, then I will enter his house and dine with him and he with me.'" Olmsted held his first Mass as bishop in his new diocese at Immaculate Heart of Mary Church in Phoenix where he celebrated and preached in Spanish. Christmas Eve found him praying the rosary in front of a Planned Parenthood center, and on January 22, 2004, he led a day of prayer and penance to mark the anniversary of Roe v. Wade.

In June 2004 Bishop Olmsted traveled to Rome on his ad limina visit. There he met with curial officials and spent some time with Pope John Paul II. Since the 1998 ad limina visit, the diocese had grown by nearly 100,000 registered Catholics. Each year approximately 2,000 catechumens and candidates were participating in the Rite of Election.

» *Bishop Olmsted with Pope John Paul II.*

» *Bishop Olmsted's installation, Saints Simon & Jude Cathedral, December 20, 2003.*
Credit: The Catholic Sun

Parish and Conventual Church Development During the Olmsted Years

Year established	Parish	City	County
2004	St. Rose Philippine Duchesne	Anthem	Maricopa
2004	Vietnamese Martyrs	Phoenix	Maricopa
2006	Our Lady of Guadalupe	Queen Creek	Maricopa
2006	Our Lady of the Angels (Franciscan Renewal Center) Conventual Church	Scottsdale	Maricopa
2008	Our Lady of Czestochowa	Phoenix	Maricopa

» *Bishop Olmsted in pith helmet at groundbreaking for St. Margaret Mary Church, Bullhead City, with Father Peter Dobrowski, pastor.*
Credit: The Catholic Sun

Pastoral Initiatives

Eschewing the idea of a "vision statement" or hard and fast pastoral plans, Bishop Olmsted drew his inspiration from the teachings of Pope John Paul II, especially from the 1997 Synod on the Americas, "Ecclesia in America"–an extended reflection and exhortation on the role of the Church in the Americas. "Ecclesia in America" became required reading for the administrative team Olmsted assembled, which included Fathers Fredrick Adamson and David Sanfilippo, as his vicars general, and Agnesian Sister Jean Steffes as chancellor. Conversion, communion and solidarity were to be the goals of his diocesan work.

» *Chancellor, Sister Jean Steffes, C.S.A., with Bishop Olmsted.*
Credit: The Catholic Sun

» *Vicar General, Father Fred Adamson, oversaw the restructuring meetings of 2008.*
Credit: *The Catholic Sun*

Restructuring

One major accomplishment of these administrators was a significant rearrangement of the diocese's civil organization from being a corporation sole, a model widely used in many American dioceses, to separately incorporated parishes, high schools and cemeteries. Father Christopher Fraser, Judicial Vicar, and Father Fredrick Adamson, Vicar General, stressed that separate incorporation better reflected the actual practice of Church governance in the Diocese of Phoenix where pastors always had the administrative authority over parish affairs. Father Adamson insisted the restructuring wasn't "being forced by any legal or financial proceedings." Concerns about the liability of the Church as a corporation sole had been on the minds of many in the diocese. Father Fraser commented, "It's irresponsible for us not to do this for the various liability issues." The new structure "safeguards the goods of the Church that are given for service." However, Father Adamson kept the focus on the spiritual dimensions of the restructuring in his various talks around the diocese. "It's more than a civil exercise," explained Father Adamson, "It's a spiritual exercise that will allow us to better understand who Christ established us to be." The reorganization process proceeded through the months of 2008, finishing up at the end of September.

Proclaiming with Faith

» *The implementation of the Extraordinary Form of the Roman Rite has gone forward under Bishop Olmsted's direction.*
Credit: *The Catholic Sun*

Bishop Olmsted brought the gift of clear-minded leadership in a number of critical areas of Church life. His early columns in *The Catholic Sun* were dedicated to clarifying church teachings on liturgy, morality and the defense of the unborn. Drawing heavily on the teaching of Pope John Paul II, Bishop Olmsted exhorted priests, religious and lay people to pursue a deeper life of prayer and personal renewal in Christ. He strongly encouraged the practice of Eucharistic adoration, already taking place in some parishes. He shied away from any ambiguity on issues such as artificial contraception and homosexuality, clearly stating the teaching of the Church and challenging critics of the Church on these issues. He reached out to Catholic traditionalists in the diocese by permitting the celebration of the Tridentine Mass in the diocese. In 2005 he established

Mater Misericordiae Mission in Phoenix for the celebration of this rite and appointed Father Kenneth Fryar of the Priestly Fraternity of St. Peter to head the mission. Fryar offered the Tridentine Mass at St. Thomas the Apostle in Phoenix, St. Cecilia Mission in Clarksdale and, on the first Sunday of the month, at All Saints Parish in Mesa. In September 2007, when Pope Benedict XVI gave permission for a wider celebration of the Latin Mass, called properly the Extraordinary Form of the Roman Rite, Bishop Olmsted helped to implement this in the Diocese of Phoenix.

Bishop Olmsted reached out to victims of sexual abuse by presiding at liturgies of healing in several parishes in various locations in the diocese. Through these Masses and the encounters they provided between victims and their pastoral leader, efforts at reconciliation began and continue.

The Primacy of the Culture of Life

Bishop Olmsted is an especially stalwart champion of pro-life issues and took a highly visible public role in calling for an end to legalized abortion in Arizona. Reflecting the teaching of Pope John Paul II in *Christifideles Laici* (1988) and *Evangelium Vitae* (1995), Olmsted maintained that of all life issues abortion was the most important since it involved the intrinsic evil of taking an innocent human life. While he pressed Catholics to take other life issues seriously, especially when they voted, he insisted the protection of unborn life supercede all other concerns. From his diocesan newspaper column, "Jesus Caritas," as well as sermons and public lectures, he proclaimed the Church's teaching on the inherent sin of abortion and called on Catholics to become more active in seeking to end this practice. Olmsted often prayed the rosary before Planned Parenthood clinics and participated in the robust demonstrations every January 22 in the state capital. He especially encouraged young people to become active in pro-life activities. He spoke clearly to Catholic politicians on the necessity of voting according to the teachings of the Church on this and other critical issues. In October 2006, just prior to off-year elections, Bishop Olmsted issued *Catholics in the Public Square*, a question and answer booklet that spoke to the responsibilities of Catholics in civic life. Insisting that the priority of the Church be the protection and promotion of the dignity of the human person, Bishop Olmsted insisted there were some non-negotiable elements to Catholic public life: protection of life in all its stages from conception to natural death; recognition and promotion of the natural structure of the family—as a union of man and woman based on marriage; and the protection of the rights of parents to educate their children. Published by the Texas-based Basilica Press, more than 100,000 copies of the booklet were made available. A second edition of *Catholics in the Public Square* was printed in the fall of 2008.

» *Bishop Olmsted at Arizona State capitol for Roe V. Wade rally.*
Credit: *The Catholic Sun*

Avondale opened. In the summer of 2006, after extensive consultation, the Diocese of Phoenix opened the third—owned and operated by the Catholic Church—mortuary in the United States at Queen of Heaven Cemetery, which had initially opened in 1978. As Phoenix's metropolitan growth continued, Holy Redeemer Cemetery on Desert Foothills Scenic Drive was laid out in 2000. All Soul's Cemetery, begun in 2004, serviced the Verde Valley area, taking in Sedona, and included a columbarium.

» *Care for the sick and dying, and providing Catholic burial grounds, is an important ministry in the Diocese of Phoenix.*
Credit: The Catholic Sun

» *Bishop Olmsted blesses Queen of Heaven Cemetery.*
Credit: The Catholic Sun

Bishop McCarthy founded the first Board of Directors of Catholic Cemeteries shortly after the Phoenix diocese originated. Monsignor Bernard Gordon was the first administrator of Catholic Cemeteries, and Monsignor William McKay its second administrator. In 1970 Gordon Mason became the general manager of Catholic Cemeteries. In April 1990 Bishop O'Brien appointed Gary L. Brown executive director.

Catholic Higher Education

Bishop Olmsted continued the ongoing effort to study the character and quality of religious education on every level and renewed Bishop O'Brien's hopes of bringing a Catholic university to the diocese. The city of Goodyear invited the University of the Incarnate Word from San Antonio into the diocese in 2006 and, with the approval of Bishop Olmsted, established an office in Goodyear in 2007. The university began offering programs, and a feasibility study for the erection of a campus in the Diocese of Phoenix began. Through Loyola University of New Orleans' Institute for Ministry Extension (LIMEX) program, a master's degree in Pastoral Studies used by several dioceses could also be earned. Other new programs were introduced to meet the growing need for Catholic higher education. In 2007 Ave Maria University, a Florida-based Catholic institution, began a Master of Theological Studies program in Phoenix. The diocese also partnered with the University of Notre Dame to make the Satellite Theological Education Program (STEP) available to local Catholics through online adult faith formation classes.

Father Charles Goraieb, then pastor of St. Henry's in Buckeye, was one of the founders of the John Paul II Resource Center for the Theology of the Body and Culture. This group dedicates itself to teaching Pope John Paul II's Theology of the Body to all levels of catechesis in the diocese as well as offering retreats and public lectures on Pope John Paul II's teachings on the dignity of women, the single Catholic life and other theological themes. In 2006 Katrina Zeno was hired as coordinator for the center. Zeno, a popular speaker, was also featured in a 13-part series on the Theology of the Body on the Eternal Word Television Network.

» *Kino Institute students celebrate their graduation, 2008.*
Credit: The Catholic Sun

The Kino Institute received its first lay director in its 32-year existence with the appointment of Dr. Barry Sargent, a Marquette University-trained theologian who came with an impressive resume in undergraduate and adult education. Sargent had taught for Kino for several years prior to his appointment to head the program and worked closely with Kino faculty member Sister Maria Celia Molina, S.N.D., and Larry Fraher to provide primary formation experience for lay leaders and diaconal candidates for the Diocese of Phoenix. The program has an active Spanish-language component. The financial recession of 2009 led to leadership changes at the Kino Institute.

Restoring the Ancient Order of the Sacraments of Initiation

» *Bishop Olmsted greeting a newly confirmed youth.*
Credit: The Catholic Sun

One area that the bishop examined carefully through broad consultation was the age at which the Sacrament of Confirmation was administered. In a pastoral letter sent to all Catholics in the diocese in May 2005, Bishop Olmsted announced a new policy adjusting the age one prepared for and received the sacrament–from 16 years of age (sophomore or junior in high school) to the age of reason often associated with students in third grade. Addressing the need for this modification in his pastoral letter, Olmsted remarked that more than "60 percent of our teens are not being confirmed...we have thousands of adults attempting to face the challenges of the modern world without the grace of confirmation to help them." Drawing on the precedent of the ancient sequence of the Sacraments of Initiation, Olmsted urged baptism be given in infancy, reconciliation in the second grade, and confirmation and first Eucharist in the third grade. The diocese phased in this policy over a three-year period.

» Bishop Olmsted has restored the order of the Rites of Initiation and moved the age of the Sacrament of Confirmation to pre-date the reception of first Holy Communion.
Credit: The Catholic Sun

Priestly Struggles

In early 2005 the problem of sex abuse resurfaced when Monsignor Dale Fushek was placed on administrative leave and then resigned as pastor of St. Timothy's. These events were felt keenly at St. Timothy's where Fushek had founded and directed Life Teen. Nonetheless, the parish continued to be a center of praise and enthusiastic worship. Nearly 4,000 parishioners returned in 2008 to celebrate the anniversary of the parish now under the leadership of new pastor Father John Spaulding. In 2007 Monsignor Fushek founded a Praise and Worship Center with Mark Dippre. These men were asked to cease this endeavor and when they persisted, they incurred excommunication.

Passing of Two Great Leaders

In 2005 the diocese also said farewell to Pope John Paul II who died on April 2. Memories of his visit to Phoenix were revived by *The Catholic Sun* and local news broadcasts, causing diocesan Catholics to remember him in their own particular way. Sorrow gave way to joy, when the cardinals elected Cardinal Joseph Ratzinger who took the name Pope Benedict XVI.

» The death of Pope John Paul II in April 2005 evoked memories of his historic visit to Phoenix in 1987.
Credit: The Catholic Sun

In June 2005 Archbishop Edward A. McCarthy passed away at the age of 87. Bishop Olmsted eulogized his predecessor, recalling that he had had the "daunting task of launching all the ministries and services of a new diocese." Bishop O'Brien noted of his passing, "He loved Phoenix. He left part of his heart here, I'm sure. When he told me he was being transferred, we both cried."

Priests and Religious for a Growing Diocese

Bishop Olsmsted worked hard to recruit vocations and bring priests from foreign lands, who are even now learning the ways of life in

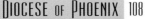

America and the Southwest. In 2007 Bishop Olmsted ordained six men to the priesthood—the largest class in 14 years. The profile of the newly-ordained was interesting. Two of them came the traditional route but most of the men entered the seminary after other careers. John Muir first felt called to the priesthood while on a Confirmation retreat in 1994. Soon after attending World Youth Day in Rome in 2000, Muir made his decision to become a priest. Paul Sullivan's favorite part of his formation was getting to know parishioners at his home parish of Resurrection in Tempe. In his early 20s Sullivan realized his call to enter the priesthood. Craig Friedley, a 49-year-old Air Force veteran, discovered his call to priesthood later in life; 40-year-old Kilian McCaffrey had worked in the automotive industry, while 30-year-old Eugene Florea had been employed by Motorola as had Mexican-born Ernesto Reynoso, age 36. Each of these men discerned the call to priestly service in a different way: devotion to Mary, Eucharistic adoration and admiration for the life and ministry of Pope John Paul II—and above all the faith and fidelity of their families.

» Six men of various backgrounds came forward to receive Holy Orders in 2007.
Credit: The Catholic Sun

Bishop Olmsted invited the Poor Clares of Perpetual Adoration to take up residence in the diocese in August 2004—thus, providing for the first time a contemplative monastery in the Diocese of Phoenix. Their residence, Our Lady of Solitude Contemplative House of Prayer in Black Canyon City, had been founded as a house of prayer by Franciscan Sister Therese Sedlock. After Sedlock died in July 2004, the property was offered to the Poor Clares, but they soon began fund-raising for a new cloister that would better suit their lives as contemplatives. In October 2006 the sisters received 40 acres of desert lands near Tonopah, Arizona, where they hope to build their enclosure.

» In August 2004 the Poor Clares of Perpetual Adoration came to the Diocese of Phoenix.
Credit: Poor Clare Sisters

In 2006 Bishop Olmsted welcomed the Dominican Sisters of Mary, Mother of the Eucharist to the diocese. This community was founded in 1997 and headquartered in Ann Arbor, Michigan. Four sisters were sent to St. Thomas the Apostle Convent in Phoenix, their first mission outside of Michigan, where they taught in the parish grade school and at St. Mary High School. In 2007 the Daughters of Mary, Mother of the Church, a religious community of women based in the Philippines, began ministry in the

Diocese of Phoenix, serving at St. Daniel School in Scottsdale. Bishop Olmsted also welcomed the Legionaries of Christ to the diocese where they began Our Lady of Guadalupe Parish in Queen Creek in August 2006. This very large religious community was founded in Mexico and has outposts in a number of American dioceses as well as a sizeable seminary in Connecticut. After much consultation, the Franciscans, who had been in the diocese since its inception, established Our Lady of the Angels Conventual Church at their Franciscan Renewal Center—the second of its kind in the United States.

Other religious orders coming into the Phoenix diocese include the Society of St. John Eudes who went to St. Jerome in Phoenix, the Apostles of Jesus who attend to St. James in Glendale, the Institute of the Incarnate Word who sent priests to Immaculate Heart of Mary in Phoenix, the Society of Our Lady of the Most Holy Trinity who went to Camp Verde, and the Priestly Fraternity of St. Peter who serve Mater Misericordiae. Priests also came from various countries around the world to serve in the Phoenix diocese, such as Mexico, the Philippines, Nigeria, Uganda, Korea and the Dominican Republic.

In early 2008 Bishop Olmsted was asked to serve as Apostolic Administrator of the Diocese of Gallup, New Mexico. On February 5, 2009, Father James Sean Wall, vicar of priests for the Diocese of Phoenix, was named Bishop of Gallup. Wall, born October 11, 1964, in Ganado, Arizona, on the Navajo Reservation, graduated from Chandler High School and Arizona State University. He attended St. John Seminary in Camarillo, California, and was ordained a priest for the Diocese of Phoenix on June 6, 1998. Wall served in several parish assignments, including St. Theresa's in Phoenix, St. Timothy's in Mesa, and St. Thomas the Apostle in Phoenix. He also served as administrator pro tem of Our Lady of Perpetual Help in Glendale. In addition to being vicar of priests, he was the director of Mount Claret Retreat Center in Phoenix. He was ordained the Bishop of Gallup on April 23, 2009.

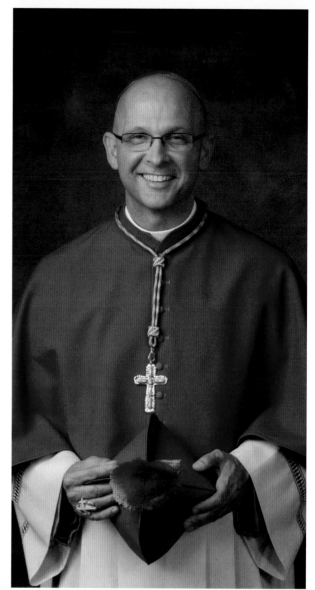

» *Bishop James Wall, a priest of the Diocese of Phoenix, was ordained Bishop of Gallup, New Mexico, on April 23, 2009.*

On February 17, 2009, Pope Benedict XVI conferred the title Chaplain to His Holiness on three priests of the Phoenix diocese: Fathers Antonio Andres Sotelo, George Edward Highberger and Thomas Francis Hever. All three were honored for their exemplary ministries in the Diocese of Phoenix. Sotelo and Highberger have worked closely with Spanish-speaking Catholics. Sotelo continues to take the sacraments to those in jail and prison. Highberger pastors St. Anthony of Padua in Wickenberg. Monsignor Hever, pastor of Our Lady of Perpetual Help, is one of the band of Irish priests who have served the diocese so well. He has worked in a number of parishes and is known for his steadfast and compassionate care for the sick and dying.

» Three new monsignori were created for the diocese on March 19, 2009: Monsignors Antonio Sotelo, George Highberger and Thomas Hever.
Credit: The Catholic Sun

The Abandonment Prayer of Charles de Foucauld

Father,
I abandon myself into your hands;
do with me what you will.
Whatever you may do,
I thank you.
I am ready for all,
I accept all.
Let only your will be done in me
and in all your creatures.
I wish no more than this,
O Lord.
Into your hands
I commend my soul;
I offer it to you,
with all the love of my heart,
for I love you, Lord,
and so need to give myself,
to surrender myself
into your hands,
without reserve,
and with boundless confidence,
for you are my Father.

Bishop Wall's episcopal ordination and the investiture of the new monsignori were occasions of joy for the Diocese of Phoenix. Many challenging and complex issues still remain for the Church: immigration, cultural values and the challenges of providing priests for the new millennium. Bishop Olmsted's faith in prayer will continue to be a source of strength and wisdom. He daily comes before the Lord to say the Prayer of Abandonment of Blessed Charles de Foucauld. As he revealed in a retrospective of his first few years in Phoenix, when he kneels before the Blessed Sacrament he adds, "Here I am, I come to do your will. If I am not doing it correctly, please let me know." Perhaps he also remembers a prayer often on the lips of St. Pius X and Blessed John XXIII, "È vostra Chiesa, O Signore." It is your Church, O Lord.

Parishes

The Diocese of Phoenix

Saints Simon & Jude Cathedral

Phoenix, Arizona

Established May 15, 1953

Saints Simon & Jude Parish was established by Bishop Daniel J. Gercke of Tucson on May 15, 1953. Father Paul P. Smith was appointed as the first pastor for 250 families. Mass was first celebrated in the Maryland School while a temporary church was built. Ground was broken for a temporary church and four classrooms on February 14, 1954. The first Mass in the church was celebrated on July 12, 1954. The temporary church was dedicated by Bishop Gercke on October 17, 1954.

Saints Simon & Jude School was founded in 1954 by Bishop Daniel J. Gercke of Tucson and Father Paul P. Smith. On August 20, 1954, four Loreto Sisters from the Order of the Institute of the Blessed Virgin Mary arrived from Navan, Ireland to staff the new school. On September 13, 1954, the first four elementary grades were opened for 200 students and staffed by the four Loreto Sisters. One grade was added each year, and by 1959, the first eighth-grade graduation ceremony was held. In 1960, a kindergarten program was added. The school had grown to 17 classrooms, a cafeteria, kitchen, and a new convent by 1963.

The groundbreaking for the church took place on September 20, 1964. The church was constructed on 17-acres of property on North 27th Avenue in Phoenix. The 1,200-seat church was dedicated by Bishop Francis J. Green of Tucson on December 11, 1966. Upon the completion of the new church, the temporary church was converted for use as the parish hall. After four months of construction, the parish dedicated a new community center in Santa Rosa on April 2, 1967.

On December 2, 1969, Pope Paul VI raised Saints Simon & Jude to the status of a Cathedral for Bishop Edward A. McCarthy and the newly established Diocese of Phoenix. The community center in Santa Rosa became the Santa Rosa Mission Chapel in 1974. Father Smith remained at the Cathedral as rector until July 1, 1976. Father Michael McGovern succeeded him as rector of the Cathedral until his departure on February 8, 1980. Father Paul Smith returned as rector in 1980 and was succeeded by Monsignor Richard Moyer.

Saints Simon & Jude Cathedral was graced by a visit from Pope John Paul II on September 14, 1987. In May 1989, Mother Teresa of Calcutta also visited the Cathedral. Monsignor Michael O'Grady served as rector of the Cathedral from 1990 to 2005. Santa Rosa Chapel was demolished in 2006, but the Santa Rosa Hall in Phoenix is still operated by the Cathedral and leased as an adult day care facility. Father Robert Clements is the current rector of the Cathedral and was appointed on July 1, 2005. The Cathedral has many ministries and organizations including RCIA, Cursillo, Legion of Mary, Marriage Preparation, Choir, Saint Vincent de Paul Society, Potter's Field Ministry, Bereavement Support, Youth Ministry, Families Remembering, and Knights of Columbus. Saints Simon and Jude Cathedral currently serves over 3,200 registered families.

ALL SAINTS
PARISH
Mesa, Arizona
Established August 26, 1972

On June 12, 1972, Father William McKay was named as pastor of a new parish in East Mesa. Bishop Edward McCarthy of Phoenix established the new parish on August 26, 1972, and approved the name of All Saints in September 1972. Early Masses for the parish were held in the Velda Rose Motel, Farnsworth Hall, Father McKay's home chapel, and Melcher's Mission Chapel.

The first Mass was celebrated by Father McKay in the new church on October 26, 1974. The dedication and blessing by Bishop McCarthy followed on February 23, 1975. The hall and parking spaces were added to the parish complex in 1975. In 1978, All Saints Parish was divided and Holy Cross Parish was established. In 1982, for the 10th Anniversary, Bishop O'Brien joined in the burning of the mortgage. Bishop's Hall was added to the parish complex a few years later.

Father McKay retired on June 30, 1995. He still remains very active at All Saints, celebrating daily and weekend Masses. He was elevated to Monsignor in early 2002, for all his dedicated years of service and many contributions to the

parish community throughout those years. Father Robert J. Caruso was appointed as pastor in 1995. All Saints Parish in Mesa currently has over 2150 registered families.

ASCENSION
PARISH
Fountain Hills, Arizona
Established September 15, 1976

More than 100 local Catholics first congregated for a Mass held in the old Community Center at the Village Bazaar on September 9, 1973, after Deacon George Clark made a written request to Bishop Edward McCarthy of Phoenix. The Church of the Ascension was established as a parish by Bishop Edward McCarthy of Phoenix on September 15, 1976. Father Paul Slanina, O.P., was appointed as the first pastor. Masses were originally held at the Community Center in Fountain Hills until 1980.

Ground was broken for a parish church building on June 10, 1979. The building included seating for more than 500 people, a private chapel, and an interim social hall. Mass was first held in the completed building on September 13, 1980. The church building was formally dedicated by Bishop James S. Rausch on May 28, 1981. This was followed by the construction of the rectory in 1984. Ground was broken for a parish hall on February 14, 1987. The Father Paul Center was completed in September 1987 and dedicated by Bishop O'Brien on January 23, 1988. Sadly, Father Slanina passed away on October 7, 1987. Father Robert Caruso was named as pastor and remained at the parish until Father Thomas O'Dea became the pastor in 1990.

In 2001, the parish purchased 14-acres of land in Fountain Hills with the intention of building a larger church facility in the near future. Father O'Dea retired in July 2003 and was succeeded by Father John T. McDonough, the current pastor. The parish has many ministries and programs including Catechetical Ministry, Music Ministry, Youth Ministry and Pastoral Care Ministry. Ascension Parish currently serves 1,100 registered families.

BLESSED SACRAMENT
PARISH

Scottsdale, Arizona
Established July 30, 1974

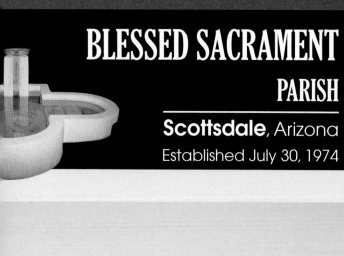

Blessed Sacrament Parish in Scottsdale was established by Bishop Edward McCarthy of Phoenix on July 30, 1974. Father Emmett J. FitzPatrick was appointed the first pastor. A 10-acre property on 64th Street was purchased prior to the parish establishment as the site of the future church. The community began celebrating Masses at Chaparral High School on September 8, 1974.

Groundbreaking for the new church took place on October 27, 1974. The building of the church, social hall and rectory was truly a community effort, with parishioners painting walls, finishing woodwork, planting trees and completing all the unexpected tasks that arose. After nearly three years of construction, the church was completed in August 1977. The first mass was held in the 750-seat church on October 1, 1977. Bishop James S. Rausch of Phoenix dedicated the church and parish complex on October 30, 1977.

In 1987, the FitzPatrick Center was constructed to add religious education classrooms and meeting space. The building was dedicated in December 1987. In 1994, additional classrooms were built for the religious education program, which now included a preschool. In 1998, the chapel and

Parish Life Center were also completed. Father Patrick Robinson is the current pastor. Ministries include Saint Vincent de Paul Society, Youth Ministry, RCIA and Catechetical Ministry. Blessed Sacrament Parish currently serves over 2,200 registered families.

BLESSED SACRAMENT
PARISH

Tolleson, Arizona

Established September 4, 1953

The Tolleson Mission had its foundations in the Franciscan and Claretian Fathers Orders who visited the small towns and villages around old Phoenix. The Claretian Fathers from Immaculate Heart of Mary came regularly to celebrate Mass. Mass was first celebrated in a frame building located in the middle of a cotton field at 92nd Avenue and Washington Street in Tolleson. Father Joseph Gamm, C.M.F., came to the mission in June 1948 and construction on the present church was soon begun. The new church was dedicated by Bishop Daniel J. Gercke of Tucson on December 12, 1949. The original frame building was then used as a hall.

Blessed Sacrament Parish in Tolleson was established on September 4, 1953. Father Joseph Gamm, C.M.F., was appointed as the first pastor. He left shortly after the parish was established and Father Francis J. Murphy became the second pastor in late 1953.

Father Murphy erected a parish rectory on North 91st Street before he left the parish in April 1956. Father George Reinweiler became pastor in September 1956. Father Alex D. Machain served as pastor from 1960 to 1969. The parish hall burned down in June 1966 and was rebuilt in 1967. A new and larger parish hall was dedicated in December 1971.

Father John Cunningham was appointed pastor in 1982. He began a major renovation of the church interior and exterior in 1982. The renovation included a remodeling of the altar, installation of skylights, new Spanish tile flooring, new dark wood ceiling, new tiled roof and bell tower, plaza entrance and the complete stuccoing of the interior and exterior of the church. The renovations were completed in 1983.

In 2006, the parish bought and refurbished an abandoned school adjacent to the church property. The building was dedicated by Bishop Thomas J. Olmsted on January 7, 2007 and named the La Casa de Maria Center for Religious Education. Father John Lankeit is the current pastor. Blessed Sacrament Parish serves over 1,200 registered families.

CHRIST THE KING

PARISH

Mesa, Arizona

Established September 19, 1959

Christ the King Parish in Mesa was established on September 19, 1959, and Father John Cullinan was appointed as the first pastor on September 21, 1959. Sunday Mass was held in the East Junior High School cafeteria until the end of 1959. In early 1960, all Masses were moved to the Mesa Knights of Columbus Hall. The Diocese of Tucson soon approved plans for a temporary church with four classrooms and the groundbreaking took place in May 1960. The first Mass was offered in the new church on December 4, 1960. The new church building and four classrooms were dedicated on January 22, 1961, by Bishop Francis J. Green.

In the fall of 1960, Catholics living at Apache Junction requested that Sunday Mass be celebrated for the 150 families living in the area. Beginning in December 1960, Mass was offered in a school building with the permission of the Apache Junction School Board. In early 1962, five acres of property were purchased in Apache Junction. Construction began on a combination church and hall in May 1962. The first Mass was celebrated in the new church on September 2, 1962. The new mission church in Apache Junction was named Saint George and placed under the care of Christ the King Parish until the establishment of the Diocese of Phoenix on December 2, 1969.

Construction on four additional classrooms and the convent began in late 1963 and was completed in 1964. Christ the King School opened in September 1964 for approximately 120 students in grades 1-4. By 1968, the school expanded to include grades 1-8. Father Thomas O'Dea became pastor in 1974. Under his leadership, a new church building and Presentation Hall were constructed. Bishop Francis J. Green of Tucson dedicated the new church and hall on November 22, 1981. The original 1962 church was eventually used to house the parish ministry offices.

Father Steven A. Kunkel became pastor in 2006. Christ the King Parish currently has approximately 2,000 registered families and over 900 parishioners active in parish ministries and organizations including Knights of Columbus, Adult Scripture Study Group, Teen Prayer Group, Bereavement Ministry and H.O.P.E. Outreach Ministry.

CORPUS CHRISTI
PARISH
Phoenix, Arizona
Established June 19, 1985

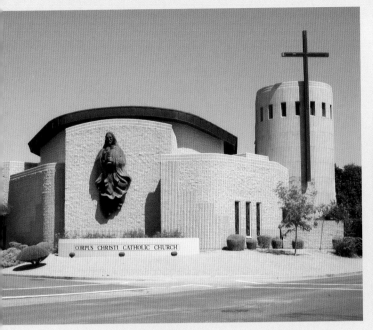

Corpus Christi Parish was established by Bishop Thomas J. O'Brien of Phoenix on June 19, 1985. Father Louis Anthony Sigman was appointed as the first pastor. Corpus Christi was established as a parish to serve the Ahwatukee area. The first Mass was celebrated at Mountain View Lutheran Church in Ahwatukee on September 14, 1985. Masses were continued there until January 21, 1989.

During the first few years, the parish grew from about 300 to nearly 1,000 families. A building fund program was successfully completed making possible the completion of the first parish facilities. These included a multi-purpose church seating 700, parish offices, six rooms for religious education classes, a meeting room for various ministries and parish organizations, and a rectory to house two priests. In 1991, seven more classrooms were added for the expanding religious education programs. The amphitheater-patio area was completed and the parish offices were enlarged.

By 1994, the parish decided it was time to build a permanent church. In January 1995, a second building fund drive was completed. Construction on the church began in March 1996 and was completed in December of 1996. The new church was dedicated by Bishop Thomas J. O'Brien of Phoenix on February 2, 1997. Father Albert Francis Hoorman is the current pastor. Corpus Christi Parish in Phoenix currently serves over 4,000 registered families.

EL CRISTO REY
PARISH

Grand Canyon, Arizona

Established 1960; March 19, 2008

El Cristo Rey was established as a parish on the South Rim of the Grand Canyon in 1960 and re-established on March 19, 2008, after an interim period of being a suppressed parish in care of Saint Joseph Parish in Williams. Father Alexander Frankoviz was appointed as the first pastor. The first Mass in the area was celebrated at the Women's Dormity Hall by Monsignor Edward Albouy from Nativity Parish in Flagstaff about 1942. Monsignor Albouy continued to visit the area once a month to say Mass and to teach Catechism to about 15 Catholic families in the local high school until 1951. Father John Faustina from Saint Joseph Parish in Williams began celebrating Mass in the lounge room of the Bright Angel Lodge on Easter Sunday in 1952. Sunday Mass became a regular event at the Bright Angel Lodge until 1960. The original Chapel and rectory were built on federal land by Father Frankoviz in 1960. The first Mass in the new chapel took place at midnight on Christmas 1960.

The first Holy Cross Priest to come to El Cristo Rey was Father Edmund Campers in September 1977. Father Campers remained until 1986 and was succeeded by Father William O'Connor, C.S.C., from 1986 to 1993. Father O'Connor renovated the interior of the Chapel and installed a new roof in 1987. Father Francis Zagorc, C.S.C., served as pastor from 1993 to 2000.

In 2002, the Chapel was renovated by 20 families of the parish and was expanded to seat nearly 100 people. Father Zagorc returned to the parish in 2002 and remained until his retirement in August 2004. Father Dindo C. (Bruno) Cuario, D.S., is the current pastor. El Cristo Rey Parish currently has 40 registered families and serves many visitors to the Grand Canyon National Park.

HOLY CROSS
PARISH

Mesa, Arizona

Established August 1, 1978

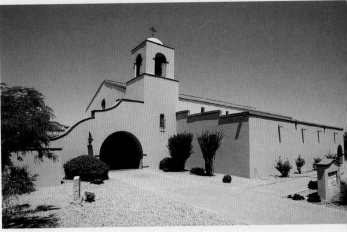

Holy Cross Parish was established on August 1, 1978, and Father William J. Mitchell was appointed as the first pastor. Eight acres of land were soon purchased at Power and Southern Roads for the construction of a church complex. Ground breaking ceremonies were held on September 14, 1980 for the 825-seat church, social hall and parish offices. Construction began on December 15, 1980 and work was completed on November 15, 1981.

The first mass was celebrated in the new Holy Cross Church on November 19, 1981, by Father Mitchell. Dedication ceremonies for the parish complex took place on March 9, 1982, with Bishop Thomas J. O'Brien officiating. A covered walkway now joins two sanctuaries and the second larger one was built in 1983 to accommodate the winter crowds.

In July 2008, Holy Cross completed renovations on the church including the retiling of the interior of the church, repainting of the church interior, and installation of a new lighting and sound systems. Decorative painting was done to enhance the mission style architecture of the church. Father Richard R. Felt is the current pastor. Holy Cross Parish has about 4,200 registered families.

HOLY FAMILY
PARISH

Phoenix, Arizona

Established January 22, 1968

Holy Family began as a mission of Saint Catherine of Siena Parish in Phoenix on October 27, 1966. Father George F. Pirrung was named as administrator of the mission. The first mass was celebrated in the cafeteria of T. G. Barr School on November 20, 1966, by Father Pirrung. Mass continued at the school cafeteria for the next several years until a church could be built.

Holy Family Mission became a parish on January 22, 1968, and Father Pirrung was named as the first pastor. Father Pirrung moved into the area and his residence on South 16th Place became the parish office and chapel. Groundbreaking for the new Holy Family Catholic Center by Bishop Edward McCarthy of Phoenix was held on April 12, 1970. The new building included a worship space, large hall, small classrooms, library and rectory on 10-acres of land located on South 24th Street.

Holy Family Parish shares its pastor with Saint Edward the Confessor Parish. Father Daniel McBride is the current canonical pastor. The parish has many ministries and services including Catechetical Ministry, RCIA, Youth Group, and Faith Formation. Holy Family Parish currently serves 600 registered families.

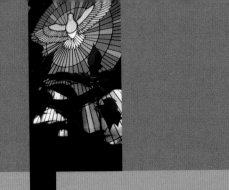

Holy Spirit Roman Catholic Parish was established on April 17, 1973. On this date, the Diocese of Phoenix bought a plot of land for a church and a priest's residence. Reverend Bernard Colton was appointed the first Pastor and given permission by Marcos de Niza High School to hold services in the drama room. The first Mass was held on Palm Sunday in 1973, and about 50 people attended. Daily Masses were held in the garage of the priest's residence. In less than a year, the parish had grown to 300 registered families. The congregation had to move out of the drama room into the gymnasium of the high school.

Plans for development of a permanent building for worship, classrooms, and social activities for the parish began, and a building committee was appointed. Reverend Michael O'Grady became Pastor in November, 1974. By early 1975 the plans were complete and Bishop Edward A. McCarthy granted permission to proceed with the project.

In May, 1975, a Mass and groundbreaking ceremony were held on the vacant lot. On July 4, 1976, the first Mass was held in the first church building. Actual dedication of the church by Bishop James S. Rausch took place on May 29, 1977, for the 1,100 registered families.

By 1984, it became evident that the worship space was inadequate. The liturgy committee met with liturgical design experts and one was hired to redesign the church. The altar was moved out on a platform and a new back drop was designed and built to display the cross. New lighting was installed and new sanctuary furniture built.

On July 1, 1991, Reverend John Hanley was assigned as Pastor. The present church was built in 2001 as a result of the Vision 2000 Building Program. The first Mass was celebrated on Christmas Day, 2001. Dedication of the building by Bishop Thomas J. O'Brien took place on Pentecost, 2002. In 2003, the parish administration building was completed. The community center was renovated and made available for parish and outside events by January, 2004. Reverend John Hanley remained Pastor for fifteen years and retired in June of 2006.

Father Thomas J. Hallsten was assigned as Parochial Administrator in July of 2006. Holy Spirit Parish currently has over 1,700 registered families.

IMMACULATE CONCEPTION

PARISH

Cottonwood, Arizona
Established 1966

In 1887 the first Catholic parish in the Verde Valley was founded. This was Holy Family in Jerome and served the people of Jerome, Clarkdale, Clemenceau and Cottonwood. As the area grew more space for worship was needed. In 1924, Saint Cecilia Mission was founded to meet the needs of the growing Clarkdale/Cottonwood community.

The booming growth of the Verde Valley continued and a few years later, the Immaculate Conception Mission was founded at Cottonwood in 1930. Father Charles Bartusch C.M.F., built the church at 421 N. Willard in Cottonwood. In 1943, Father John Atucha, C.M.F., a priest from Spain, added the sacristy to the church himself. Father Driscoll established the first Catholic Youth Organization (CYO) and built the recreation hall in 1953. Priests lived in a rented residence in Clarkdale until the rectory was built in 1955.

The first Parish Council, elected in 1965 updated the sanctuary by providing a new altar, lecterns and acolyte benches. In 1966, Immaculate Conception Church was separated from Clarkdale and for all intents and purposes was a separate parish. Father John J. Hannon was the first pastor. Saint Cecelia became its mission on September 23, 1971.

As times changed and the mines were closed, Immaculate Conception became the primary church in the valley with Saint Cecilia serving as its mission. In the late 1990s, both churches outgrew the rapid population growth in the valley. The Diocese of Phoenix purchased enough land to build a new church, grade school and high school. Saint Joseph Montessori School opened on August 21, 2006, with 60 students. The school originally opened as a Montessori school that was not affiliated with the diocese in 2005. The school was under renovation when school began on August 21, 2006, and classes were temporarily held at the Immaculate Conception chapel. The school still follows the Montessori model of teaching only for preschool and kindergarten.

A temporary church in portable buildings was constructed and opened in 2002. Father David J. Kelash is the current pastor. The church seats approximately 400 people and is now more than 95% occupied at all Masses. Immaculate Conception Parish currently has 900 registered families.

Immaculate Heart of Mary Parish was established by Bishop Daniel J. Gercke of Tucson on December 12, 1924. The parish was served by the Claretian Fathers and Father Antimo G. Nebreda, C.M.F., was appointed the first pastor on October 24, 1925. Father Nebreda was to coordinate his efforts in forming a community and building a school, church and rectory. Plans for the parish buildings began in 1926.

Immaculate Heart of Mary School was opened in 1926 by the Immaculate Heart Sisters. After two years work on the school and rectory, ground was broken for the church on January 10, 1928. Mass was being celebrated in the basement of the school at this time. Bishop Gercke came to Phoenix to dedicate the new church on December 15, 1928. Father Nebreda remained at the parish until June 1939. In 1951, a gymnasium was added to the school and dedicated on July 8, 1951. The school was closed in May 1969.

The parish has served the Spanish speaking community since its inception. For many decades, Immaculate Heart of Mary was the only parish to offer masses in Spanish. In the fall of 1959, work began to establish the first permanent Cursillo Center in the United States at Immaculate Heart of Mary. Father Alonso Duran, C.M.F., initiated the project and the parish was to have the first permanent center for Cursillos on the first floor of the rectory. The movement grew in the following years and a national publication for the Cursillo movement began at Immaculate Heart of Mary. The Claretian Fathers continued to serve the parish until November 5, 1970.

Immaculate Heart of Mary is the second oldest church in Phoenix. In 1996, Immaculate Heart of Mary Church was named as a historical site and listed on the National Register of Historic Places. In 1997, the gymnasium building was remodeled and converted into a parish hall. The parish hall was dedicated in October 1997. A tragic fire on April 17, 2000 destroyed most of the interior of the church. Following a $3 million restoration project, the church was rededicated by Bishop Thomas J. O'Brien of Phoenix on March 24, 2002.

On February 18, 2006, through the invitation of Bishop Thomas J. Olmsted, the Institute of Incarnate World was given the pastoral care of Immaculate Heart of Mary parish in downtown Phoenix. The Institute of Incarnate Word also oversees a second parish, Saint Anthony. Immaculate Heart of Mary is a "national parish" established by the Diocese of Phoenix for the extensive Mexican population living in the city.

The parishioners greeted the Institute of the Incarnate Word and the two priests assigned to the parishes with great joy. The Institute assigned Fr. Humberto Villa, recently parochial vicar in New Bedford, Massachusetts, as pastor and newly ordained, Fr. Librado Godinez, a native of Mexico, as the parochial vicar. The predominantly Mexican parishes will keep the priests busy with 16 Masses on weekends and 7,000-8,000 people attending Mass on an average Sunday. Father Walter Alfredo Frutades, I.V.E., is the current pastor.

MOST HOLY TRINITY
PARISH
Phoenix, Arizona
Established November 1, 1951

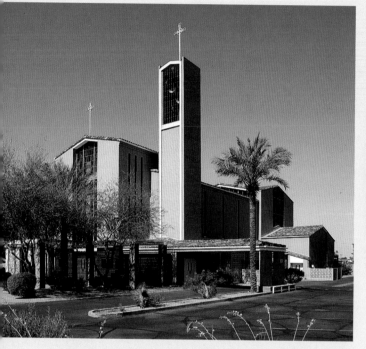

In the spring of 1942, Mass was celebrated by the Jesuit Fathers for 23 people in an old rented butcher shop. The building was sold later in 1942, forcing those faithful Catholics to use the Schmitt home for Sunday Mass. As their number increased, three acres of land on 7th Street were acquired for the construction of a small chapel called Our Lady of the Wayside Mission. The first Mass in the chapel was celebrated on December 8, 1943. A parish hall was constructed in 1948 and later named McHugh Hall.

Most Holy Trinity Parish was established on November 1, 1951. Father (later Monsignor) Neil P. McHugh was appointed as the first pastor. Most Holy Trinity School was founded in September 1953 by the Sisters of Notre Dame de Namur from Reading, Ohio. The school opened with 129 students in grades 1-6 and a staff of four Sisters. Grade 7 was added for the 1954-1955 school year and grade 8 for the 1955-1956 school year. Construction of the present church building was completed in late 1957 and dedicated on December 8, 1957. The rectory was completed in 1962 and a convent in 1967. The old Our Lady of the Wayside mission chapel was also converted for use as the Saint Thomas Aquinas Hall. Additions to the school building were made during 1966-1969 including a new library. The Sisters of Notre Dame de Namur remained at the school until 1976.

Monsignor McHugh served the parish until 1986. The Dominican Fathers were invited to staff the parish in 1988. They brought to Most Holy Trinity Parish the renewing spirit of Vatican II, and the parish experienced a dramatic increase in lay involvement in the parish. Responding to the need to evangelize our youth, in 2003 the Saint Augustine Youth Center was built. During this time, the parish also became a multi-cultural community, welcoming a Spanish community and a Vietnamese community. The Disciples of Hope assumed leadership of the parish on July 1, 2003. Father Alphonsus Bakyil, S.O.L.T., is the current pastor. Ministries include Life Teen, Ministry of Care, Hispanic Ministry, and RCIA. Most Holy Trinity Parish currently serves over 850 registered families.

OUR LADY OF CZESTOCHOWA
PARISH

Phoenix, Arizona
Established March 19, 2008

The early history of the Polish mission began with Father Grzegorz Kotnis from the Pauline Order organizing Holy Mass in Polish once a month from 1978 to 1986, with the help of Father Richard Ciesniewski. In September 1986, Father Edward Wanat from the Salvatorian Order began celebrating Mass in Polish at Brophy Chapel once a month and later in Saint Theresa Parish once a week with help from Father (later Monsignor) John McMahon. At this time, the Polish community numbered 300 people. Father Stanislaw Pieczara of the Salvatorian Order continued Polish Masses at Saint Theresa from 1987 to 1992. Father Klemens Pepel cared for the Polish community at Saint Theresa from December 1992 to January 1995.

In 1993, Bishop Thomas J. O'Brien agreed that the Polish community should start efforts towards the purchase of a church building. On January 22, 1995, Father Klemens Dabrowski from the Society of Christ Fathers came to Phoenix to serve the Polish community. The Polish Apostolate was established by Bishop O'Brien on April 22, 1995.

On October 18, 1996, a former Christian Science church building was purchased as a new place for the Polish Apostolate on North 7th Street in Phoenix. The first Mass was celebrated on December 22, 1996. The church was remodeled and the dedication by Bishop O'Brien took place on May 24, 1997 to Our Lady of Czestochowa.

Our Lady of Czestochowa Mission was established by Bishop O'Brien on July 18, 2000. The Diocese of Phoenix purchased a church located on West Country Gables Drive for the mission on March 16, 2006. The first mass in the new church was celebrated on March 25, 2006. Bishop Thomas J. Olmsted elevated Our Lady of Czestochowa to become a parish on March 19, 2008. Father Eugeniusz Bolda, S. Chr., was named the founding pastor and had served at the mission since September 2000. The parish has many ministries and services including Children's Choir, Catechetical Ministry, Music Ministry, Rosary Society, Knights of Columbus, and Saint Monica Senior Club. Our Lady of Czestochowa Parish currently serves 650 registered families.

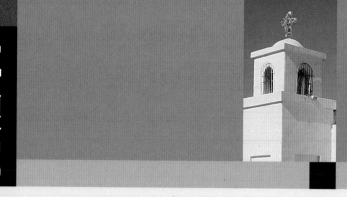

OUR LADY OF GUADALUPE

PARISH

Guadalupe, Arizona
Established April 28, 1970

A small group of Yaqui Indians, lead by a Catholic priest, migrated up into Arizona and were taken in by the Tohono O'odham Indians. The Franciscans at Saint Mary Mission brought them to Tempe and Father Lucius Zittier, O.F.M., began ministering to the needs of the Yaqui Indians in 1904. By 1910, the area where the Yaqui Indians lived was needed for farming and they were evicted. Father Zittier was able to secure 40-acres, donated by the Haynes family, for the Yaqui Indians in Guadalupe. The Yaqui Indians relocated from Tempe to Guadalupe by June 1910.

The Yaqui Indians, under the direction of Father Zittier, built an adobe church in 1912 that they called the Templo Mayor. The church became a mission of Our Lady of Mount Carmel Parish in Tempe in 1932. The adobe towers were added to the church during the 1940's.

The Yaqui Indians built another smaller structure next to the church in 1948. It was named the Templo Menor and used as a social hall. From 1916 until 1960, there was only intermittent care of the Templo Mayor and a priest from Our Lady of Mount Carmel came on Sundays to say a Mass. In 1960, a Franciscan named Father Fidelis Kuban decided to use Guadalupe as a home base for his Trailer Mission. The church was expanded and

renovated in 1967. A parish center was also built in 1967.

Our Lady of Guadalupe Parish was established by Bishop Edward McCarthy of Phoenix on April 28, 1970. Father James Kelly was appointed the first pastor. The historic church was proclaimed the Shrine of Our Lady of Guadalupe by Bishop McCarthy on May 7, 1972. In 1972, the church was renovated and a rectory was built. The Franciscan Fathers took over administration of the parish in the summer of 1973. A fire destroyed most of the church on April 22, 1974. Only the adobe walls and the two towers remained after the fire. The church was rebuilt in 1975 and included raising the height of the walls with a new dome added over the altar area. Mass was held in the Templo Menor during the reconstruction. Father Joseph A. Baur, O.F.M., is the current parochial administrator. Ministries include Music Ministry, Religious Education, Catechetical Ministry, and Baptism/Marriage Preparation. Our Lady of Guadalupe Parish serves over 1,000 registered families.

OUR LADY OF GUADALUPE

PARISH

Queen Creek, Arizona

Established June 20, 2006

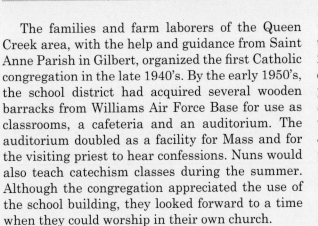

The families and farm laborers of the Queen Creek area, with the help and guidance from Saint Anne Parish in Gilbert, organized the first Catholic congregation in the late 1940's. By the early 1950's, the school district had acquired several wooden barracks from Williams Air Force Base for use as classrooms, a cafeteria and an auditorium. The auditorium doubled as a facility for Mass and for the visiting priest to hear confessions. Nuns would also teach catechism classes during the summer. Although the congregation appreciated the use of the school building, they looked forward to a time when they could worship in their own church.

In 1960, the members started raising money for a building fund. Father Joseph N. Patterson of Chandler helped with the purchase of property and Father Charles O'Hern of Gilbert helped acquire a barracks building from Williams Air Force Base. The barracks building was moved to the site on the north side of Ocotillo Road where the chapel still stands today. By 1975, the chapel building was deemed unsafe and new fundraising efforts were started. In 1988, seven acres of land was purchased across the street for a new multi-purpose building. Father Douglas Lorig was appointed as the first administrator on July 1, 1988. Groundbreaking on the new facility took place in July 1988 for use as a worship space and hall to seat up to 400 people. The new church and hall were dedicated on December 12, 1988. The old chapel was converted into classrooms and ministries space.

Our Lady of Guadalupe Mission began to grow to over 1,200 families around 2006. With this burgeoning population came calls for a dedicated parish, a place of worship offering the Catholic sacraments and ministries. Our Lady of Guadalupe Mission was elevated to parish status by Bishop Thomas J. Olmsted of Phoenix on June 20, 2006. The new parish was administered by the Legionaries of Christ, Father Michael Shannon was appointed as the first pastor on August 15, 2006. The current pastor is Father Thomas Moylan, L.C. Ministries and organizations include Youth Ministry, RCIA, Cursillo, Ministry of Care, Spanish Prayer Group, and Knights of Columbus. Our Lady of Guadalupe Parish currently serves 2,000 registered families.

OUR LADY OF JOY
PARISH
Carefree, Arizona
Established November 14, 1972

In 1964, some 25 Catholic families came together for Mass at the Carefree Inn. A visiting priest said Mass for these founding families. Our Lady of Joy was soon founded as a mission of Our Lady of Perpetual Help in Scottsdale. By 1970, the mission included 70 families and grew to over 100 families just two years later.

Our Lady of Joy Parish was established by Bishop Edward McCarthy of Phoenix on November 14, 1972. Father John P. Doran was appointed as the first pastor. The first building fund allowed for the purchase of 10 acres that had formerly been used as a dumping ground. The dedication of a new multi-purpose building by Bishop McCarthy took place on December 1, 1974. The building included a worship space, offices, and a small priest's residence. By 1980, the number of children in the parish had grown to about 50. In order to offer Religious Education classes, a construction trailer was added to the parish grounds. The trailer provided room for classes and additional office space.

By 1985, the parish had grown to 320 families and plans for a permanent church were begun. The new church was completed in early 1988. The original multi-purpose building was renovated for use as a parish hall and parish office. In 1991, a permanent rectory was built just uphill from the church. The parish hall was also remodeled into a meeting room, four permanent classrooms, and offices.

In 1995, the church was expanded and a new Parish Center was erected. In 1997, the Administration Building was built to house the growing parish staff. Following these projects, the Atrium and the Teen Center were also constructed. The original parish hall was again remodeled as the Children's Center to house a Preschool and Child Care facilities. Father Patrick Farley is the pastoral administrator. Ministries and services include RCIA, Outreach, Faith Formation, Stewardship, Gift Shop, and Music and Liturgy. Our Lady of Joy Parish currently has 3,400 registered families.

OUR LADY OF LOURDES

PARISH (Our Lady of Lourdes & Prince of Peace Church)

Sun City West, Arizona
Established January 16, 1979

Our Lady of Lourdes
Church

Prince of Peace Church

Our Lady of Lourdes Parish in Sun City West was established by Bishop James Rausch of Phoenix on January 16, 1979. Father Vincent J. Nevulis was appointed as the first pastor. The parish's first home was the R.H. Johnson Social Hall. The first Mass in the new parish was celebrated at the Johnson Social Hall by Father Nevulis on April 1, 1979 and regular Masses continued there until 1982. Father Nevulis rented a furnished house on Prospect Drive and celebrated daily Masses at his residence.

Ground was broken for Madonna Hall, the first permanent church structure built in Sun City West, on February 8, 1981 and dedicated by Bishop Thomas J. O'Brien of Phoenix on February 11, 1982. Madonna Hall served as both the church and parish activity center.

Father Cornelius Moynihan was named pastor in 1985. Plans began in earnest to build a church adjacent to Madonna Hall. Ground was broken for the new church on December 13, 1987. The first Mass was celebrated in the church on November 10, 1988. Bishop O'Brien dedicated the new church on February 26, 1989. Father Moynihan retired in 1993 and Father Michael Minogue was appointed as pastor.

In 1994, the Diocese of Phoenix announced plans for a second church to be built as a "sister church" to Our Lady of Lourdes. The unique concept of one parish with two churches was born. From October 1994, until the dedication of Prince of Peace Church, additional Sunday Masses were held at Palm Ridge Recreation Center in Sun City West. Construction on Prince of Peace began in summer 1997 and the 1400-seat church was dedicated by Bishop Thomas O'Brien of Phoenix on April 18, 1999. Father David M. Ostler is the current pastor. Ministries and organization include Saint Vincent de Paul Society, Westside Food Bank, Women's Guild, Men's Club, Catholic Daughters and Knights of Columbus, and Prison Ministry. Our Lady of Lourdes and Prince of Peace currently serve over 3,300 registered families.

OUR LADY OF MOUNT CARMEL PARISH

Tempe, Arizona
Established June 14, 1932

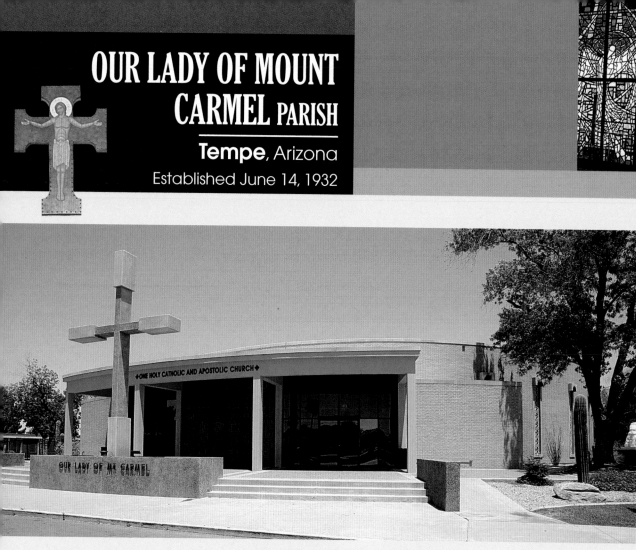

In 1876, Father (later Monsignor) Edouard Gerard saw the need for a chapel in Tempe. Local Catholics began constructing an adobe building in 1877. In 1880, the little chapel was completed and dedicated to Our Lady of Mount Carmel. Father Gerard served the chapel until 1891. Franciscan Fathers from Phoenix took over in 1895. In 1902, Father Severin Westhoff, O.F.M., bought property for a new church at Eighth and College Street. The new church was dedicated in 1903. From 1925 to 1932, the Tempe mission was known as Saint Mary Mission and served by Claretian priests from Immaculate Heart of Mary in Phoenix.

On June 14, 1932, Saint Mary Mission in Tempe was given the status of a parish by Bishop Daniel J. Gercke of Tucson. The new parish was renamed Our Lady of Mount Carmel and Father James Peter Davis (later Archbishop of San Juan de Puerto Rico and Archbishop of Santa Fe) was appointed the first pastor. Our Lady of Mount Carmel School in Tempe opened September 8, 1945 with two classrooms for 75 students. The school started with grades 1-3 and a faculty of the Sisters of Charity of the Blessed Virgin Mary of Dubuque, Iowa. Classes were held in a temporary classroom arrangement in the basement of the old Mount Carmel Church. In 1950, a four classroom building was erected and the school was expanded to included grades 1-8. In 1957, the school was moved to its present location and built in stages from 1957 to 1960.

In 1956, the Hughes family donated 10-acres on Rural Road to the parish and a new school, social hall and convent were all built by 1960. The social hall was dedicated on February 9, 1958 and services were held at both the church and hall until 1962. In 1962, the parish sold the old church to the Newman Catholic Student Center at Arizona State University. Masses were held at the social hall until late 1968. A new church was completed at the Rural Road property in December 1968. The 1000-seat church was dedicated by Bishop Francis J. Green of Tucson on May 11, 1969.

Father John Bonavitacola is the parochial administrator. Ministries and organizations include Catechetical Ministry, Youth Ministry, RCIA, and Children's Choir. Our Lady of Mount Carmel Parish currently serves 2,700 registered families.

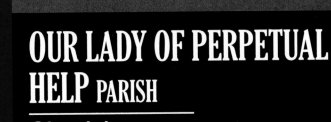

OUR LADY OF PERPETUAL HELP PARISH

Glendale, Arizona
Established February 11, 1947

The parish had its beginnings as a small mission under the auspices of the Franciscan Fathers from Saint Mary Parish in Phoenix. The Claretian Fathers of Immaculate Heart of Mary Parish in Phoenix took over the mission about 1928. Masses were held in a small adobe church named in honor of Saint Joseph. The adobe church was completed in 1933 and destroyed by fire in 1936. The adobe church was rebuilt again in 1938 as Our Lady of Perpetual Help Mission.

Our Lady of Perpetual Help Parish was established on February 11, 1947, with over 650 families. Father (later Monsignor) James E. McFaddan was appointed the first pastor. Our Lady of Perpetual Help School was established by Father Charles Towner and three Sisters of Notre Dame de Namur in September 1950.

In 1972, land was donated by the Sinnett family and was sold to finance the building of a new church. The new church was dedicated by Bishop Edward McCarthy of Phoenix on October 21, 1973. The adobe church became a center for religious education classes and social activities. The old church has been restored and is now known as Our Lady of Guadalupe Chapel.

Father Michael D. Accinni Rienhardt is the current pastor. Our Lady of Perpetual Help Parish in Glendale serves over 3,300 registered families.

In 1923, three lots were purchased on the southeast corner of Brown and 1st Streets in Scottsdale, but it was 10 years before a church was erected. The first Mass took place in 1924 at a vacant store in Scottsdale and celebrated by Father Antimo G. Nebreda, a Claretian priest. Masses were celebrated in the store, the Old Coronado School (known as the Little Red Schoolhouse) and the Morales home. A building fund was begun in 1930 by Father Manuel Almuedo, who served the mission from 1929 to 1931. In 1932, Father James Peter Davis (later Archbishop of San Juan de Puerto Rico and Archbishop of Santa Fe) from Our Lady of Mount Carmel in Tempe was assigned to the mission. The 150-seat adobe mission church was completed in October 1933. The first Mass was celebrated in the church on October 14, 1933.

Our Lady of Perpetual Help was established as a parish on October 8, 1948. Father James Mulvihill was appointed the first pastor. He replaced the old flooring and installed a Communion railing, new altars and statues in the church. In 1952, Father (later Monsignor) Eugene Maguire was appointed as pastor. The adobe church could no longer handle the 194 families and 10-acres of property were bought in 1954. The new church could seat 600 people and the first Mass was held on December 23, 1956. The old adobe church was used for meetings for many years before becoming the home of the Scottsdale Symphony Orchestra in 1977.

The Sisters of Charity of Seton Hill from Greensburg, Pennsylvania sent three Sisters to help Father Eugene Maguire open Our Lady of Perpetual Help School on September 10, 1956, for 87 students. By 1962, the 17-room school was completed and 720 children were attending classes. On April 2, 1978, Father Maguire rejoiced as the present church on the corner of Miller and Main Street was blessed and dedicated. The original church became the parish hall. Monsignor Maguire retired in 1993. Father William Healy was the pastor from 1993 to 2000.

The school offices and classrooms are newly renovated and a multipurpose building with a gym is in the plans. The original mission, now called the Old Adobe Mission, is being restored thanks to the Restoration Committee and 60 volunteers. Monsignor Thomas F. Hever has been pastor since 2000. Our Lady of Perpetual Help Parish serves over 2,500 registered families.

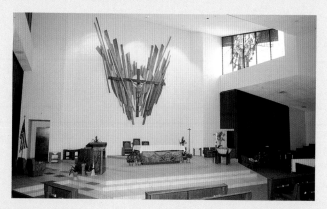

OUR LADY OF THE ANGELS
CONVENTUAL CHURCH
Scottsdale, Arizona
Established February 26, 2006

(formerly Casa Chapel/ Franciscan Renewal Center)

Originally founded by the Franciscan Friars in 1951, the Casa de Paz y Bien Franciscan Renewal Center was located on a 25-acre private desert site between the Camelback and Mummy Mountains in Scottsdale. The original buildings of the center were built in 1945 as the second Paradise Valley resort, called Echo Lodge. The property was renamed Kachina Lodge in 1947.

Father Owen da Silva, O.F.M., looking for a retreat site at the request of Bishop Daniel Gercke of Tucson, purchased the Kachina Lodge and 25-acres for the Franciscans in 1951. It was named Casa de Paz y Bien Franciscan Retreat. The first retreat was held in the fall of 1951 and staffed by the Franciscan friars of the Santa Barbara Province. The name was simplified as the Franciscan Renewal Center in the 1970's. The main chapel retained the name, Casa de Paz y Bien. The Casa Chapel provided seating for 200 people and Sunday Masses were offered regularly.

Our Lady of the Angels Conventual Church at the Franciscan Renewal Center became a parish on February 26, 2006, and was dedicated on February 26, 2006. It was with great joy that the Franciscan community announced that the Franciscan Renewal

Center's chapel received this new status in the Diocese of Phoenix. The Casa Chapel was changed from its previous classification as a semi-private oratory to the status of a conventual church. The classification of conventual church is unique in the diocese. The church will continue to belong to and be guided by the Franciscan community, while continuing their cooperative partnership with the mission of the Diocese of Phoenix. Reverend Laurence P. Dolan, O.F.M., is the founding and current rector of the parish. Our Lady of the Angels Conventual Church serves 700 families.

OUR LADY OF THE LAKE
PARISH

Lake Havasu City, Arizona

Established May 10, 1969

Our Lady of the Lake was selected as the name of the church in Lake Havasu City by Bishop Bernard Espelage, O.F.M., of Gallup. Early Masses took place in an old army mess hall. Father John Sullivan, pastor of Saint Mary Parish in Kingman, began holding weekly Mass at the Lake Havasu City mission in 1965. Father Cyril Levy began serving the people of Lake Havasu City as a mission in 1967. Father Joseph Brackett became the first administrator in-residence at the mission in 1968.

Father Brackett, with the assistance of about 35 local families and a substantial gift from the Catholic Church Extension Society of Chicago built the first church and rectory in 1968. About 8-acres of land near Lake Havasu were provided for the mission church by Robert P. McCulloch Sr., the founder of Lake Havasu City. The church seated 150 worshipers in folding chairs and also served as recreation hall and meeting room. Our Lady of the Lake was established as a parish on May 10, 1969, with Father Brackett as the founding pastor.

The groundbreaking for a new church of Our Lady of the Lake took place in September 1972. The new church could accommodate nearly 700 people for worship. The new church was dedicated on March 25, 1974, by Bishop Edward McCarthy of Phoenix.

The groundbreaking for the present church building took place in April 2003. On October 3, 2004, the church was dedicated. On that day a formal dedication of the new church was celebrated by Bishop Thomas Olmsted of Phoenix. Father Chauncey K. Winkler, the current pastor, arrived in July 2007. Ministries include a very active Saint Vincent de Paul Society, Community Soup Kitchen and many more ministries and organisations. Our Lady of the Lake Parish currently serves approximately 2,500 registered families.

OUR LADY OF THE VALLEY PARISH

Phoenix, Arizona

Established July 24, 1973

Bishop Edward McCarthy decreed the erection of Our Lady of the Valley Parish on July 24, 1973. Prior to the acquisition of the current parish property daily Mass, parish business and Baptisms for the young parish took place in the home of founding pastor Father James Kelly on 33rd Avenue. Weekend Masses were celebrated in the cafeteria of Desert Foothills School across the street from Father Kelly's house. Besides the school, several area Protestant churches opened their doors to Our Lady of the Valley weekend Masses until the community established a home of its own.

Bishop McCarthy broke ground for Our Lady of the Valley Church on February 9, 1975 and celebrated the Sacrament of Confirmation for the parish youth at Greenway High School. The multi-purpose facility opened its doors for the first time the weekend of March 27-28, 1976. Our Lady of the Valley Church was dedicated May 9, 1976.

Today, the parish has been paired with Saint Raphael Parish in Glendale and Father Edward J. Kaminski, C.S.C., is the pastor of both parishes. The parish has many ministries and programs that include RCIA, Youth Ministry, Pastoral Care, Catechetical Ministry and Social Outreach. Our Lady of the Valley Parish currently has about 600 registered families.

QUEEN OF PEACE
PARISH

Mesa, Arizona
Established November 1, 1934

(formerly Sacred Heart Parish & Saint Mary, Queen of Peace Parish)

The Franciscan Fathers at Saint Mary Parish in Phoenix established the Sacred Heart Mission in 1908 on the corner of Second Street and Country Club Drive in Mesa. The Franciscans served the community until 1932, when the Missionary Sons of the Immaculate Heart of Mary took over the mission. Sacred Heart in Mesa was established as a parish on November 1, 1934. Father Vincent Mestre became the first pastor.

A mission school was opened in the fall of 1940, under the guidance of the Sisters of the Precious Blood. The school, along with its 85 students in grades 1-4, was moved to its present location on MacDonald Street in 1942. In 1947, a new church and the school building were constructed and the parish name was changed from Sacred Heart to Saint Mary, Queen of Peace. The name was eventually shortened to Queen of Peace Parish. The Sisters of the Precious Blood continued at the school until 1981.

The parish hall was added in 1968 and Madonna Hall was built in 1977 and used by the school for assemblies, plays, music lessons, meetings, and the lunchroom. Over the past twenty years, many building projects and renovation projects have taken place at Queen of Peace including the building of a large parish office and the Antonio Perri Center, remodeling of the rectory, renovation of the church interior and installation of the Ten Commandments Monument.

Queen of Peace was served by the Society of the Divine Savior until 2005. After more than 20 years of religious guidance by the Salvatorian Fathers, the parish and school were placed under the supervision of diocesan priests. Father Charles Goraieb is the current pastor of Queen of Peace Parish. Plans for a major renovation of the parish campus including the conversion of the Perri Center into a state-of-the-art elementary school, the building of a new parish hall and parish offices were begun in 2008. Queen of Peace Parish currently has over 3,000 registered families.

RESURRECTION
PARISH

Tempe, Arizona

Established March 29, 1970

Resurrection Parish in Tempe was established on March 29, 1970. Father Philip J. Poirier was appointed as the first pastor. Resurrection was the first parish established by Bishop Edward J. McCarthy in the new Diocese of Phoenix. The new parish began with 380 families.

The first Masses were held on Easter Sunday in the assembly room at Mesa Community College. Hospitality was also offered by the King of Glory Lutheran Church and the Lutheran sanctuary was the site for confessions and special services which allowed for an ecumenical touch to the new parish until its own buildings were constructed. The site of the new church was selected as 7.7 acres of land north of Southern Ave from Evergreen Street to the Canal. The first rectory was a house at Huntington Drive and Evergreen. The groundbreaking for the first church building was held April 11, 1971. The first Mass in the new church was celebrated on April 2, 1972, and dedication ceremonies were held on April 23, 1972.

In 1979, the parish constructed a new social hall, administrative wing, education building, and storage area attached to the church. In March 1984,

an expansion of the church was begun to create seating for 200 more people. The church expansion was completed in 1985. Father Poirier remained pastor until July 8, 1986. Father Charles Parker was appointed the second pastor on August 1, 1986. Father (later Monsignor) Thomas F. Hever became the third pastor on July 1, 1989. A renovation of the church interior took place in honor of the parish's 25th anniversary and was completed in 1995. Succeeding pastors were Father Leo Brogan, Father Fredrick Adamson, V.G., and Father Steven Kunkel.

Work began on the Resurrection Memorial Gardens in spring of 2006. The gardens were completed in time for Bishop Thomas Olmsted to bless them on September 2, 2006, when he installed Father Joseph P. McGaffin as pastor. On July 30, 2007, the church sustained major monsoon damage both to the roof and water damage to the interior. Weekend masses were moved to Philip Hall and construction began to restore the church on June 25, 2008. The dedication of the new Church was celebrated on March 15, 2009.

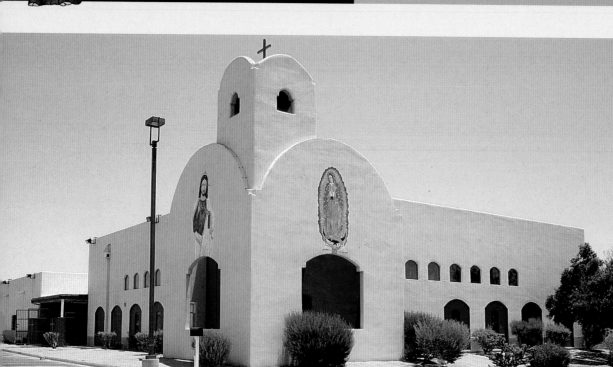

During the 1930s and 1940s, residents of the Golden Gate barrio in Phoenix began holding Mass in their homes, an old store and in a vacant lot with benches. Father Albert Braun, O.F.M., came to the area in 1940. Sacred Heart was established as a mission in March 1954. Father Albert Braun, O.F.M., was appointed as the first pastor. Permission was granted from the Congregation of the Religious to elevate Sacred Heart to become a territorial movable parish on November 16, 1959. Bishop Francis J. Green of Tucson signed the formal Decree of Establishment on September 13, 1962.

The two missions of the parish, Saint Mary Magdalene Chapel and Santa Rita Chapel had been founded in 1953. A third mission chapel, Saint John the Baptist was later established but closed in September 1973. Early Masses were originally held in an army barracks located on 17th Street. The original brick church was dedicated on October 14, 1956. Sacred Heart Center was built in 1957 and followed by the construction of Sacred Heart School in 1959. The school was run by the Sisters of the Precious Blood and the Benedictine Sisters until 1964.

The Golden Gate area was severely impacted by the airport expansion in 1970s. The city bought the old church, school and rectory in 1985 to make way for the Sky Harbor Center. Christmas Mass in 1985 was the final ceremony closing the old church. The old school and rectory were eventually torn down but the old church was renovated for use as a community center. The remaining chapels of Saint Mary Magdalene and Santa Rita thrived in the subsequent years. Many relocated people traveled to these chapels.

In 1987, the location for a new parish church was found on 12th Street and Buckeye. Construction on the new Sacred Heart Church began on October 6, 1989 and was completed in 1990. Saint Mary Magdalene Chapel and Santa Rita Chapel were closed as a result. The new church has a seating capacity for 300 people and has a small social hall adjacent to it. Father Timothy Conlon, O.S.C., is canonical pastor and Annie Conway is the parish life coordinator. Sacred Heart Parish currently serves over 450 registered families.

Sacred Heart Parish in Prescott was established by Bishop John Baptiste Salpointe in the year 1877. Sacred Heart was the first parish established in what would later become the Diocese of Phoenix. Father Michael Murphy was appointed as the first pastor. The first resident pastor was Father F. C. Becker from 1878 to 1879. Mass was celebrated in a house on North Marina Street and a room served as a chapel from 1878 to 1894. This small chapel was dedicated to the Sacred Heart of Jesus. Father Alfred Quetu became pastor in 1889 and began construction on a brick church on North Marina Street on May 22, 1891. Mass continued at the chapel until 1894. Mass was held in the basement of the new church from 1894 until February 17, 1895. The new church was dedicated by Bishop Peter Bourgade on February 1, 1896. The original chapel was sold and the house later burned down. Father Quetu remained at Sacred Heart until 1908.

On September 6, 1878, three Sisters of Saint Joseph of Carondelet opened a hospital on Alarcon and Willis Streets. A school was opened in the back of the building for Catholic children called the Little Pioneer School of the West. In 1886, the hospital was closed and Saint Joseph Academy was opened in its place. In 1890, the Academy moved to a larger house on North Marina Street. Saint Joseph Academy was relocated to a new building on 10-acres of property and opened in September 1904 for students in grades 1-12.

In 1915, the Claretian Missionary Fathers assumed responsibility for the parish and built a two-story rectory. The Chapel of the Immaculate Heart of Mary was established by the Claretians in 1920. The Chapel was located on South Marina Street but was moved in 1935 to McCormick and Goodwin Streets. Lightning struck the church in 1930 and destroyed the steeple. In 1948, the old church was remodeled and stained glass windows were installed. The parish purchased a portion of the Academy property and built a school in 1956. Sacred Heart School was opened in September 1956 by the Sisters of Saint Joseph. Saint Joseph Academy became a high school. The Sisters closed the Academy in 1966. In 1967, the Chapel of the Immaculate Heart of Mary was also closed and torn down. The Sisters of Saint Joseph of Carondelet left the parish in 1972 and were replaced by the Loreto Sisters.

The Academy property was purchased by the parish for a new church and parish center. The first Mass in the new church was held March 16, 1969. The new church and parish center were dedicated on June 13, 1969. The old church was sold to the Prescott Fine Arts Association in 1969. The Blessed Sacrament Chapel was built in 1995 and the Precious Blood Adoration Chapel was built in 1996. In 2004, the Blessed Sacrament Chapel was relocated to the newly remodeled chapel in the church. Father Daryl Olds, C.M.F., is the current pastor. Sacred Heart Parish in Prescott currently serves over 3,100 registered families.

SAINT AGNES
PARISH

Phoenix, Arizona

Established March 19, 1940

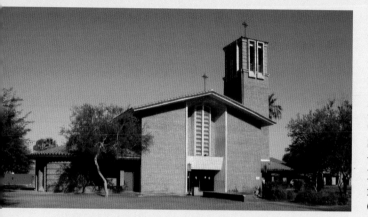

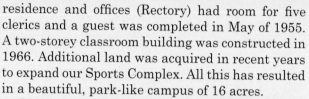

Saint Agnes Parish was established by the Most Reverend Daniel Gercke, Bishop of Tucson on March 19, 1940. Reverend (later Monsignor) Robert J. Donohue was appointed as the first pastor, a position he would hold for 32 years. The first Mass was held in a building built as a grocery store at Sixteenth and Yale Streets until almost 10 acres of property was purchased on 24th Street near McDowell Road. The first church (now Donohoe Hall) was dedicated on the 27th of April, 1941. Saint Agnes School opened on September 20th, 1943 and was staffed by the Sisters of Charity of the Blessed Virgin Mary from Dubuque, Iowa. Construction of the new school building began in January of 1945 and was dedicated by Bishop Gercke on April 18th, 1946. The school was expanded over the years 1945-48. At its peak, Saint Agnes School enrolled over 1000 children.

As growth continued at a phenomenal rate, plans for a new church were drawn up by one of the premier architectural firms of mid-century Phoenix, Weaver and Drover. The new church was a grand edifice of steel and brick. Saint Agnes measures 218 feet long with an overall width of 80 feet. The total cost including landscaping and furnishings of the new Saint Agnes Church was $378,000. With a seating capacity of 1140 worshipers, the Church of Saint Agnes was solemnly dedicated by James Francis Cardinal McIntyre, Archbishop of Los Angeles on the 11th of October, 1953. The Bell in the tower which was raised 75 feet into the desert sky and weighs over two tons, was consecrated with the name Gabriel by Arizona's brand new Auxiliary Bishop (later Ordinary of the Diocese of Tucson), the Most Reverend Francis Green. Saint Agnes soon after would boast of one of the finest organs in the state, and Aeolian Skinner made in Boston, planned in the baroque style. The priests'

residence and offices (Rectory) had room for five clerics and a guest was completed in May of 1955. A two-storey classroom building was constructed in 1966. Additional land was acquired in recent years to expand our Sports Complex. All this has resulted in a beautiful, park-like campus of 16 acres.

In 1969, the Diocese of Phoenix was erected by Pope Paul VI. Soon afterward in 1971, the Carmelite Order took on the pastoral and temporal care of Saint Agnes as Monsignor Donohoe was appointed to the Arizona Interfaith Council. Father Murray Phelan, O. Carm. served as Pastor from 1972-1981, followed in succession by Carmelite Fathers: Roy Ontiveros, 1981-1990; Tiernan O'Callaghan, 1990-2003, Michael Sgarioto, 2003-2005; Peter Liuzzi, 2005-2008. The current pastor, Father Bradley Peterson, O. Carm. was a parishioner at Saint Agnes from 1974-1985, serving in the folk group and liturgy committee. In 1985 he entered the Carmelites and was ordained priest in Saint Agnes Church by Bishop Thomas O'Brien in 1992. Today, Saint Agnes remains a beautiful Church and School with modern sports facilities, including state-of-the-art baseball and softball fields.

Saint Agnes Parish is richly blessed with families and persons of diverse ages and backgrounds. Some of the original members still provide our historical foundation. Many of their families and descendants are here, along with parishioners transplanted from colder parts of the United States. In recent decades, Saint Agnes has received new parishioners from as near as Mexico and Latin America, and as far as Africa, India, and Asia. Our variety helps Saint Agnes embody the universal Church in culture and history. Over the principal entrance of the church is found the image of Saint Agnes, the teenage virgin and martyr of Christian antiquity with a lamb in her arms. Written next to her are Saint Paul's words, *"The weak things of the world hath God chosen that He may confound the strong"* (I Cor. 1:27).

SAINT ANDREW THE APOSTLE PARISH

Chandler, Arizona

Established June 21, 1985

Saint Andrew the Apostle Parish in Chandler was established by Bishop Thomas J. O'Brien of Phoenix on June 21, 1985. Father Joseph I. Hennessy was appointed as the first pastor. Father Hennessey visited Saint Mary, Holy Spirit, and Saint Timothy Parishes, asking who would want to join a new faith community. It would be nearly seven months before the community of Saint Andrew the Apostle first celebrated Mass for 130 families in the cafeteria at Kyrene Junior High School on January 26, 1986. The parish grew and moved their Masses to the new cafeteria at Seton High School on August 10, 1986.

Ground was broken by Bishop Thomas J. O'Brien of Phoenix for a social hall on May 10, 1987. The parish social hall was built to serve as the worship and event center. The administrative offices and the bell tower were also built. The first Mass was celebrated in the parish hall on Palm Sunday 1988. The building was dedicated by Bishop O'Brien on December 11, 1988.

The groundbreaking for a building expansion to house classrooms for religious education and office space took place on August 5, 1990. An open house in the new building was held on January 27, 1991. As the parish grew, so did the need for a permanent church building and construction was begun on a new church in 1996. In October 1996, the parish community celebrated its first mass in the new church. The new church was dedicated by Bishop O'Brien on November 30, 1996.

In late 1999, the parish initiated a capital campaign to build a permanent home for the Youth Ministry and Adult Faith Enrichment programs. On March 28, 2004, Bishop Thomas J. Olmsted of Phoenix dedicated these key additions to the parish facilities. Father John R. Coleman is the current pastor. There are many ministries and organizations including Adult Formation, Young Adult Ministry, RCIA, Yesterday's Kids, and Emmaus. Saint Andrew the Apostle Parish currently has over 4,100 registered families.

145

SAINT ANNE
PARISH
Gilbert, Arizona
Established October 22, 1943

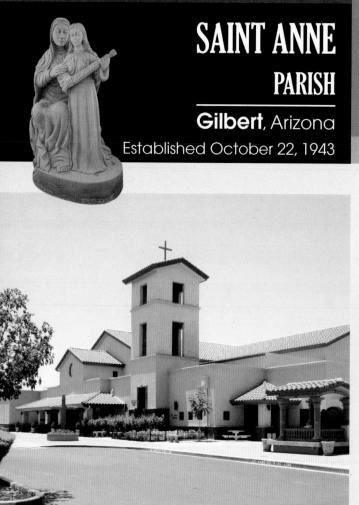

In 1936, Father Vincent Mestres built a small adobe church on West Bruce Street with a $3,000 donation from the Catholic Church Extension Society. On November 22, 1936, Father Vincent Mestres celebrated the first Mass in the new adobe church. In 1938, Father Joseph N. Patterson became administrator and had the back wall of the church torn down to add a sacristy and altar. The church now seated 70 people and Mass was celebrated by Father Patterson every Sunday as a mission of Saint Mary Parish in Chandler.

Saint Anne Parish in Gilbert was established on October 22, 1943. Father Godfrey Fontaine was appointed the first pastor. Father Loyola O'Dougherty succeeded him in 1947. The Dominican Sisters from Adrian, Michigan arrived about 1948 and opened a school for grades kindergarten to 4th grade. Father William Collins became pastor in November 1949 and was succeeded by Father John Cullinan in 1952. Father Cullinan obtained a barracks building and moved it to the property adjacent to the church where it served as a social hall. Father Cornelius Moynihan became pastor in March 1954 and was succeded by Father Bernard O'Boyle in 1956. The Dominican Sisters were stationed elsewhere in 1958, resulting in the closure of the school.

Father Vincent J. Nevulis became pastor in 1968 and began plans for a new church. The last Mass in the adobe church was celebrated on March 21, 1971, and it was torn down. Ground was broken for a new church on March 28, 1971 and the dedication by Bishop Edward McCarthy on August 1, 1971. Father Raul Morales became pastor in 1985 and after 3 years of planning, ground was broken on a multi-purpose church building in June 1988. The first Mass in the new church took place on February 25, 1989 and the dedication by Bishop O'Brien took place on April 30, 1989. Perpetual Adoration was started at the parish in January 1993. A new sanctuary was dedicated by Bishop O'Brien on April 21, 1998. Father Gregory J. Schlarb is the current pastor. Saint Anne Parish in Gilbert currently serves 4,500 registered families.

SAINT ANTHONY
PARISH

Phoenix, Arizona

Established January 3, 1943

Saint Anthony Parish in Phoenix was established by Bishop Daniel Gercke of Tucson on January 3, 1943. Father Antonius Bandres, C.M.F., was appointed as the first pastor. Before being elevated to a parish, Saint Anthony was a mission of Immaculate Heart of Mary and was first located at 7th Avenue and Buckeye near where Phoenix Memorial Hospital now stands. Some of the founding parishioners included the Miramon, Orabuena, and Escalante Families. Construction of the parish hall began in April 1944. The parish hall was used as a temporary church and dedicated by Bishop Gercke in September 10, 1944. A rectory was also dedicated in May 1945.

Construction on the church began in November 1946. The first Mass was held in the new church in March 1948 and the dedication was held on April 1948. The immense new three-nave church rises over the original parish hall, seats 480 and includes a 100-foot tower. Father Bandres oversaw construction of the current church and he is said to have based the design on a church in his home town of Spain. The basement of the church became the social hall of the parish. A new rectory was also built in 1957. In 1970 the parish community united to build the current parish hall. Ground was broken in 1971 and dedicated in 1974.

The church was badly damaged by a fire on December 11, 1994. The altar and pulpit were destroyed in the fire and the church suffered major smoke damage. Renovations of the church interior and a new roof were completed in 1995. The parish hall was used as a temporary church during the restoration. The parish community worked together to rebuild the space to its current configuration.

The parish has many ministries and programs including RCIA, Saint Vincent de Paul Society, Marriage Preparation, Young Adult Group, Encentros, and Guadalupanas. Saint Anthony Parish currently serves over 1,160 registered families. Father Walter Alfredo Frutades, I.V.E., is the current pastor.

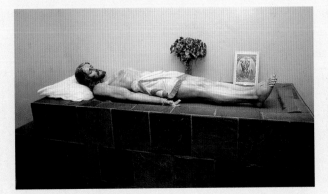

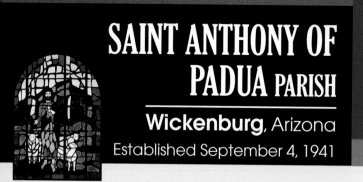

SAINT ANTHONY OF PADUA PARISH

Wickenburg, Arizona

Established September 4, 1941

Saint Anthony's Church was built in 1903 on land that had been donated by Henry Wickenburg in 1901. There were few Catholic families in the town and Mass was celebrated monthly by Franciscans from Saint Mary Parish in Phoenix. On September 18, 1923, lightning stuck the steeple and the church caught fire. The steeple, roof and ceiling were damaged by the fire and reconstruction began December 22, 1923. The church was rebuilt and the addition of two towers and a sacristy room were completed in 1924. From 1925 to 1941, the mission was served by priests from Sacred Heart in Prescott.

The parish was established on September 4, 1941 by Bishop Daniel J. Gercke of Tucson and named for Saint Anthony of Padua. The first resident pastor was Father Albert Knier in 1941. Saint Anthony Church was built of adobe and served the community for over half a century. The time came when the parish decided to replace it with a new edifice. The new church was built in 1957 and the first Mass celebrated at midnight on Christmas 1957. The new church was dedicated by Bishop Gercke on February 23, 1958. The old Saint Anthony adobe building was used as a catechetical center until 1968.

Father D. F. O'Sullivan was pastor from 1947 to 1975. During his pastorate, not only was the new church constructed in 1957 but a rectory addition was built in 1964. O'Sullivan Hall was built on the site of the original church in 1968. Father Thomas Boyle became pastor in 1976. The interior of the church was soon renovated and was followed by the construction of the convent and Padua Learning Center in 1979. Father John Vogt became the pastor in 1995 and the Good Shepherd of the Desert Church in Congress became a mission of Saint Anthony's. Between 1995 and 2003, the parish renovated the Center for Religious Education building and added new lighting and air conditioning to the church.

Father Brian Bell became pastor upon Father Vogt's retirement in July 2003 and served until September 2005. During this time, the church was renovated and redecorated with a "mission atmosphere" adding decorative painting, a brick patio and Mary's Garden. Father (later Monsignor) George E. Highberger became pastor in 2005 and has continued the parish renovations by modernizing the halls, offices, classrooms and Saint Vincent de Paul Pantry. Saint Anthony of Padua Parish currently serves over 550 registered families.

SAINT AUGUSTINE
PARISH

Phoenix, Arizona
Established July 16, 1970

Saint Augustine Parish was established by Bishop McCarthy on July 16, 1970, due to the rapid growth of the Maryvale area. Father William I. Reid was appointed as the first pastor. The first Mass was held in Madonna Hall at Bourgade High School on July 12, 1970. The parishioners continued to attend Masses at Desert Sands Junior High School until a permanent multi-purpose church building was completed in September 1972.

As the community and its needs increased, the religious education facility was added to the church complex in 1978. A parish office complex was added in 1985. A new parish social hall was also built in 2003.

The parish has a wide variety of ministries and parish organizations including Saint Vincent de Paul Society, Youth Group, Ministry of Care, Knights of Columbus, Pastoral Council, Financial Council, Charismatic Prayer Group and Guadalupanas. Father Carlos A. Gomez was appointed pastor in 2006. Saint Augustine Parish currently has 3,500 registered families.

SAINT BENEDICT
PARISH

Phoenix, Arizona

Established October 29, 1985

Saint Benedict Parish was established on October 29, 1985 in Chandler and Father Lan S. Sherwood became the first pastor. The parish began with 79 families meeting in an office building in November 1985. The first multi-purpose building was completed in October 1988. In 1993, Father Patrick Robinson arrived as pastor and served the parish for the next 5 years. In October 1996, two classroom buildings and an administration building were added to accommodate more than 800 families who were now attending. Father Dennis O'Rourke arrived as the next pastor in 1998.

Considering the impending shortage of priests plus the demographics of the Chandler-Ahwatukee area, Bishop Thomas J. O'Brien in 2001 decided it would be the best use of resources to move Saint Benedict's two miles from its present location to property next to Saint John Bosco Interparish School. As part of the "Today's Children, Tomorrow's Leaders" campaign in the late 1990s, the school was built as one of two new elementary schools in the Diocese of Phoenix. The school was finally opened in 2001 for grades K-8 as an Interparish school with support from Corpus Christi, Saint Benedict, Saint Andrew and Holy Spirit Parishes. In 2004, Saint John Bosco became a Diocesan school and associated with Saint Benedict Parish. In 2005, a Pre-kindergarten was added through the generosity of Father Hoorman at Corpus Christi.

The Chandler property was sold in May 2003 to the Valley Unitarian Universalist Church, who gave the parish up to 8 months to move out. In early January 2004, the parish moved into temporary facilities at the multipurpose room of Saint John Bosco School and remained there for 51 weeks. The parish offices were moved into trailers at the new Phoenix site.

Construction of the new multi-purpose church building was completed in early December 2004. The church dedication was held by Bishop Olmsted on December 16, 2004. The first Mass in the new building took place on December 24, 2004. Father O'Rourke remained at the parish until January 1, 2006. Father Gary R. Regula was appointed as the current pastor on June 1, 2006. Saint Benedict Parish in Phoenix currently has 1,250 registered families.

SAINT BERNADETTE
PARISH

Scottsdale, Arizona

Established January 1, 1995

Saint Bernadette Parish in Scottsdale was established by Bishop Thomas J. O'Brien on January 1, 1995. Father Richard R. Felt was appointed as the first pastor. The north Scottsdale parish was formed from what was originally part of Blessed Sacrament Parish in Scottsdale.

The first Mass celebrated in the new parish was held in the auditorium of the Desert Shadows Middle School in Scottsdale on January 7, 1995. Over 250 parishioners were in attendance for the first Mass. Masses were held at the school until October 31, 1998.

The present parish center was built on the parish property at North 60th Street and Kings and completed in October 1998. Masses were moved from the school auditorium to the new church following its dedication by Bishop Thomas O'Brien of Phoenix November 1, 1998.

As part of the "Today's Children, Tomorrow's Leaders" campaign in the late 1990s, the Pope John XXIII Interparish School was built as one of two new elementary schools in the Diocese of Phoenix. The Diocesan plan to build the school was officially announced on May 21, 1998, and the groundbreaking took place on November 28, 1998. Pope John XXIII Catholic School was opened on August 24, 1999, for grades K-8. The Interparish school was built with support from Saint Bernadette, Saint Joan of Arc, Our Lady of Joy, and Blessed Sacrament Parishes.

Saint Bernadette Parish has many ministries and organizations to include Life Teen, Youth Ministry, Adult Formation, Initiation Ministry, Catechetical Ministry, Ministers of Care, Perpetual Adoration and Saint Vincent de Paul Ministry. Father Peter Rossa is the current pastor. Saint Bernadette Parish in Scottsdale currently serves over 1550 registered families.

SAINT BERNARD OF CLAIRVAUX PARISH

Scottsdale, Arizona

Established July 1, 1994

Saint Bernard of Clairvaux Parish was established on July 1, 1994, by Bishop Thomas J. O'Brien of Phoenix. Father John J. Vogt was appointed as the first pastor. Sunday Mass was celebrated for the first few years in a rented space located at Mountainside Middle School. Father Vogt remained at the parish until 1995 and was succeeded as pastor by Father Robert Voss in July 1995.

The parish purchased ten acres of property in Scottsdale and first constructed a small office and chapel before breaking ground for the parish's first church building on January 1, 1998. The 25,000 square foot church was completed and dedicated by Bishop Thomas O'Brien on March 25, 1999. Father Voss served as pastor of Saint Bernard until April 2005.

Father Brian Bell became pastor in September 2005. The parish began a new Capital Campaign in October 2006 and formed a building committee for the construction of a Parish Social Hall in the near future. Saint Bernard of Clairvaux Parish currently has over 1,200 registered families.

SAINT BRIDGET
PARISH
Mesa, Arizona
Established June 19, 1985

Saint Bridget Parish was established on June 19, 1985 with Father John F. Cunningham appointed as the founding pastor. The first Mass was held on November 17, 1985, at the MacArthur Elementary School in Mesa. The parish began with 550 households in November 1985. Construction on the Parish Center and rectory began that December and the first Mass in the Parish Center was held on July 26, 1987. After a year of construction, Bishop Thomas J. O'Brien came to dedicate the new Parish Center on October 1, 1987.

Saint Bridget Church not only serves as a place of worship, but as a showcase of Indian and Southwestern art. The plaza features 15 huge monolithic stones from New Mexico that serve as Stations of the Cross. Bronze reliefs depicting the Stations of the Cross decorate 14 of the stones. In the center of the Plaza there is a 3 jet fountain to complete this unique prayer space.

In March 1991, the Reverend Bernard G. Collins Center for Religious Education was dedicated to serve the parish's critical need for classrooms and a parish hall. The two-level building contained eight classrooms, a conference room, library and a social hall.

Father W. Scott Brubaker became the second pastor on July 1, 2002. There have been some changes in recent years to the parish complex including the creation of a chapel for meditation and prayer, a new office, and a Spirituality Center. Saint Bridget Parish currently has over 1,400 registered families.

SAINT CATHERINE OF SIENA PARISH

Phoenix, Arizona
Established May 22, 1946

Saint Catherine of Siena Parish was established by Bishop Daniel J. Gercke of Tucson on May 22, 1946. Father George M. Feeney was appointed as the first pastor and took up residence in the parish on February 1, 1947. The first Mass in the new parish was celebrated in the cafeteria of the Roosevelt School on February 2, 1947. Masses were said for the next several months in Roosevelt School and the community room at the Neighborhood House on Seventh Street and Southern.

The first Mass in the church, an old army barracks building remodeled and redecorated by the parishioners, was celebrated on November 1, 1947. The church was dedicated by Bishop Gercke on April 4, 1948. In 1948, the Mother Seton Sisters of Charity began the religious education of the children of the parish. Three members of the Seton Sisters opened Saint Catherine of Siena School in 1949 with almost 100 students in grades 1-4. The school added a new classroom each year until the new upper grades building was completed in 1953. Father Palmer Plourde was pastor from 1955 to 1959. It was during this time the present church was built on the West side of South Central across from the first church and dedicated by Bishop Francis J. Green of Tucson in 1958. Father Richard Costigan was pastor from 1959 to 1969. During his pastorate, a new convent was built and later

became the rectory. Father Bernard Colton became pastor in 1969.

In 1978, a new wing was added to the school for grades K-4. The old barracks were removed and a new hall was built where the old church once stood. In 1985, a new office complex was built onto the rectory with four new offices and a workroom. In the 1990s, the Nazareth Gift Shop was added to the church and the Teen Center was purchased in 1999. In 2007, the Stations of the Cross were enlarged and a new baptismal font was installed in the church. In 2008, the parish began installing stained glass windows in the church. Father Alonso Saenz is the current pastor. Saint Catherine of Siena Parish currently serves 4,500 registered families.

SAINT CHARLES BORROMEO PARISH

Peoria, Arizona

Established January 22, 1968

(formerly Santo Nino de Atocha Mission)

In 1910, Masses were celebrated at a one room church built on the northeast corner of 83rd Avenue and Cactus Road. The mission chapel was called Santo Nino de Atocha and was originally a mission of Saint Mary Parish in Phoenix. Mass was celebrated on a very irregular schedule and the chapel was torn down in 1920. From 1920 to 1930, Masses were held in the home of Santiago Salazar in Peoria. During the years 1930 to 1935, Masses were held at the San Jose Mission in Glendale by Father Ambrosio Trabert and no services took place in Peoria.

About 1935, Father Juan Atucha Gorostiaga, C.M.F., began soliciting funds for the purchase of an old adobe store building on Monroe Street and the first Mass was celebrated there in 1936. All research tends to confirm that the name Saint Charles Borromeo was bestowed by Father Juan Atucha at the time he began using the old store building for worship. Father Leo Gattas remodeled the old store and made it into a church complete with steeple. The Peoria church became a mission of Our Lady of Perpetual Help in Glendale with about 50 registered families in the 1940's.

In 1961, 54-acres were purchased by Father Francis Bechtel for the purpose of constructing a new church in Peoria. Construction on a new church facility began on July 8, 1963. The structure was to be a multi-purpose building consisting of a sanctuary, a nave seating 400 people, rectory, classrooms, convent, kitchen and social hall. The first Mass was celebrated in the new church on December 8, 1963. Bishop Francis Green of Tucson appointed Father Francis C. Long as administrator on September 15, 1965.

Saint Charles Borromeo Mission was elevated to parish status by Bishop Green on January 22, 1968. Father Francis Long was appointed the first pastor of the new parish of 329 registered families.

New classrooms were dedicated on September 4, 1990 and a renovation of the church sanctuary was also completed on December 31, 1990. In 2008, the church is being renovated with improvements such as the repainting of the church interior, a new roof, refinished pews, a new altar and the installation of new stained glass windows. The parish has many ministries and organizations including Bible Study, Choir, Fiesta Committee, High School Ministry, Knights of Columbus, Marriage Preparation, Ministry of Care, RCIA, Rosary Prayer Group, Social Committee, Saint Vincent de Paul Society and Women's Guild. Father Loren Gonzales is the current pastor. Saint Charles Borromeo Parish serves over 760 registered families.

SAINT CLARE OF ASSISI
PARISH

Surprise, Arizona
Established July 1, 2000

The parish history began when the area was still part of Santa Teresita Parish in El Mirage and of Our Lady of Lourdes Parish in Sun City West whose pastor, Father Moynihan arranged for the first Masses at Happy Trails Resort in 1988 on Saturdays at 4:00pm. A Sunday Mass was then added at 9:00am in Sun Village and in 1990 a third Mass at 11:00am in Arizona Traditions Community. Retired priests took care of the spiritual needs as the three communities started to build the local Catholic community and raise money for a new parish. Religious education programs for the children began under the leadership of Margaret and Mike Planeta in their home with guidance from Father David Kelash, pastor of Santa Teresita Parish.

Most Reverend Thomas J. O'Brien chose the name, Saint Clare of Assisi, and established the parish on July 1, 2000. He appointed Father John Coleman as the founding pastor. For ten months three weekend Masses were held at the Kingswood Parke Elementary School in Surprise. Later, in the summer of 2001, two temporary buildings were placed on 12.5 acres owned by the Diocese of Phoenix at the corner of Bell Road and Cotton Lane. The larger building seated 480 people for Mass and the smaller building became the offices and conference rooms. The larger building also served many other purposes including the religious education programs.

Father Hans P. Ruygt was appointed by Bishop O'Brien to lead the parish on July 1, 2002, and to carry out a building program. Thousands of parishioners rallied together to raise funds and to assess the needs of the parish. They determined that the first need was for a permanent church. They conducted several capital campaigns. On August 12, 2006, the day after the Feast of the patroness, Saint Clare of Assisi, Most Reverend Thomas J. Olmsted, Bishop of Phoenix, gathered the parishioners, with Father Coleman, Father Ruygt and several other priests and deacons and civic leaders for the Blessing and Groundbreaking for the new church. Site work and grading were completed in 2007 and the parking lot was expanded. Construction on the church began in January 2008. Meanwhile the parish numbers grew rapidly reaching 2600 parish families and 500 children in the religious education programs for children and teens. Many other lay ministries also flourished. Hundreds of people had to sit outside listening to ground speakers for Saturday and Sunday Masses on many weekend because they didn't fit inside the church.

It was a glorious day when parishioners moved into the new church and celebrated the first Mass on Christmas Eve 2008 at 4:00pm. The parishioners had no permanent furnishings and no tile on the floor but they finally had a roof over their heads and were able to accommodate the large crowds which often reached 1,000 people. The city limited the parish to seating 1,400 people because parking will need to expand again before they can seat the full 2000 people.

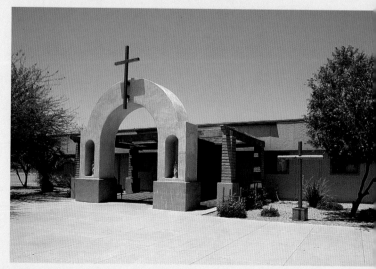

Saint Clement of Rome Parish was established by Bishop Edward A. McCarthy of Phoenix on December 1, 1970. Father Harry R. Morgan was appointed the first pastor.

Father Morgan had arrived in Sun City to start a new parish in Sun City on October 23, 1970, and was joined by almost 200 local Catholics. Daily Masses began at the rectory on Tropicana Circle. The first Sunday Mass was celebrated at Sunland Memorial Chapel on November 1, 1970.

In 1971, a 6-acre site was purchased for the parish. On November 29, 1971, daily Mass at the Rectory was suspended because it was unable to accommodate the large numbers attending. In December 1971, a building committee was formed to proceed with plans for a new church and social hall. Father William Waldron became pastor in May 1972 and daily Masses were resumed at Sunland Memorial Chapel on June 17, 1972. The groundbreaking for the church and social hall took place on May 31, 1973. The first Mass was celebrated in the social hall on December 22, 1973, and the first Mass in the new church building took place for 700 people on April 14, 1974. The new church was completed in March 1974 and dedicated on June 16, 1974. A new rectory was completed in May 1975.

By 1983, the adult care center was added to Saint Clement Parish through the auspices of Interfaith Services. The parish hall was enlarged in September 1983 and completed by January 1984. In 1993, Father Waldron stepped down and Father Theodore Breslin became pastor. A choir area was added to the church in 1994. Father Breslin passed away in 1994. Father Earl D'Eon served as pastor until his retirement on June 30, 2004. Father John Slobig has been pastor since July 1, 2004. Saint Clement of Rome Parish currently serves over 1,800 registered families.

SAINT DANIEL THE PROPHET PARISH

Scottsdale, Arizona

Established May 13, 1961

Saint Daniel the Prophet Parish was established by Bishop Francis J. Green of Tucson on May 13, 1961. Father Paul G. Lawrence was appointed the first pastor. The parish was named in honor of retired Bishop Daniel J. Gercke of Tucson. The first Mass in the new parish was celebrated in the cafeteria of the Motorola Plant on August 20, 1961 for 647 parishioners. Mass was continued at the Motorola cafeteria for the next 10 months. Construction on six schoolrooms and a temporary church was begun in April 1962. The fist Mass in the church was held in October 1962.

The school and temporary church were completed in 1963. Saint Daniel the Prophet School was opened in September 1963 for 150 students enrolled in grades K-3. The school was staffed by three Sisters of Saint Dominic from Adrian, Michigan. The two lots and home north of the church were purchased for the rectory in January 1965. In September 1965, the temporary church was enlarged. In January 1966, a two-story school building was completed with room for classrooms and a parish social hall. By 1969, the convent was completed and the school had expanded to include grades K-8. In 1974, the Dominican Sisters withdrew from the parish and

school. Several orders of religious continued, over the years, to operate the school. In August 1988, the Sisters of Charity of Seton Hill took over the administration of the school. Today, the school has lay administrators.

Plans for a new church were begun by Father Louis Sigman in 1978. Groundbreaking for the church took place on October 3, 1979 and the building was dedicated by Bishop James Rausch of Phoenix on February 13, 1981. The church included a 900-seat sanctuary, a 100-seat chapel and two courtyards.

Construction on a shrine at the parish was begun in 2006 and Bishop Thomas J. Olmsted of Phoenix dedicated the new Saint Joseph the Worker Shrine on February 4, 2007. In the summer of 2007, the parish welcomed the Daughters of Mary Sisters. Father Thaddeus M. McGuire has been pastor since July 1, 2004. Ministries include Catechetical Ministry, Liturgy and Music, Youth Ministry, RCIA, and Respect Life. Saint Daniel the Prophet Parish in Scottsdale currently serves 1,500 registered families.

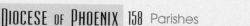

SAINT EDWARD THE CONFESSOR PARISH

Phoenix, Arizona

Established September 15, 1976

On September 15, 1976, Bishop Edward A. McCarthy of Phoenix officially signed the decree establishing a new parish on the southeast side of Phoenix and part of western Tempe. Father Andre Boulanger was appointed to be the first pastor. After some consultation with the people of the newly established parish, Father Boulanger asked that the new parish be named Saint Edward the Confessor in honor of Bishop Edward McCarthy.

The new parish was constructed on five acres of property on East Southern Avenue, where the parish had purchased a building to serve as the rectory. The parish had the vision to build a modest but attractive church that would seat up to 500 people, include a few classrooms and also office space for the parish staff. Father Patrick Ratchford was appointed to succeed Father Boulanger as pastor in 1978.

Groundbreaking for the parish was held on October 15, 1978. Sunday Mass was held in a multi-purpose building at Nevitt Elementary School until the new church was completed.

The first official mass in Saint Edward the Confessor Church was held on Thanksgiving Day, 1979. The church was officially dedicated by Bishop James S. Rausch of Phoenix on October 11, 1980. By 1980, the parish had grown to over 375 families.

Saint Edward the Confessor has several ministries and programs including RCIA, Youth Ministry and Saint Vincent de Paul Society. The parish shares its canonical pastor, Father Daniel McBride, with Holy Family Parish in Phoenix. Saint Edward the Confessor Parish currently has over 150 registered families.

159

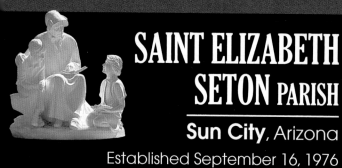

SAINT ELIZABETH SETON PARISH

Sun City, Arizona

Established September 16, 1976

On September 16, 1976, Bishop Edward McCarthy officially announced the formation of a third parish in Sun City, named Saint Elizabeth Seton Parish. Father Paul P. Smith was appointed as the first pastor for about 300 families. The new parish site was reserved at 98th Ave. and West Palmeras Drive. Daily Mass was celebrated at Saint Clement Parish, and weekend Masses were celebrated at Sunland Memorial Chapel and the social hall of the Bell Recreation Center until a church could be built.

Groundbreaking for the church and hall took place in May 1978. The first Mass in the new church was celebrated by Bishop James Rausch of Phoenix on July 14, 1979. Bishop Rausch dedicated the church and hall on October 2a1, 1979. Father Henry Hodges became the second pastor on February 8, 1980, followed by Father Matt Feit in January 1987 and Father Joseph Gillespie in 1992. Under Father Gillespie, the Deacon Tone Room and library were built adjacent to the Hall. Father Joseph Gillespie retired in June 2000.

Father Franklin L. Bartel has been pastor since July 2000. During Father Bartel's first year as

pastor, a reorganization of the parish took place as well as some remodeling of the church. Since 2004, much space has been converted into classrooms and meeting rooms. Ministries include RCIA, Ministry of Care, Knights of Columbus, Religious Education, Seton Society, Legion of Mary, Music Ministry and Liturgical Ministries. Saint Elizabeth Seton Parish currently serves over 2,200 registered families.

In the spring of 1962, Father Samuel J. Wilson, pastor of Immaculate Conception in Cottonwood, informed two Camp Verde Catholics that Bishop Bernard Espelage, O.F.M., of Gallup wanted to find a suitable place for Sunday Mass in Camp Verde. In 1962, Bishop Espelage approved the present church site and purchase of 9.45 acres on which Saint Frances Cabrini Church now stands. A grant from Catholic Church Extension Society enabled work to begin on the church.

The only place available for Mass in Camp Verde was the jail. Father Wilson came each Sunday from Cottonwood. The first Mass at the jail was celebrated on June 3, 1962, for 14 people. The Monroe house on the access road to Phoenix was soon rented and Father Wilson moved there in July 1962, as the first resident priest. In 1963, Father Wilson rented an apartment in the barracks building behind the hotel. The living room was large enough to become the permanent chapel, with living quarters in the rear. Father Wilson remained as pastor until June 1964. He was succeeded by Father Clement Hageman from 1964 to 1965, Father James Burns 1965 to 1966, Father Philip Reiser from 1966 to 1970, and Father Anthony Schwartz from 1970 to 1971. Father Reiser returned again in 1971.

Saint Frances Cabrini Church had seating for 70 people and was completed by Summer 1964. The first Mass was celebrated in August 1964. The front entrance of the church was built in 1968. Saint Frances Cabrini was privileged to be the first church dedicated in the newly formed Diocese of Phoenix by Bishop Edward A. McCarthy on February 22, 1970. An addition to the church that expanded the sanctuary was dedicated on June 11, 1972. The church was painted and the bell tower erected in 1986 while Fr. Michael L. Diskin was pastor.

Father Reynaldo Clutario Jr., S.O.L.T., is the current pastor. Ministries and services include Catechetical Ministry, Jail Ministry, Bereavement Ministry, Ladies Guild and RCIA. Saint Frances Cabrini Parish currently serves 250 registered families.

SAINT FRANCIS OF ASSISI PARISH

Bagdad, Arizona

Established 1959

The Bagdad mission was originally served by the Claretian Fathers from Prescott and priests from Flagstaff who would celebrate Mass on Saturday in the Bagdad Community Church. Saint Francis of Assisi Church was built in 1947 and 1948. The church was dedicated in 1949 by Bishop Bernard Espelage of Gallup and Father Gerard Laskowski became the mission's first administrator.

Father Laskowski added a confessional and entryway to the church between 1953 and 1955. Saint Francis of Assisi was established as a parish in 1959. Father J. Sylvester Krotoszynski was named the founding pastor and served from April 1956 to September 1977. A church annex for educational and social activities was dedicated by Bishop Edward McCarthy of Phoenix on November 21, 1971. Father Vincent Doherty, S.J., was pastor from 1979 to 1985. A new parish hall was built in 1984 and named Doherty Hall after Father Doherty. A new rectory was also built in 1988.

Bagdad is a mining community owned by the Freeport McMoran Mine Company. Families can only rent a home here so many buy homes out of town. This causes many people to be absent on the weekends and low Mass attendance at times. The parish is in the process of upgrading the church sacristy and religious education classes began in September 2008. Father Leonardo J. Vargas is the current pastor. Saint Francis of Assisi Parish currently serves over 35 registered families.

SAINT FRANCIS
PARISH

Seligman, Arizona

Established 1940

Saint Francis Mission can trace its roots back to sometime before 1923 when the first church building was started. In 1940, Bishop Bernard T. Espelage, O.F.M., of Gallup, New Mexico elevated the mission to become a parish. The first parish administrator was Father Patrick Burke. Saint Anne in Ash Fork became a mission of the parish.

Father William Stauble became pastor in July 1982. A fire destroyed the rectory and part of the original church in January 1983. The parish immediately began plans to build a new church and construction began in 1983. The new church building was dedicated in October 1984 and included a rectory and meeting hall. Father Stauble remained at the parish until December 1, 1985. Father Dindo C. (Bruno) Cuario, D.S., is the current pastor. Saint Francis Parish currently serves 65 registered families.

SAINT FRANCIS XAVIER
PARISH
Phoenix, Arizona
Established December 19, 1928

In early 1928, Ellen Brophy called upon the Jesuits to build a college. She donated 25 acres of land and the funds to build the college. Ground was broken in January 1928 and the chapel completed in April 1928. Brophy College Preparatory opened in September 1928. Saint Francis Xavier Parish in Phoenix was established by Bishop Daniel Gercke of Tucson on December 19, 1928. Father Felix Rossetti, S.J., was appointed the first pastor for 158 families. The first Mass took place in Brophy Chapel at Midnight on Christmas 1928. Masses continued to be held in the Chapel.

Due to the depression years, Brophy College Preparatory closed and the parish took over the campus in 1935. Saint Francis Xavier School was opened in 1936 by the Sisters of Charity of the Blessed Virgin Mary of Dubuque for 120 students. The parish also founded Xavier College Preparatory, a girls' high school, in 1943. In 1952, the grade school was moved to a new building when Brophy College Preparatory was reopened and given the existing campus. The parish kept 10 acres but had to find new homes for the grade school, girls' high school, convent and the church. In 1953, a capital campaign began to expand the new grade school, build the girls' high school and convent. The expansion of the grade school, the building of a convent, and the purchase of land for the girls' high school took place in 1953. The girl's high school was built in

1956. After 31 years of services in Brophy Chapel, the first parish church was completed in 1959 and dedicated by Bishop Gercke on December 6, 1959.

In 1989, the church received its first repainting. The parish purchased a house just north of the parish for religious education classes in 1999. In 2000, the Jesuits moved into a nearby house and the old rectory was converted into the parish offices. A restoration of the church took place in 2005. A capital campaign was launched in the fall of 2007 to fulfill the parish vision of a new school, parish hall and parish center complex. Father Daniel J. Sullivan, S.J., has been pastor since 2006. Saint Francis Xavier Parish serves 4,100 registered families.

SAINT GABRIEL THE ARCHANGEL PARISH

Cave Creek, Arizona

Established July 1, 2002

Saint Gabriel the Archangel Parish was established by Bishop Thomas J. O'Brien of Phoenix on July 1, 2002. Father John D. Spaulding was appointed as the first pastor. The parish has grown over its short years from a small parish worshipping at a local school to even outgrowing the 450-person sanctuary where Mass was celebrated until 2008.

Saint Gabriel the Archangel Parish finally broke ground on a large multi-purpose building that includes a worship space/parish hall seating 800 and parish offices on September 8, 2007. The multi-purpose hall was completed in April 2008. The old church building is now used as the parish hall for ministries and classrooms. Renovation of the parish hall was begun on October 21, 2008 and completed in December 2008.

Father Dennis O'Rourke is the current pastor. The parish has many ministries and organizations including Adult Formation, Life Teen, RCIA, Junior High Ministry, Youth Formation, Saint Vincent de Paul, Outreach, Choir, and Boy Scouts. Saint Gabriel the Archangel Parish currently serves 1,500 registered families.

SAINT GERMAINE

PARISH

Prescott Valley, Arizona

Established October 15, 1984

The Prescott Valley Mission began on June 10, 1979, when about 60 people attended the first Mass at the Prescott Valley Cultural Center. On November 23, 1980, the first shovel full of dirt was turned over at the groundbreaking for Saint Germaine Mission in Prescott Valley. Father Philip Reiser was named as the mission's first administrator.

Parishoners submitted potential names for this new mission and Saint Germaine of Pibrac was chosen. The first Mass was celebrated in the mission church on June 14, 1981. The formal dedication of the church was held on March 28, 1982. Bishop Thomas J. O'Brien of Phoenix established Saint Germaine as a parish on October 15, 1984, and named Father Philip Reiser as the first pastor.

As the Parish grew, the religious education classrooms were built in 1984. Father Philip Reiser returned as pastor in 1986. In 1987, construction began on the parish hall and it was dedicated on May 21, 1989. The parish hall was officially named Reiser Hall in honor of Father Reiser. In 1993, Father Reiser left due to poor health and Father Michael Shay became pastor on July 1, 1993. Father Shay was instrumental in updating the decor of the church.

Father Gerald Yeager became pastor on July 1, 1994. A new rectory was soon completed in November 1994. On July 1, 1998, Father Yeager retired and Father John "J.R." Shetler became pastor. During his time at Saint Germaine, the Healing Garden and Perpetual Adoration Chapel were erected. Father John Shetler was transferred on July 1, 2005, and Father Daniel Vollmer became the pastor. The parish initiated a Spanish Mass on weekends the first weekend of October 2006 and began plans for the proposed building of a new church in July 2007. Saint Germaine Parish currently has over 800 registered families.

SAINT GREGORY
PARISH
Phoenix, Arizona
Established March 6, 1947

Saint Gregory Parish in Phoenix was established by Bishop Daniel J. Gercke of Tucson on March 6, 1947. Father (later Monsignor) Bernard L. Gordon was appointed the first pastor. The first Mass in the parish was celebrated for 400 families at the Arizona State Fairgrounds on March 30, 1947. Masses were continued at the Fairgrounds and at Whitney-Murphy Funeral Home chapel. In 1947, five acres of property at 18th Avenue and Osborn Road were purchased and an army barracks building was moved to the site. The remodeling of the barracks was completed on November 23, 1947, and served as a temporary church. Groundbreaking for a church took place on July 7, 1947. The new 375-seat church was dedicated on April 4, 1948.

Father Gordon invited the Mother General of the Institute of the Blessed Virgin Mary to visit Saint Gregory Parish in 1948 and she agreed to send sisters to form a school faculty. Saint Gregory School opened in September 1949 with 110 students in grades 1-4. The school housed three classrooms and was located on 18th Avenue. Construction began immediately to add a wing of classrooms and office. In September 1951, a third classroom building enclosing the courtyard was completed. A western wing of classrooms was completed in September 1954 and a two-story addition in February 1958.

A parish complex was constructed that also included a convent, cafeteria, rectory, and permanent church by March 1957. The groundbreaking of the new church took place on March 4, 1956. The new 1000-seat church was dedicated by Bishop Gercke of Tucson on March 10, 1957. In 1997, the school purchased a building to house a library, computer lab and meeting room. The Pre-K program was begun in 2002.

In 2000, the priests of the Congregation of Holy Cross accepted the invitation of Bishop Thomas O'Brien to take over the operation and administration of the parish. Father John Dougherty, C.S.C., has been pastor since 2000. Under his pastorate, a new baptistery was constructed near the church entrance and the outside prayer garden was remodeled. The Holy Cross Fathers left in June 2009. Father Emile C. Pelletier is the current pastor. Ministries and organizations include RCIA, Catechetical Ministry, Youth Ministry, Ministry of Care, Hispanic Ministry, and Saint Vincent de Paul Society. Saint Gregory Parish currently serves 1,150 registered families.

SAINT HELEN
PARISH

Glendale, Arizona

Established July 30, 1974

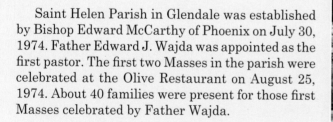

Saint Helen Parish in Glendale was established by Bishop Edward McCarthy of Phoenix on July 30, 1974. Father Edward J. Wajda was appointed as the first pastor. The first two Masses in the parish were celebrated at the Olive Restaurant on August 25, 1974. About 40 families were present for those first Masses celebrated by Father Wajda.

By 1977, Saint Helen Parish had grown to 420 families and construction on a new church building was begun. The first Mass in the new church was held on May 7, 1978. Bishop James Rausch of Phoenix dedicated the new church building on September 14, 1978, the feast of Saint Helen of the Cross. On December 12, 1991, the Adoration Chapel was dedicated and named after Our Lady of Guadalupe and continues to offer Perpetual Eucharistic Adoration.

Father R. Bruce Downs was appointed as pastor in 2007. Saint Helen Parish has many ministries and organizations including Adult Formation, Youth Ministry, Grief Support, Senior Adults Ministry and Baptism Preparation. The parish campus consists of the main church, offices, religious education building, social center and a teen center. Saint Helen Parish in Glendale currently serves 2,600 registered families.

SAINT HENRY
PARISH
Buckeye, Arizona
Established May 5, 1956

Before the first adobe church, Mass in Buckeye was celebrated in the Pablo Perez home on Centre Street. Mass was not celebrated on a regular basis at this time, but only when a priest managed to make it to Buckeye. The adobe church was dedicated in 1906 and Saint Henry's became a Franciscan Mission attached to Saint Mary Parish of Phoenix.

The old adobe church was condemned in 1936, however members of Saint Henry's held services there for another 10 years. Father Raymond Martinez broke ground for the new brick church on land donated by the Mulville family. Father Joseph Gamm was the last pastor of the adobe church and first pastor of the new brick church built in the fall of 1947. Father Gamm remained until 1953 and was replaced by Father Francis Murphy.

Saint Henry Mission became a parish on May 5, 1956. Father Cornelius Moynihan was appointed as the first pastor. Father Coleman Casey became pastor in 1960, followed by Father Francis Bechtel in 1962. Father Eugene O'Carroll served as pastor from 1973 to 1981. Plans for a larger church began in 1979 and the groundbreaking for the present church was held on Easter Sunday, 1980. The present church is built around the old church and

was dedicated by Bishop James Rausch of Phoenix on April 26, 1981. The old church was converted for use as a parish hall and classroom space.

Father William J. Kosco was appointed pastor in 2006. The parish has many ministries and organizations including Catechetical Ministry, Youth Ministry, Music Ministry, and Saint Vincent de Paul: Ozanam House. Saint Henry Parish currently serves 950 registered families.

SAINT JAMES
PARISH
Glendale, Arizona
Established June 2, 1982

Saint James Parish in Glendale was established by Bishop Thomas J. O'Brien of Phoenix on June 2, 1982. Father Matthias Feit was appointed as the first pastor. The parish was named after Saint James the Greater in honor of the late Bishop James Rausch of Phoenix. Saint James' first parish building was the rectory. The parish began using the Park Meadows School to celebrate Sunday Masses on September 12, 1982, for about 300 families.

In July 1983, Father Wayne Goulet was appointed the second pastor. Under his direction, plans for the construction of a new church building began. Ground breaking for the new church facility was held on April 29, 1984, and officiated by Bishop Thomas J. O'Brien of Phoenix. The first Mass was celebrated in the new church on December 24, 1984. The new facility included the church, chapel, small administration wing, social hall and space for religious education classes.

Within two and a half years, the parish had very active ministries including Music, Hospitality, Youth Group, Women's Group, and Saint Vincent De Paul Society. Since the parish grew rapidly, the Parish Service Building was built in 1991.

In September 1987, Father Ken Van De Ven was appointed the new pastor and served until April 2005. In April 2005, Father Robert S. Aliunzi, A. J., was appointed as pastor. Saint James the Greater Parish currently serves 1,300 registered families.

SAINT JEROME
PARISH

Phoenix, Arizona

Established May 12, 1962

Saint Jerome Parish was established on May 12, 1962 by Bishop Francis J. Green of Tucson. Father Michael F. McGovern was appointed as the first pastor. The first Mass in the parish was celebrated in August 1962 at the Cholla School cafeteria, with 800 people in attendance. Construction on a parish hall and school began with the groundbreaking in February 1963. The first Mass in the parish hall was held on August 5, 1963. The building was dedicated by Bishop Green of Tucson on April 5, 1964.

Saint Jerome School was opened in September 1965 by the Sisters of Loreto from Ireland for grades K-3. Construction on the school facilities was completed and additional classrooms were added in December 1967. In May 1971, the school was expanded to include grades K-8.

Father McGovern left the parish in 1975 and Father (later Monsignor) Richard Moyer became pastor in June 1975. The groundbreaking for the new church took place in September 1978. The new church facility was completed in December 1979 and included administration, multi-purpose and nursery facilities. The new church seated 950 people with the option to close off the nave into a smaller chapel for 250 people. Father Moyer remained at the parish until July 1984. Father Frank Zappitelli was pastor from 1984 to 1990.

Father Pierre Hissey was appointed pastor in March 1995 and served the parish for 10 years. Father Andres Arango, eud., was appointed as the current pastor in September 2005. Ministries and programs at Saint Jerome include Catholic Faith Formation, Life Teen, Development Council, Knights of Columbus, Little Rock Scripture Study, Respect Life, Saint Vincent de Paul Society, Youth Ministry, Senior's Group, Homebound Ministry, Family Ministry and Vacation Bible School. Saint Jerome Parish currently has 2,200 registered families.

SAINT JOACHIM & SAINT ANNE PARISH

Sun City, Arizona
Established March 18, 1961

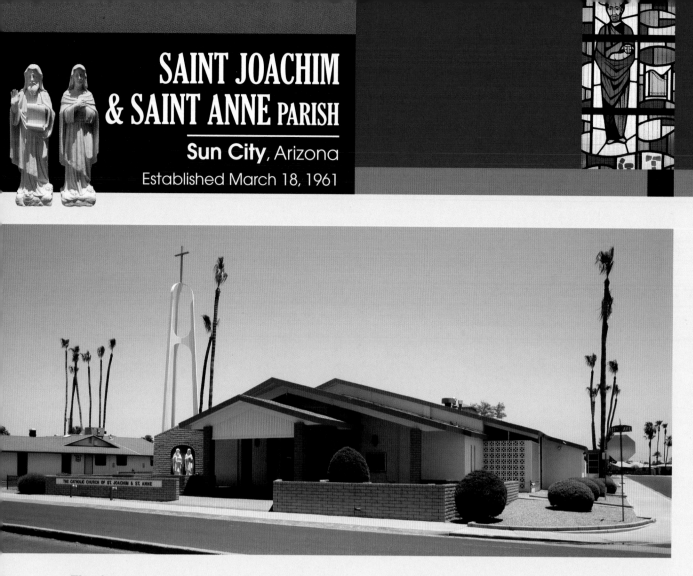

The formation of Saint Joachim Parish began when the Saint Anne's Guild was formed to discuss the needs for a Catholic church in Youngtown on October 30, 1957. The Guild was renamed the Youngtown Catholic Society in 1958. On May 1, 1959, Father Francis Bechtel met with the Youngtown Catholic Society to begin plans for a proposed Catholic church. On October 16, 1960, the first Mass was celebrated in the Youngtown Clubhouse by Father Bechtel for 197 people. In early 1961, property in Sun City was purchased for the future parish. Masses continued to be held at the Youngtown Clubhouse and later in the Sun City Community Hall.

Saint Joachim Parish was established by Bishop Francis Green of Tucson on March 18, 1961. Father Palmer Plourde was appointed the first pastor. The first Mass in the new parish was celebrated at the Sun City Community Hall on March 26, 1961. The church groundbreaking took place on August 13, 1961, and the rectory was completed in September 1961. Masses were transferred to the Town Hall in September 1961. The first Mass in the church was celebrated on December 24, 1961. The dedication by Bishop Francis Green of Tucson took place on January 16, 1963. In 1969, the church was expanded by adding wings and a new vestibule. A Shrine to Our Lady of Lourdes was also built in April 1974. Father Plourde remained as pastor until 1975.

The Blessed Family name was completed with the addition of Saint Anne to the parish name. The parish became Saint Joachim and Saint Anne Parish on July 26, 1979. Father Frank Simlik became pastor in July 1989. A renovation of Saint Anne Hall was completed in March 1996 and was followed by the restoration of the Shrine by Eagle Scouts in May 1999. In July 2002, Father Mark Harrington became pastor and the church altar was remodeled one month later. Additional remodeling of the church was completed in June 2004. Father John L. Ebbesmier has been pastor since July 2007. Saint Joachim and Saint Anne Parish currently serve 1,200 registered families.

SAINT JOAN OF ARC
PARISH

Phoenix, Arizona
Established July 12, 1979

Saint Joan of Arc Parish was established by Bishop James Rausch of Phoenix on July 12, 1979. Father Robert D. Skagen was appointed as the first pastor. The parish's name had been chosen at an organizational meeting attended by about 30-40 residents a week later.

The first official mass for Saint Joan of Arc parishioners was held at Larkspur Elementary School on July 22, 1979. Weekend Masses were held at Greenway Middle School and daily Mass in the rectory on Waltann Lane until construction of the parish multi-purpose building was completed. The new church was first used for Mass on May 2, 1981. The church building was officially dedicated by Bishop Thomas J. O'Brien of Phoenix on May 30, 1982.

Plans for a permanent church began in 1989. After 10 long years, the parish finally completed $4.5 million in new construction and realized its dream by moving into their permanent church. The permanent sanctuary was dedicated on November 6, 1999, by Bishop Thomas J. O'Brien of Phoenix. Saint Joan of Arc Parish has many ministries and programs including Saint Vincent de Paul Society, Hispanic Ministry, Seniors Ministry, Health Care Ministry, and RCIA. Father Donald Kline is the current pastor. Saint Joan of Arc Parish currently serves over 2800 registered families.

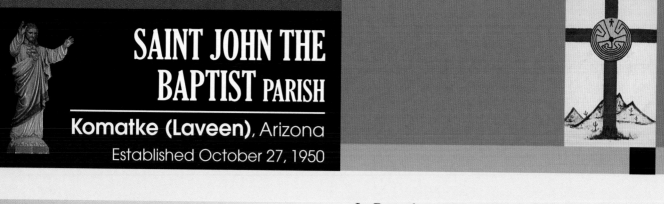

SAINT JOHN THE BAPTIST PARISH

Komatke (Laveen), Arizona
Established October 27, 1950

The mission to the Pima Indians on the Gila River Reservation dates back to 1896 under the guidance of Father Novatus Benzing, O.F.M. Franciscan priests from Saint Mary's, Phoenix, built a small chapel in the summer of 1897 and dedicated it to Saint John the Baptist. Saint John the Baptist School opened in 1899. Fire destroyed the chapel in 1900 and a larger chapel was built. The Franciscans administered and staffed the school until 1901, when the Sisters of Saint Joseph of Carondelet from Los Angeles arrived and also established a boarding school. Construction on the church was begun in late 1901 and dedicated on September 29, 1903. A monastery for the priests was built in 1908. Saint John the Baptist was officially established as a mission in 1910 by the Franciscans. Father Justin Deutsch, O.F.M., had arrived in 1901 and remained at the mission until 1918. He was responsible for the construction of the school dormitories, convent, new church, and dining hall. A fire destroyed most of the church in 1922. The original adobe walls survived the fire and the church was rebuilt. Saint John the Baptist was established as a parish on October 27, 1950 by Bishop Daniel J. Gercke of Tucson.

The Sisters of Saint Joseph of Carondelet continued to staff the school until 1930. The Sisters of Saint Joseph of Orange from California staffed the school from 1931 until December 1935.

In December 1935, the first Franciscan Sisters of Christian Charity from Manitowoc, Wisconsin arrived to staff the school. In 1943, the school was expanded to grades 1-12. The high school was closed in 1975. The Christian Brothers of the San Francisco Province arrived to help the Franciscan Sisters staff the school in 1980. Saint John the Baptist School was closed in 1990 due to financial difficulties and low enrollment. Both the Franciscan Sisters and Christian Brothers remained until 1990. Most of the school buildings were sadly burned down by vandals between 1990 and 2007.

Saint John the Baptist is the mother parish to four Native American Missions. Saint Francis of Assisi Mission in the Pima-Maricopa Indian Community was established in 1880. Saint Catherine Mission in Santa Cruz was established in 1919. Saint Paschal Baylon Chapel in Lehi was established about 1989. San Lucy Mission in Gila Bend became a mission of Saint John the Baptist Parish about 1999 and was previously a mission church of Saint Michael Parish in Gila Bend for many years. The Franciscan Fathers remained at the parish until 1984. Father James F. O'Brien, S.J., became pastor in 1984. Deacon James Trant is the current parish life coordinator. Father Dale Jamison, O.F.M., is the canonical pastor. Father Jamison began directing the Diocese of Phoenix Native American Ministry in October 2006. Saint John the Baptist Parish in Komatke (Laveen) currently serves over 150 registered families.

SAINT JOHN VIANNEY
PARISH

Goodyear, Arizona

Established April 28, 1956

Saint John Vianney Parish in Goodyear was established on April 28, 1956. Father Francis S. Murphy was appointed as the first pastor. The parish began in the 1950's when the first church was constructed. The first church continued to be used until a new church was built. Father Thomas Zurcher, C.S.C., was pastor from 1981 until July 1990. During his tenure, construction on the new church was begun in 1989 and completed in 1990. Father Joseph Corpora, C.S.C., was appointed pastor in 1990.

Saint John Vianney School was established in 1992 and began with a preschool and each year another grade was added. By 2001, the school has expanded to serve the children from preschool through eighth grade. The Salesian Sisters of Saint John Bosco, also known as the Daughters of Mary Help of Christians, came to serve the parish and school in July 1995. New buildings were constructed for the school and dedicated by Bishop Thomas O'Brien of Phoenix on December 7, 1997. In May 1998, the Cindy Moreno Youth Center was moved to Lakin Park and established as the Saint John Bosco Center for the after school program run by the Salesian Sisters. The Salesian Sisters had been providing religious education classes there since 1996.

Father Joseph Corpora remained as pastor until June 2002. In 2003, the 10-acre Lakin Park property was donated to the parish by Chuck Lakin.

A renovation of the church followed in June 2007, with a permanent sanctuary platform and permanent pews installed. Father John A. Herman, C.S.C., is the current pastor. The parish has many ministries and organizations including Outreach Ministry, Catechetical Ministry, Liturgy and Environment, and Youth Ministry. Saint John Vianney currently serves over 2,000 registered families.

175

SAINT JOSEPH
PARISH

Williams, Arizona

Established 1928

(formerly Sacred Heart Mission)

Saint Joseph Parish in Williams was established in 1928 by Bishop Daniel J. Gercke of Tucson. The founding pastor was Father Joseph Tremblay. The parish was originally named Sacred Heart Mission and began in 1895 under the direction of Father Joseph Freri of Flagstaff. The first church was built in 1896 and was located on the corner of Third Street and Sheridan. The mission had outside priests come through once a month to celebrate Mass. Father (later Monsignor) Edward Albouy was appointed as administrator from 1914 to 1916.

During the 1930s, an addition was added to the front of the church to enlarge the sanctuary and sacristy. An enclosed hallway was later added to connect the church to the rectory. Father Tremblay remained as pastor until 1940. In the 1950s, the Santa Fe Railroad donated the present property to the church. The present church was built in 1958 and the first mass was celebrated by Father John Faustina on December 24, 1958. Father Faustina remained at Saint Joseph until 1980.

Father Larry Weidner became pastor in 1987 and oversaw the remodeling of church interior and the addition of stained glass windows in October 1988. Additional stained glass windows and a parish hall were added during the 1990s. A former classroom was also remodeled into the parish chapel in 2002. Additional renovations and restoration of the church also took place in 2004 and 2006. Father Dindo C. (Bruno) Cuario, D.S., was appointed as pastor in 2006. Saint Joseph Parish currently serves 200 registered families.

SAINT LOUIS THE KING
PARISH
Glendale, Arizona
Established May 12, 1962

On May 12, 1962, Bishop Francis Green of Tucson established a new parish in Glendale to serve the growing population in the Northwest valley. Bishop Green placed the parish under the patronage of St. Louis, King of France to honor the early French missionaries of Arizona. The parish was able to use the Catalina School auditorium for Masses for 17 months until their church could be completed.

Under the founding pastor, Father (later Monsignor) James E. McFadden, ground was broken for the Church and school buildings on March 3, 1963. The new parish facility was dedicated by Bishop Green on April 5, 1964. The parish complex included six classrooms and a parish hall to serve a temporary church seating 700 people.

Saint Louis the King Elementary School was opened in September 1965 and staffed by the Sisters of Humility of Mary from Ottumwa, Iowa. The Sisters remained at the school until the early 1970s. The convent building was soon converted into parish offices, religious education classrooms, and meeting rooms. Father McFadden served the parish for 20 years, building a spirit of community and lay participation in all areas.

Since July 2004, a resident pastor is no longer assigned to St. Louis the King and Bishop Thomas Olmsted appointed a Canonical Pastor to serve the parish. Because of changing demographics of the parish boundaries, a Mass in Spanish and a ministry to Hispanics were added to the parish in 2005. Father Michael L. Diskin is the canonical pastor of the parish. Saint Louis the King Parish currently serves over 1,150 registered families.

SAINT LUKE
PARISH
Phoenix, Arizona
Established January 15, 1985

Saint Luke Parish in Phoenix was established by Bishop Thomas O'Brien on January 15, 1985. Father Richard A. Milligan was appointed as the first pastor. The first weekday Mass was held in the double garage of Father Milligan's parish residence on January 29, 1985. The parish named it the "Carport Cathedral" and daily Mass was held there for the next two years. The first Sunday Mass was held in the Village Meadows School auditorium on February 3, 1985 and Sunday Masses continued there for the next two years.

The site for a church had been purchased by the Diocese at Beardsley and 7th Avenue in Phoenix. Ground was broken for the church by Bishop O'Brien on September 6, 1986. The building plans opted for a building with a chapel, sanctuary, kitchen and cry room/meeting room. An addition held a reception area with an adjoining work room, a parish office, and a religious education office. A courtyard, meditation garden and rectory were also included in the plans. The first Mass was held in the new church on April 18, 1987. The dedication of the church complex by Bishop O'Brien took place on October 25, 1987.

By October 1989, the parish membership continued to grow and the parish began plans and fundraising for a parish hall. In 1992, the parish decided on an activity center and fundraising efforts continued. The groundbreaking for the activity center took place on January 15, 1995, and the building was dedicated on September 10, 1995.

Father Richard A. Milligan remains pastor to this day. Saint Luke parish currently serves 1,050 registered families.

SAINT MARGARET MARY
PARISH

Bullhead City, Arizona

Established May 11, 1947

The first Catholic chapel in the area was purchased in 1940 by Father Leo Oelmann in what is now "Davis Camp." Prior to that, Masses had been offered in the gold mining town of Oatman on Route 66 whenever a priest came through. A single room in Father Oelmann's house served as the chapel for the almost 60 Catholic families working on Davis Dam. In January 1947, a gift of $2,000 from the Catholic Church Extension Society enabled ground breaking for a church at Davis Dam (also known as Davis City) on leased government land. The name Saint Margaret Mary Mission was selected by the Society. Bishop Bernard T. Espelage, O.F.M., of Gallup established the parish on May 11, 1947.

On April 20, 1976, Bishop Edward McCarthy of Phoenix signed the decree officially establishing Saint Margaret Mary as a parish in a new location with almost 400 registered families. Father John Sullivan purchased six acres of property for the parish on North Oatman Road on May 12, 1978. On November 12, 1980, the Department of the Interior notified Bishop James S. Rausch of Phoenix that the lease on the old church property would not be renewed.

Ground was broken by Father Dominc Candappa for a combination church on May 24, 1981. The first mass was celebrated on February 2, 1982, and the church was dedicated by Bishop Thomas J. O'Brien on April 25, 1982. Father Candappa also dedicated a parish hall-classroom complex on January 25,

1985. A new rectory was built in 1991. Five additional acres were added to the parish property in August 1996.

On February 27, 2008, ground was broken for a new church by Bishop Thomas J. Olmsted of Phoenix on February 27, 2008. Father Peter P. Dobrowski has been pastor since June 12, 1991. Ministries include Saint Vincent de Paul Society, Catechetical Ministry, Youth Ministry, and Family Ministry. Saint Margaret Mary Parish currently serves 1,350 registered families.

SAINT MARGARET

PARISH

Tempe, Arizona

Established June 21, 1972

(originally Saint Margaret Mary Alacoque Mission)

In the early 1950s, a Catholic community started to build a mission to Queen of Peace in Mesa called Saint Margaret Mary Alacoque. Masses were held in the home of Virgina Campos in Victory Acres. The mission church was built in 1953 and funded by the Catholic Church Extension Society. Father Laurence A. Florez came to the mission in 1970 and was living in a room built on the west side of the church for a year that later became the sacristy. In 1972, a house across from the church became the rectory for several years.

Saint Margaret Parish was established by Bishop Edward McCarthy of Phoenix on June 21, 1972. Father Laurence A. Florez was appointed the first pastor. At that time, the parish celebrated two Masses in both Spanish and English. Father Florez also purchased two properties for parking purposes. Father Florez remained as pastor until 1980. Father Henry Perez was appointed the second pastor in September 1980 and was responsible for the original frosted-glass windows in the church being replaced by 14 stained glass windows between 1981 and 1983. By 1981, the parish had grown to over 300 families.

Saint Margaret became a parish without a resident priest on July 1, 1993, with Father Marcel Salinas appointed as canonical pastor and Deacon Frank Galarza as parish life coordinator. Father Charles Goraieb is the current canonical pastor. The parish has several ministries and services that include RCIA, Cristo Rey, Liturgy, Quinceañeras, and Religious Education classes. Saint Margaret Parish currently has over 1,000 registered families.

Saint Maria Goretti Parish in Scottsdale was established June 14, 1967 by Bishop Francis Green of Tucson. Father Thomas J. Lambert was appointed the first pastor. A 10 acre parcel of land at Granite Reef and Rose Lane had been previously purchased. This was to remain the site of the present parish buildings.

The first Mass was celebrated at Saguaro High School Cafeteria on July 23, 1967. A multi-purpose building was the first building constructed and was ready for use by late 1968. It served all parish functions until the church was finished. Father Aloysius McCaughey was appointed as the second pastor in early 1969. The church was finally completed in 1972 and the first Mass in the new church was celebrated on December 24, 1972. The original multi-purpose building was also named Lambert Hall after the founding pastor.

To accommodate the growing parish, Piper Hall and the chapel were constructed between 1990 and 1992. The parish offices were refurbished at that time. Since 2006, the parish has added stained glass windows in the chapel. Father Douglas Lorig is the current pastor. Ministries and organizations include Faith Formation, Youth Ministry, Outreach,

Parish Life and Stewardship. Saint Maria Goretti Parish currently serves 1,300 registered families.

Saint Mark Parish in Phoenix was established by Bishop Daniel Gercke of Tucson on March 2, 1946. Father Claude Riffel, O.F.M., was appointed the first pastor and purchased property for a new church. On August 16, 1946, Father Victor Herring, O.F.M., became pastor and was succeeded by Father John F. McMorran, O.F.M., on August 9, 1947. Father McMorran acquired and dismantled a POW army barracks building. The barracks was reassembled on the new property at South 20th and East Mohave and became a temporary church. The first Mass was celebrated on October 12, 1947.

Father Thomas More Schneider, O.F.M., became pastor in August 1951 and purchased property on East Adams Street for a new church. On December 12, 1951, ground was broken for the church. About six months prior to the completion of the new structure, the parish vacated the Mohave site and worshipped in the Longfellow School. The church was completed on August 21, 1952, and dedicated by Bishop Gercke on November 2, 1952. Father Giles Valcovich, O.F.M., became pastor in 1954 and became interested in building a school.

The parish purchased 13-acres of property on 30th Street. Ground was broken for the new school

and hall on September 21, 1958. Saint Mark School and Parish Hall were completed and opened in September of 1959 by the Sisters of the Precious Blood. A convent was built for the Sisters in 1960. On April 4, 1962, the church building on Adams Street was sold. Masses were moved to the new parish hall/church building in July 1962. In 1969, the Diocese invited the Salvatorian Fathers to be administrators of the parish. Saint Mark School closed on May 30, 1983, due to financial difficulties. Father Jorge G. Gonzalez is the current parochial administrator. Saint Mark Parish currently serves over 700 registered families.

SAINT MARTIN DE PORRES PARISH

Phoenix, Arizona

Established April 18, 1973

In 1970, when Father Raymond Gillis was assigned to Saint Catherine of Siena in Phoenix, he was invited to say Mass at a home on 35th Avenue. Father Gillis soon learned of the need for a Catholic church in the neighborhood. Through a donation made by the von Wrangell family, a multi-purpose church building was begun. Bishop Edward McCarthy of Phoenix broke ground for the new church center, named the Ann and Carl von Wrangell Building, in 1971.

Saint Martin de Porres was established as a parish by Bishop McCarthy on April 18, 1973. The new church center was dedicated in the summer of 1973. Each Sunday the building was used as a church and during the week it served as a senior center, free clinic, recreational center, and city service office. In 1973, Father Gillis was appointed as the parish administrator. Father Henry R. Wasielewski was appointed the first pastor in 1974.

In 1978, Father T. Eamon Barden was installed as the new pastor. During his first year, Father Barden moved the clinic into a trailer behind the church, consolidated the city offices, stopped the recreation program, and continued the weekly meetings for seniors. All other rooms were used for catechetical classes and church programs. Sunday Masses and the revised uses of the building continued for the next 12 years. When Father Raymond Ritari was appointed pastor in 1990, the clinic and city satellite office were closed and he opened up the hall and altar area into one large worship space.

Father Ritari was transferred in 1994 because of a shortage of priests and Bishop O'Brien installed Deacon Jose Olivarez as Pastoral Life Coordinator. Under Deacon Olivarez, the floor of the church was tiled in ceramic and a sanctuary was added with small shrines along the walls. Stained glass windows were also installed and a wall was built to enclose the old altar area.

In 2005, Deacon Olivarez retired and Sister Dorothy Deger, S.N.D. de N., took over as the Pastoral Life Coordinator. Sister Dorothy has since moved a trailer behind the church for office space and installed windows on the wall of the old altar space to create a crying room. A new roof for the church has also been installed. Father David Sanfilippo is the current canonical pastor. Saint Martin de Porres Parish currently serves over 755 registered families.

SAINT MARY BASILICA

Phoenix, Arizona

Dedicated June 24, 1881

The first Masses in Phoenix were conducted by priests from Florence in the home of Jesus Otero from 1872-1881. Father (later Monsignor) Edouard Gerard began the construction of the first Catholic Church in Phoenix at Third Street and Monroe in 1880. The church was dedicated by Bishop Jean Baptiste Salpointe on June 24, 1881, with Father Gerard traveling from Florence to minister to the Phoenician Catholics. Saint Mary's has been known by several names including Sacred Heart of Mary and Immaculate Heart of Mary. Father Joseph Bloise arrived in 1882 and was the first resident pastor. Father Francoise Jouvenceau became pastor in 1887 and invited the Sisters of Mercy to help found a school in August 1892. The Sisters of Mercy continued teaching until 1903 and were replaced by the Sisters of the Precious Blood.

In December 1895, the Franciscan Friars agreed to staff the parish and the first friars arrived on January 12, 1896. Father Novatus Benzing, O.F.M., became pastor in July 1896. By 1902 the church was in need of repairs and enlargement. The old adobe church was torn down and construction of the basement of the new church began in 1902. The basement church was dedicated under the patronage of the Immaculate Conception of the

Blessed Virgin Mary by Bishop Henri Granjon of Tucson on February 11, 1903. Construction of the upper church began in July 1913 and was completed on December 31, 1914. The church was dedicated by Bishop Granjon on February 11, 1915. In January 1916, the parish was entrusted to the newly created Franciscan Province of Santa Barbara.

A minor renovation of the church took place in 1958. On September 6, 1976, the church was named a historic site by the Arizona Historical Society and was placed on the National Register of Historic Places on November 29, 1978. On the

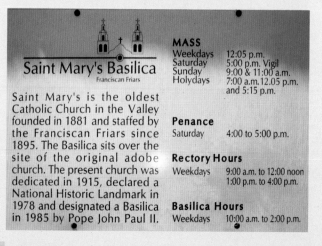

Saint Mary's Basilica
Franciscan Friars

Saint Mary's is the oldest Catholic Church in the Valley founded in 1881 and staffed by the Franciscan Friars since 1895. The Basilica sits over the site of the original adobe church. The present church was dedicated in 1915, declared a National Historic Landmark in 1978 and designated a Basilica in 1985 by Pope John Paul II.

MASS
Weekdays	12:05 p.m.
Saturday	5:00 p.m. Vigil
Sunday	9:00 & 11:00 a.m.
Holydays	7:00 a.m. 12.05 p.m. and 5:15 p.m.

Penance
| Saturday | 4:00 to 5:00 p.m. |

Rectory Hours
| Weekdays | 9:00 a.m. to 12:00 noon 1:00 p.m. to 4:00 p.m. |

Basilica Hours
| Weekdays | 10:00 a.m. to 2:00 p.m. |

occasion of the 100th anniversary in 1981, Father Howard Hall began a fundraising program for the renovation of the church. Father Warren Rouse, O.F.M., became pastor in August 1982, finished restoring the church and edited a history of the parish titled "100 Years: The Franciscans and St. Mary's Basilica." The former friars' oratory adjacent to the sanctuary was transformed into a chapel dedicated to the Blessed Sacrament and a new tabernacle was purchased in 1986. The church was consecrated by Bishop Thomas J. O'Brien on February 6, 1985. On September 2, 1985, Pope John Paul II solemnly proclaimed the church of the Immaculate Conception of the Blessed Virgin Mary to be a Minor Basilica. The public ceremony was in the form of a Vesper Service held on December 8, 1985. Pope John Paul II visited Saint Mary Basilica on September 14, 1987.

In October 1993, the frosted window panes in the chapel were replaced with stained glass windows to

enhance the chapel. In May 1998, the chapel was dedicated to Our Lady of Guadalupe. On September 11, 2003, Fr. Vincent J. Mesi, O.F.M., arrived as rector of the Basilica. Since 2003, the upper stained glass windows depicting the life of Mary were releaded, the dome of the Basilica was made more structurally sound, and the Franciscan Friary was updated and remodeled. The Bells of Saint Mary, after 25 years of not ringing, were electrified and now the original bells of the Basilica ring as a call to worship. Saint Mary Basilica currently serves 900 registered families.

SAINT MARY MAGDALENE
PARISH
Gilbert, Arizona
Established July 1, 2002

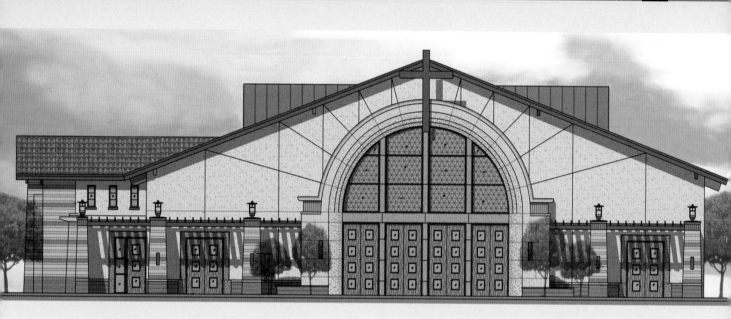

Saint Mary Magdalene Parish was established by Bishop Thomas J. O'Brien of Phoenix on July 1, 2002. Father John F. Cunningham was appointed as the first pastor. The first Masses in the parish were celebrated Labor Day Weekend in early September 2002. The parish held Masses for three years at Williams Elementary School at Williams Air Field. The parish was able to secure a place to worship at Gateway Pointe Elementary School and the first Masses were held there on August 5, 2006.

The parish office is located on South Recker Road, where the administration of the parish takes place and adult education sessions are held. Religious education classes and teen groups meet at Gateway Pointe Elementary School. The parish currently owns 20 acres of land on Williams Field Road in Gilbert, where the parish will build its permanent church complex.

Saint Mary Magdalene Parish hopes to break ground for a multi-purpose complex to house the parish offices, classrooms and worship space by June 2009. The parish will then begin efforts to build a permanent church and elementary school in the near future. Father Gregory A. Menegay is the current pastor. The parish has many ministries and organizations including the Knights of Columbus, Ladies Auxiliary, Peace and Justice Committee, Stewardship Committee, Saint Vincent de Paul Society, Respect Life Ministry, and RCIA. Saint Mary Magdalene Parish currently serves over 1,600 registered families.

SAINT MARY
PARISH
Chandler, Arizona
Established December 10, 1937

On March 30, 1915, Father Lucius Zittier, a Franciscan Father, celebrated Mass in Chandler for the first time in the Koch family home. Priests ministered to the Chandler area came from Our Lady of Mount Carmel in Tempe and Immaculate Heart of Mary in Phoenix. Masses were celebrated in the Koch home and the old American Legion Hall.

The church basement was built by Father James Peter Davis (later Archbishop of San Juan de Puerto Rico and Archbishop of Santa Fe) when Chandler was a mission of Tempe and used as a church until 1936. The mission was served by priests from Sacred Heart (later Queen of Peace) in Mesa from 1932 to 1937. The church was completed by Father Vincent Mestre in 1936 and the basement of the church was used as a hall.

Saint Mary Parish in Chandler was established by Bishop Daniel Gercke of Tucson on December 10, 1937. Father Vincent Mestre was appointed the first pastor. Father Joseph N. Patterson became pastor in 1938. In 1941, the old Koch home was purchased and later remodeled as the first convent. Four adobe classrooms for the school were built in 1944 and blessed by Bishop Gercke. The Sisters of Charity have been associated with the school since its inception. Father Patterson and parishioner, Joe Martinez, built the first four classrooms for 123 students when the school opened in September 1944. More classrooms were added in the late 1940's for grades 1-8. In 1953, a building was built

for Seton High School. Father Patterson remained at the parish until 1958.

The Basha family was responsible for the construction of a new school. Ground was broken on March 7, 1963 and the new building, renamed Saint Mary-Basha School, was dedicated by Bishop Francis Green of Tucson on December 13, 1964. The original school was demolished to make room for parking. Thanks to donations by the Weinberg and Quarty families, a new convent was built in 1966 and a rectory in 1968. Construction on the new church began in 1975. The building was completed in October 1976 and was dedicated by Bishop James Rausch of Phoenix on October 9, 1977.

Father Daniel McBride is the current pastor. Ministries include Saint Vincent de Paul, Altar Society, Respect Life, Knights of Columbus, Hispanic Ministry, Ministry of Care, Senior Adult Group, and Las Guadaluopanas. Saint Mary Parish in Chandler currently serves 4,700 registered families.

SAINT MARY PARISH

Kingman, Arizona

Established 1906

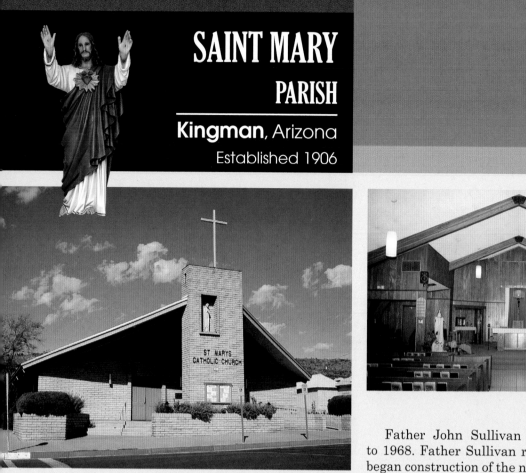

Catholic missionaries visited the Kingman area prior to 1890. In 1892, missionary priests would stay with the Lynch and Mulligan families and celebrate Mass. Masses were also held in the courthouse and old Kingman schoolhouse. Kingman became a station in 1895. Father Cyprian Vabre wrote to Bishop Henry Granjon of Tucson in March 1901 about the need for a church in Kingman. Saint Mary Parish was established in 1906 and Father Vabre was the first pastor until 1914. Construction on the church began in June 1906 and was completed May 25, 1907. The church was dedicated on September 22, 1906. The first Mass was celebrated on May 26, 1907.

Father (later Monsignor) Edward Albouy was the first resident pastor from 1914 to 1918 and built the rectory. Father Joseph Hootsman was pastor from 1918 to 1930 and he remodeled the old church. The former Greystone Inn was converted into Saint Mary School on the lower level and the convent on the second floor. Despite not being completely renovated, the school opened on September 5, 1944, with 60 students in grades K-4. The school was dedicated by Bishop Bernard Espelage, O.F.M., of Gallup on September 12, 1944. In 1945, grades 5-6 were added. In 1948, the convent on the 2nd floor of the school was converted into classrooms for grades 7-8 and a parish hall. On February 17, 1966, ground was broken for the new school across the street from the new church. The new school was dedicated by Bishop Espelage on September 18, 1966.

Father John Sullivan was pastor from 1965 to 1968. Father Sullivan razed the old school and began construction of the new church at that site in 1966. The church was dedicated October 29, 1967, by Bishop Espelage. The old church became Saint Mary Hall. The Dominican Sisters remained until 1970. Franciscan Sisters from Milwaukee staffed the school from 1970 to 1973. The Congregation of the Precious Blood staffed the school from 1981 to 1985, when the school, rectory and convent all closed. The old church was placed on the National Historic Register in 1986 and restored in 1988. In 1989, the school was remodeled as the parish center.

The old church was refurbished for use as a church museum/gift shop in 1991 and later became a classroom/meeting space. The old church was renovated again in October 2006 and the Perpetual Adoration Chapel was dedicated. Father Matthew Krempel is the current pastoral administrator. Saint Mary Parish serves 1,350 registered families.

SAINT MATTHEW
PARISH
Phoenix, Arizona
Established December 20, 1939

Saint Matthew Parish was established by Bishop Daniel J. Gercke of Tucson on December 20, 1939. Father Willard David Kinney was appointed the first pastor. The first Mass in the parish was held in the Capitol School auditorium. Construction on the church building was begun in 1940 and the first Mass in the new church was Midnight Mass, Christmas 1940. Bishop Gercke dedicated the new church on December 29, 1940.

Saint Matthew School was opened in September 1943 by the Sisters of Charity of the Blessed Virgin Mary from Dubuque, Iowa. That first year there were 64 boys and girls in grades 1-4. In 1944, 150 children attended eight grades. The school was begun in barracks-type buildings located where the school playground and parking lot are now located. The present school building was completed in the mid 1940's. The Franciscan Sisters of Joliet, Illinois and the Sisters of Charity of the Blessed Virgin Mary served as teachers and administrators of the school until 1999.

Father Kinney left in 1949 to become a Trappist monk and Father Paul Lawrence was appointed the second pastor on September 14, 1949. Under his leadership, the convent and rectory were built. In 1961, Father Thomas Lambert was appointed as pastor. Father William Mitchell became administrator in 1962 and was responsible for establishing the CCD program at Saint Matthew's. In 1964, Father Francis Murphy was appointed

pastor and moved ahead with an improvement program and reorganization of parish societies. Father Cornelius Moynihan was pastor from 1969 to 1972 and succeeded by Father Thomas O'Dea. The Marist Fathers took over the administration of the parish in 1974 and remained until 1993. Father Raymond J. Ritari was appointed pastor in 1994.

Since 1993, there have been two phases of renovation to the church and installation of a new plaza and fountain. The parish hall collapsed and a new hall, named San Juan Diego Hall, was completed in 2001. The former convent has also been converted into the Centro Soledad Faith Development Center. Father Raymond J. Ritari is the current pastor. Ministries include Faith Formation, Social Outreach, Pastoral Ministry, Adult Prayer Group, and Young Adult Groups. Saint Matthew Parish currently serves 1,200 registered families.

SAINT MICHAEL
PARISH
Gila Bend, Arizona
Established September 6, 1963

Saint Michael was originally a mission of Saint Henry Parish in Buckeye. The first church building used by the mission was built in 1937. Saint Michael's Chapel was built in 1951 and used as the mission church. In 1961, one of the four trailer missions of the Diocese was headquartered at Gila Bend by Father William T. Byrne. Because of the presence of the trailer mission priest, the Gila Bend area developed sufficiently to warrant the status of a parish with a resident pastor.

Saint Michael Parish in Gila Bend was established on September 6, 1963. Father Andrew Strednak was appointed the first pastor. Ground was broken for the present church on March 3, 1964 and the first Mass was held there April 23, 1964. The new church was dedicated by Bishop Francis Green of Tucson on June 4, 1964. Father Andrew L. Strednak remained as pastor until 1967 and was succeeded by Father Joseph Joniko from 1967-1968, Father George Connelly from 1968-1969, Father Henry Hodges from 1969-1970, and Father Alan Malone from 1970-1972.

By the 1980s, a shortage in priests allowed for Sister Maria Lucinda Lopez, C.S.J., to become pastoral administrator in 1986. She was responsible for starting the parish's first youth ministry for the

230 families. Masses were celebrated each Sunday by Father David Meyers, S.J., from Guadalupe in 1988. Father Frank Gallagher, S.J., from Brophy College Preparatory in Phoenix, celebrated Masses for the parish in 1990. Today, the parish has a Catechetical Ministry and Father Kieran Kleczewski is the parochial administrator. Saint Michael Parish in Gila Bend currently serves 75 registered families.

SAINT PATRICK

PARISH

Scottsdale, Arizona

Established May 25, 1980

Saint Patrick Parish was established by Bishop James S. Rausch of Phoenix on May 25, 1980. Father Brian A. Fenlon was appointed as the first pastor for the 60 families in the parish. The first Sunday Liturgy was celebrated on May 25, 1980 at Scottsdale Country Club.

The parish soon outgrew that space and Sunday Mass was held at Cochise School until 1985, when the first multi-use facility was completed. Bishop Thomas J. O'Brien dedicated the new facility on March 17, 1985. This first building contained the worship space with seating for 600, parish offices and three meeting rooms.

Father Eric Tellez has been pastor since 1995. The parish soon began to quickly outgrow its multi-use facility and in 1997, the Building Steering Committee was formed. A campaign to build a new Worship Center for the parish began and construction on a new worship center was completed in 2002. The first Mass in the new Worship Center was held on September 4, 2002. The new facility contained a main sanctuary with seating for 1,200, the Daily Mass Chapel has a capacity for 160 people, meeting space, and a courtyard for outdoor community events.

In 2007, a new Administration and Conference Center was built which added office space, storage space, flexible meeting space, a chapel, and a pastoral office for parish staff and volunteers. In April 2008, the multi-use building was remodeled and rededicated as the Fenlon Hospitality Center. Saint Patrick Parish in Scottsdale currently serves 4,000 registered families.

SAINT PAUL
PARISH
Phoenix, Arizona
Established August 26, 1976

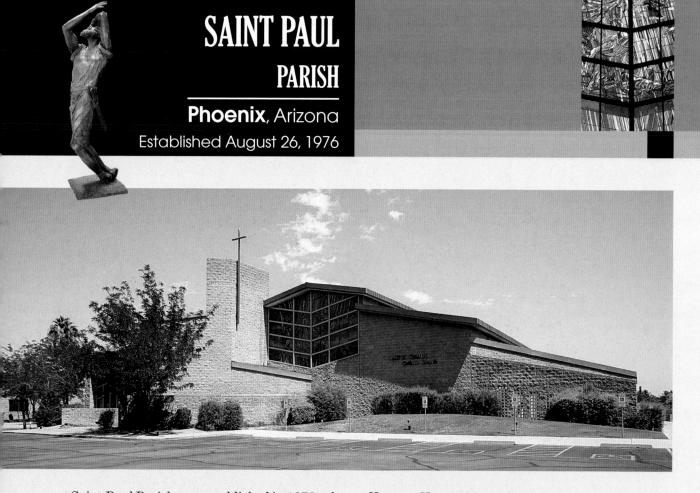

Saint Paul Parish was established in 1976, when the development committee of the Diocese decided that the Moon Valley area was ready for a parish for 200 Catholic families. Bishop Edward A. McCarthy of Phoenix established the parish on August 26, 1976. Father Harold P. Graf was appointed as the first pastor. The first Mass was celebrated in the cafeteria of Moon Mountain School on October 17, 1976. At that time, a mobile home served as the rectory for almost two years.

In 1978, ten acres of land was purchased at the present location in Phoenix. A multi-purpose building to house a parish hall, four classrooms, chapel, rectory and outdoor ramada with bell tower was completed in October 1979. The first Mass was celebrated on October 13, 1979. The new parish multi-purpose facility was dedicated by Bishop James Rausch on June 29, 1980. Father Eugene O'Carroll became pastor in 1981.

In January 1986, the building fund got under way to construct the present church building. Bishop Thomas J. O'Brien of Phoenix formally broke ground for the building in June 1986. The new church was dedicated on January 25, 1987.

In January 2002, the groundbreaking for a new parish hall took place. The building was dedicated O'Carroll Hall, in honor of Father Eugene O'Carroll, on October 5, 2002. Father O'Carroll retired on July 1, 2008, after 27 years as pastor. The parish has many ministries and organizations including Harvest House, Men's Club, Saint Vincent de Paul Society, Widows' Support Group and Women's Guild. Father Michael J. Straley is the current pastor. Saint Paul Parish currently serves over 1,950 registered families.

Saint Peter Parish in Bapchule was established by Bishop Daniel J. Gercke of Tucson on October 27, 1950. Father Hubert Mounier, O.F.M., was appointed the first pastor. Saint Peter Parish is the mother parish to five Native American Missions, four in the Gila River Indian Community and one in the Ak-Chin Indian Community. Saint Anthony Mission in Sacaton was established in 1916. Holy Family Mission in Blackwater was established in 1918. Saint Francis Mission in Ak-Chin was established in 1922. Saint Anne Mission in Santan was established in 1937. Our Lady of Victory Mission in Sacaton Flats was established in about 1941.

The Franciscan Fathers of the Santa Barbara Province continued as administrators of the parish until 1992. Since 1992, permanent deacons have served the parish. In 2009, the school has a number of Franciscan Sisters still dedicated to teaching the Pima Indians on the Gila River Reservation. The school has also been blessed by generous benefactors and friends including baseball legend, Joe Garagiola, Sr. Father Dale Jamison, O.F.M., Native American Ministry Director, is the parochial administrator. Saint Peter Parish in Bapchule currently serves 150 registered families.

Beginning in 1873, priests from Assumption Parish in Florence began visiting the Pima Indians on the Gila River Reservation. These visits from diocesan priests continued through the 1890's. The old adobe church was built about 1920. Saint Peter Mission was first established in 1929 by Franciscan Fathers from the Santa Barbara Province in Oakland, California. The Franciscans also began ministering to the Sacaton, Blackwater and Ak-Chin missions in 1929.

Saint Peter Mission School in Bapchule was opened in 1923 and staffed by lay teachers until 1931. The Sisters of Saint Joseph of Orange from Orange, California staffed the school from 1932-1935. In December 1935, the first Franciscan Sisters of Christian Charity from Manitowoc, Wisconsin arrived to staff the school.

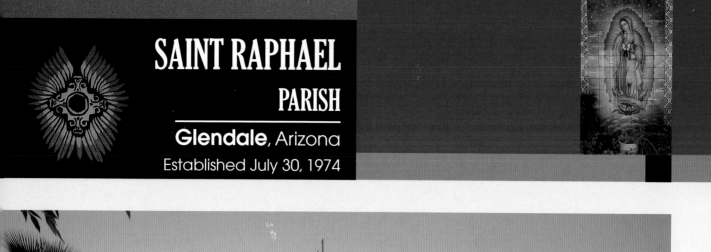

SAINT RAPHAEL

PARISH

Glendale, Arizona

Established July 30, 1974

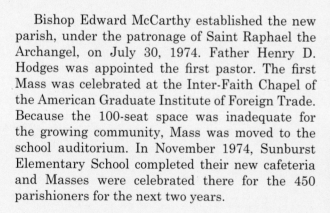

Bishop Edward McCarthy established the new parish, under the patronage of Saint Raphael the Archangel, on July 30, 1974. Father Henry D. Hodges was appointed the first pastor. The first Mass was celebrated at the Inter-Faith Chapel of the American Graduate Institute of Foreign Trade. Because the 100-seat space was inadequate for the growing community, Mass was moved to the school auditorium. In November 1974, Sunburst Elementary School completed their new cafeteria and Masses were celebrated there for the 450 parishioners for the next two years.

The first Mass was celebrated in the new church on November 20, 1976. Bishop James Rausch formally dedicated the church on October 24, 1977. In 1980, the care of the parish was entrusted to the Carmelite Order. The Carmelite Fathers served the parish community over the next 16 years until 1996. A special moment of grace for the parish community occurred in 1999. Saint Raphael Church was designated as a stop for the national pilgrimage of the relics of the great Carmelite mystic, Saint Therese of Lisieux on December 22-23, 1999.

Parish growth continued with the construction of the education building in 1982 and the administrative

building in 1989. In 1995, the decision was made to build a parish hall. The parish hall was dedicated by Bishop Thomas O'Brien in 1998. The parish Community hopes to renovate the worship space in the near future.

Today, the parish has been paired with Our Lady of the Valley Parish in Phoenix and Father Edward J. Kaminski, C.S.C., is the pastor of both parishes. The parish has many ministries and programs that include RCIA, Youth Ministry, Pastoral Care, Catechetical Ministry and Social Outreach. Saint Raphael Parish currently has about 600 registered families.

SAINT ROSE PHILIPPINE DUCHESNE PARISH

Anthem, Arizona

Established September 1, 2004

Before the small desert town of New River had any neighboring communities, Catholics of the area gathered for their first Mass in a public school gymnasium on April 9, 1983. Father Valentine L. Boyle, O. Carm., was appointed administrator of this small Catholic community in 1985. A building fund was started in 1985 and Mary Aguire donated five acres of land for a future church and related buildings in 1987. The community was established as Good Shepherd, a mission of Saint Luke Parish in 1988.

By 1992, the mission was able to complete a multi-use church building. Good Shepherd Church was dedicated in May 1993 and additions were made to the church in 1997. By the time Father Boyle retired in 2003, the area had begun to experience rapid population growth. On New River's border, the planned community of Anthem was outgrowing all expectations. Mass was first celebrated at the Anthem Community Center in 2002 for 450 people. Catholics also gathered in Anthem for many social events and religious education classes. Deacon James Fogel provided support and administration for the Catholic community in Anthem.

Saint Rose Philippine Duchesne Parish in Anthem was established on September 1, 2004. Good Shepherd Church in New River became a mission of the new parish and Father John Coleman was appointed as the founding pastor. Masses were celebrated at Gavilan Peak Elementary School in Anthem until the Spirituality Center was completed

in July 2009. Prior to the creation of the parish, the Diocese decided to buy 24 acres of property in Anthem. Plans for a church, multipurpose spirituality center and a school were begun. Father Mark E. Harrington became pastor in 2007 and St. Rose Philippine Duchesne parish serves 1,000 registered families with a staff of 5 and has 39 active ministries.

SAINT STEVEN

PARISH

Sun Lakes, Arizona

Established May 20, 1988

Saint Steven Parish in Sun Lakes was established by Bishop Thomas J. O'Brien on May 20, 1988. Father Emmett J. FitzPatrick was appointed as the first pastor. The parish was originally a mission of Saint Mary Parish in Chandler. The parish celebrated the groundbreaking of the church in February 1990. The first Mass in the new church was celebrated on August 15, 1990. Bishop Thomas O'Brien of Phoenix dedicated Saint Steven Church on November 4, 1990.

In 1994, the complex was expanded to include a new social hall with meeting rooms, a storage area and a large Great Room. This construction completed the enclosure of the Spanish style courtyard around a beautiful fountain. In 1995, the parish purchased a new rectory location in the Oakwood area of Sun Lakes, just minutes from the church complex. In 1997, the population growth in the southeast Chandler area necessitated an expansion of the church's seating capacity and two wings were added on each side of the main sanctuary. The church now seats 800 people.

Father FitzPatrick, passed away in October 2004. Bishop Thomas Olmsted appointed Father L. Pierre Hissey as the second pastor of the parish, and presided over Father Hissey's installation ceremony on February 26, 2005. Saint Steven Parish currently serves 1,600 registered families.

SAINT THERESA
PARISH
Phoenix, Arizona
Established August 5, 1955

On August 5th 1955, Bishop Daniel J. Gercke of Tucson erected a new parish to meet the needs of Catholics in what was then the far northeastern edge of Phoenix. The parish was placed under the patronage of Saint Theresa, the Little Flower, with Father George Feeney as its first pastor. The parish area, encompassing the southern slopes of Camelback Mountain, was largely citrus and date palm groves at the time of its founding. The neighborhoods of Arcadia, Orangedale and west Scottsdale were to grow exponentially in the coming years – as did parish membership, active parish organizations and Saint Theresa Catholic School, founded in 1957 and initially staffed by the Sisters of Charity of Seton Hill.

Construction of the original church, the rectory, the convent and a portion of the school was completed just four months after the parish was established. Following Father Feeney's accidental death in 1961, Father Theodore Radtke was appointed pastor. Parish membership, the school building (and enrollment) continued to flourish: by 1964, there were 872 students in the school's 17 classrooms. A ramada was constructed in the quadrangle of the school to accommodate Sunday "overflow" Masses, since the parish community had already outgrown its original church building.

Succeeding Father Radtke as pastor in 1968, Father John J. McMahon set about organizing the parishioners into neighborhood groups, continued construction of the school facilities, acquired additional land and embarked on a master plan for the parish campus. On May 25, 1975, a new church and parish center with a gym and meeting rooms was dedicated by Bishop McCarthy. The former church, now to be known as Father Feeney Hall, became a social hall. Following his coordination of Pope John Paul II's pastoral visit to Phoenix in 1987, Father McMahon was honored with the title of Monsignor.

Upon Monsignor McMahon's retirement in 1991, Father Charles G. Kieffer was appointed the fourth pastor of Saint Theresa. Parish members became increasingly involved in outreach ministries to those in need and the homeless, as well as spiritual opportunities like Taizé Prayer and Centering Prayer. In the 1990's and into the new millennium, eleven men entered seminary, one woman entered religious life. Five first Masses were celebrated by newly-ordained parishioners. A successful capital campaign in 1997 led to a series of phased-in improvements to the parish campus, including a complete renovation of Father Feeney Hall and school classrooms, the addition of Our Lady of Guadalupe Courtyard, a new church baptistery and a commercial kitchen for the parish center (now the Monsignor McMahon Center). A new preschool building, currently being designed, is the final phase of the campaign. Additional improvements in recent years include campus security gates, new granite and travertine sanctuary appointments, a state-of-the-art organ and piano for the church and campus landscaping.

Now an urban parish and school in East Central Phoenix, Saint Theresa celebrated its Golden Jubilee in 2005 and continues to be a vibrant faith community of approximately 2,800 families, with over 70 active ministries and a school serving more than 600 students.

SAINT THOMAS AQUINAS PARISH

Avondale, Arizona

Established June 20, 1975

Saint Thomas Aquinas started as a mission and was the first Church built in Litchfield Park. From 1913 to 1925, Saint Mary's Basilica in Phoenix operated the mission. Masses were said in the Serrano home in 1918. The property for the church was sold to the Diocese by the Litchfield family. The Serrano and Litchfield families were instrumental in getting the mission church built and construction began in 1919. The church was completed in October 1923.

Father Cubillo, a Claretian priest from Immaculate Heart of Mary, ran the mission from 1925 until 1943. Priests from Our Lady of Perpetual Help in Glendale looked after the mission from 1943 until 1954, when it became a mission church of Saint John Vianney Parish in Goodyear. Father Francis Murphy was administrator of the mission from 1954 until 1972.

The old mission church seated only 125 people and the growth in the area demanded a larger church. In 1973, 3.7 acres were purchased for a new church and Saint Thomas Aquinas became a parish on June 20, 1975. Father T. Eamon Barden was the first pastor. An activity Center that seated 200 was built at the new parish site in 1976. The original church was sold in 1983 and Mass was held in the Activity Center. Construction on the new 725-seat church began in April 1985. The first Mass was held on December 15, 1985, and the church was dedicated by Bishop Thomas J. O'Brien

on February 23, 1986. The Activity Center was renamed the Aquinas Center in 1995.

Due to the immense population growth of the area, the parish decided to sell the church in Litchfield Park and build a new Saint Thomas Aquinas Church in Avondale. The Avondale property was purchased in 1999, and the new church was dedicated in December 2003. Saint Thomas Aquinas School was opened in 2003 for grades P-8. Father Kieran Kleczewski has been pastor since 1998. Ministries and organizations include Saint Vincent de Paul, Ministry of Care, RCIA, Youth Ministry, Respect Life, and Bible Study. Saint Thomas Aquinas Parish currently serves 5,500 registered families.

SAINT THOMAS MORE
PARISH

Glendale, Arizona
Established July 1, 1997

Saint Thomas More Parish was established by Bishop Thomas O'Brien of Phoenix on July 1, 1997. Father James F. Turner was appointed as the first pastor. While awaiting the completion of the local elementary school where weekend masses would be held, daily masses were held in parishioner's homes with groups of neighbors in order to spread the word about the new parish. This continued until a temporary building was placed on the 13-acre church property on Utopia Road. The first weekend Mass was held on October 4, 1997 at Copper Creek Elementary School with approximately 200 families attending.

In June 1998, a parish building committee was formed and began to explore the idea of building a permanent church. In August 1998, a modular building was placed on the parish property to become the office and multi-purpose room/chapel and daily mass was now celebrated in the modular building. In March 1999, the first Capital Campaign was begun to raise funds for the construction of the church facilities. The plan was to construct a church and an office building to house a growing staff. In 1999, there were about 900 families registered in the parish.

Construction on a new church and administration building began on December 28, 2001. On November 1, 2002, the parish office moved into the new Administration Building. On December 12, 2002, the first Mass was held in the new church building which was still under construction. The new church and altar were dedicated by Bishop Thomas O'Brien of Phoenix on February 1, 2003. Construction on the parish hall began in August 2007 and the building was blessed on October 25, 2008. Father James F. Turner is the current pastor. Ministries and organizations include Christian Formation, RCIA, Youth Ministry, Pastoral Care, Saint Vincent de Paul Society, and Knights of Columbus. Saint Thomas More Parish currently serves nearly 4,000 registered families.

SAINT THOMAS THE APOSTLE PARISH

Phoenix, Arizona

Established October 11, 1950

Saint Thomas the Apostle Parish was established by Bishop Daniel J. Gercke of Tucson on October 11, 1950. Father John P. Doran was appointed the first pastor on November 6, 1950. A 10-acre plot at 24th Street and Campbell Avenue had been purchased prior to the establishment of the parish. A little red brick house on the grounds was used as the first rectory. Sunday Masses began in November 1950 at the Madison School auditorium for 250 families. Soon after, an army barracks building was used as a temporary chapel.

The church groundbreaking took place on January 14, 1951, and the first Mass was held on June 24, 1951. The new church was completed on September 23, 1951, and dedicated by Bishop Gercke on December 21, 1951. Saint Thomas the Apostle School was opened on September 8th, 1953, by four Sisters of Saint Benedict from Duluth, Minnesota. There were 230 students enrolled in grades 1-6 that first year. The old barracks, now used as a cafeteria/hall, was renovated in December 1954. A new convent was built in 1957. Other religious communities have served the school including the Sisters of the Precious Blood, Sisters of Saint Francis, Sisters of Divine Providence, Sisters of Saint Joseph, Sisters of Notre Dame, Sisters of the Immaculate Heart of Mary, Sisters of Charity of the Blessed Virgin Mary and the Dominican Sisters.

On August 15, 1959, ground was broken for a new church. The first Mass in the new church was held on December 8, 1960 and dedicated by Bishop

Francis J. Green of Tucson on December 18, 1960. The old barracks were torn down and the first church building became the parish hall. During the 1990s, the convent became the Spirituality Center, a perpetual adoration chapel was built, and the rectory was renovated. The convent was later restored to house the Dominican Sisters. The parish is renovating the interior of the church at present. Father John D. Ehrich is the current pastor. Saint Thomas the Apostle Parish serves over 3,200 registered families.

SAINT TIMOTHY
PARISH

Mesa, Arizona

Established March 1, 1978

Saint Timothy Parish was established by Bishop James S. Rausch of Phoenix on March 1, 1978. Father Ronald P. Simon was appointed as the first pastor. Groundbreaking for the church and parish center was held on March 16, 1980. The church was dedicated by Bishop Thomas O'Brien of Phoenix on the Feast of Saint Timothy, January 26, 1982.

Much symbolism has been incorporated into the church's design, including the triple shepherd's crook that rises from the baptismal font, through the ceiling and is topped with an 18-foot cross. The area behind the altar features a vibrant "Salvation's History" mural and the sculpture originally behind the altar was moved to the side walls.

The facility's underground design was creatively used to help cut utility costs and to provide a large facility on a small six-acre piece of land. The church campus has expanded to include the Father Marcel Salinas Blessed Sacrament Chapel, Children's Center and amphitheater. Father Dale Fushek was named as pastor in 1985.

Saint Timothy Catholic Academy was established in 2000 by Monsignor Dale Fushek. Classes began in August 2000 with the first Kindergarten class. The following year, 100 students in grades 1-6 were attending the school. With a desire to meet the needs of junior high students, a committee searched and found a new site for the Academy.

A Lutheran church building was purchased and remodeled during the summer of 2004. Classes began in August 2004 at the current school site.

Today, Saint Timothy Parish has nearly 100 active ministries including Adult Formation, Catechetical Ministry, RCIA, Sanctity of Life, Grief and Bereavement, and Life Teen.

Father John D. Spaulding was named as pastor in 2005. Saint Timothy Parish currently serves over 3,700 registered families.

SAINT VINCENT DE PAUL PARISH

Phoenix, Arizona

Established January 26, 1957

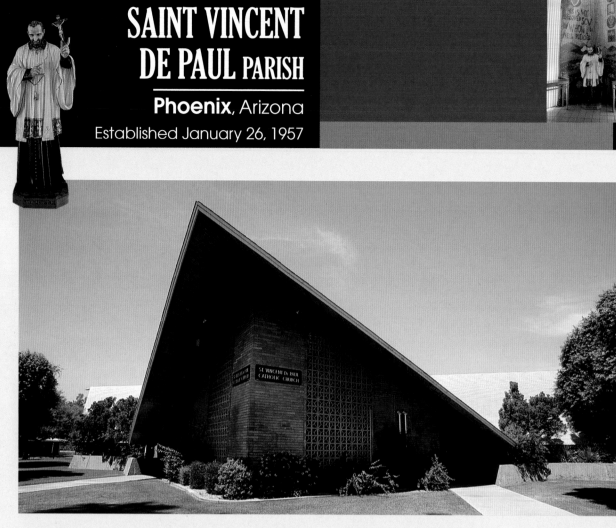

Saint Vincent de Paul Parish was established by Bishop Daniel J. Gercke of Tucson on January 26, 1957. The Vincentian Fathers were placed in charge of the parish and Father Philip LeFevre, C.M., was appointed as the first pastor. Father LeFevre arrived on February 27, 1957, and a temporary residence was rented on West Indian School Road. The first Sunday Mass was celebrated at the Phoenix Coliseum on March 31, 1957. Ground was broken for the present parish hall, used then as the temporary church, on November 9, 1957. The first Mass was a Midnight Mass on December 25, 1957, in the unfinished building. An addition to the temporary church was built in June 1958.

On June 15, 1958, the parish purchased 15-acres of property at 51st Avenue and Osborn Road where the permanent church would be erected. Father John Sharpe, C.M., was appointed the second pastor on February 6, 1959. Ground was broken for two new school buildings on April 19, 1959. The school occupied one of the buildings, and Mass was celebrated in the other. Saint Vincent de Paul School was opened in September 1959, by four Daughters of Charity and one lay teacher serving students in grades 1-5. In 1960, a second first grade class was added, along with a sixth grade. Grade 7 was added in 1961 and grade eight in 1962. In 1966, the school added a Kindergarten.

The groundbreaking for the present church building took place on June 19, 1959 and the first Mass in the new church was celebrated in April 1960. The church was dedicated in September 1960. The mosaic in the vestibule was completed by the school children and dedicated in June 1964. The parish hall and two classrooms were added in 1970.

In 1978, the church interior was remodeled and a new altar installed. The remodeling of the church was completed on September 30, 1978. The new rectory and office building were completed in April 1981. Father Kilian McCaffrey is the pastoral administrator. There are many ministries at the parish including Catechetical Ministry, Christian Formation, Youth Ministry, Adult Formation, and Spanish Prayer Group. Saint Vincent de Paul Parish currently serves over 2,300 registered families.

SAINT WILLIAM
PARISH

Cashion, Arizona
Established August 7, 1973

Saint William Mission in Cashion began back in the late 1960's, when Edna Henline and other local Catholics decided to build a chapel. The chapel was built on 109th Avenue and Mohave. Saint William was a mission of Blessed Sacrament Parish in Tolleson. Bishop Edward McCarthy of Phoenix appointed Father Frank Gelskey as full-time administrator of the mission on July 1, 1972.

Saint William Mission in Cashion was elevated to parish status by Bishop Edward McCarthy on August 7, 1973. Father Frank L. Gelskey was appointed as the first pastor. A day care center was soon purchased by the parish and converted into the original chapel. Father Gelskey submitted a request to Bishop McCarthy to allow the Missionary Sisters of the Sacred Heart from Mexico to minister to the parishioners. These sisters organized religious instruction, visitations for families and the homebound, and directed parish organizations. On December 13, 1974, Father Gelskey resigned because of poor health.

Due to increasing numbers, the parish outgrew its church building. A Southern Baptist Church on 111th Avenue and Third Street decided to sell its buildings including a 300-seat chapel, classrooms, and a parish hall. The church was purchased on September 8, 1981. On June 14, 1982, the house next to the church was bought and converted into the rectory. After the needed renovations, Bishop O'Brien dedicated the church in 1982.

Father Joseph Briceno was appointed pastor on July 1, 1985. The Sacred Heart Sisters also left the parish and returned to Mexico. Over the next few years, Saint William Church was remodeled. Father Tom Bielawa, S.D.S., was named administrator on July 1, 1992. Father Loren Gonzales was pastor from July 2002 until June 2005. Father Mario Garcia-Icedo has been pastor since June 2005. Ministries include Legion of Mary, Religious Education, and Saint Vincent de Paul Society. Saint William Parish currently serves 500 registered families.

SAN FRANCISCO DE ASÍS PARISH
Flagstaff, Arizona
Established July 1, 1997

Nativity of the Blessed Virgin Mary Chapel

Our Lady of Guadalupe Chapel

San Francisco de Asís Parish was established by Bishop Thomas O'Brien of Phoenix on July 1, 1997. Father Douglas J. Nohava was appointed as the first pastor. San Francisco de Asís Parish was formed by consolidating three Flagstaff parishes and a campus ministry into one new parish and included Nativity of the Blessed Virgin Mary Parish, Our Lady of Guadalupe Parish, Saint Pius X Parish and Holy Trinity Newman Center at Northern Arizona University. The process of consolidation of the former parishes, Catholic school, and Newman Center continued over the next 10 years.

The name of the parish school was changed from Saint Mary School to San Francisco de Asís School to reflect its direct relationship with the parish in September 2007. The school originally started as a one-room cabin in 1895. In 1899, the Sisters of Loretto of Nernix, Kentucky relocated to Flagstaff to operate the school and it was renamed Saint Anthony School. In 1911, Saint Anthony's new multi-story school building was erected. Our Lady of Guadalupe School opened in 1953 and soon after, Nativity Parish built the current school building and renamed it Saint Mary School. The two schools were merged in 1976.

The first Catholic Mass in Flagstaff by Father F. X. Gubitosi, a Jesuit from Prescott, at the home of P. J. Brennan on February 4, 1887. The first Catholic Church in Flagstaff was built in 1888 and the first Mass in the new Church of the Nativity was celebrated on December 25, 1888. Nativity of

the Blessed Virgin Mary Parish was established in 1891. Our Lady of Guadalupe Church was built in 1926 and a new Nativity Church was completed in 1930. The first Newman Club was formed at North Arizona State Teachers College in 1930. The Newman Center was formed as a mission of Our Lady of Guadalupe in the 1950s. Saint Pius X Church was built in 1958 and a new church was completed in 1969. Holy Trinity Newman Center moved to NAU campus in 1962. Nativity of the Blessed Virgin Mary has been a Chapel since 1997. Our Lady of Guadalupe has been a Chapel since 1997 and underwent an interior restoration in 2007. Holy Trinity Newman Center at NAU is still used for special events.

Father Nohava died on October 8, 1998. Father Michael Straley became pastor on July 1, 1999. The parish purchased 105-acres of land on McMillan Mesa in Flagstaff for a new 1,000-seat church, school, fellowship hall, and administrative center in November 2003. Bishop Thomas Olmsted officiated at the ground breaking ceremony for the new parish complex in the summer of 2008. Father Patrick Mowrer has been pastor since July 1, 2004. Ministries include Ministry of Care, Music Ministry, RCIA, and Youth Ministry. San Francisco de Asís Parish serves 2,000 registered families.

Saint Pius X Church

SANTA TERESITA
PARISH
El Mirage, Arizona
Established January 22, 1968

Priests from Our Lady of Perpetual Help in Glendale first came to El Mirage in the late 1940's. Father Francis Long and Father Palmer Plourde were among the clergy that came weekly and ministered to the homesteaders. Most people attended Sunday Mass at the old El Mirage Theater. A small parcel of land at the southwest corner of Verbena and Ventura Streets was acquired on August 3, 1952. Father Francis Long spoke with Bishop Francis Green of Tucson to seek his permission to establish a mission at El Mirage. Bishop Green gave his blessing and money to help start the mission.

Father Long and the people of El Mirage chose the name of Santa Teresita for the mission. In 1953, the church was built on the property at Verbena and Ventura Streets. As the town grew in population, so did the need for more seating capacity. The parishioners knocked down walls and erected new ones to accommodate the parish growth. Throughout the years, new sections have been added to the front and south ends of the church. In 1954, Father Plourde acquired an altar, containing a relic of Saint Therese of Lisieux, for the newly built church. In the early 1960s, a rectory was built for the priests.

Santa Teresita was established as a parish on January 22, 1968. Father Paul Mattingly was appointed as the first pastor. The parish center was built in 1978 and was named after Father Francis O'Reilly. Property was purchased across from the church in 1988. A multi-purpose hall was completed 6 months later and named Nazareth Hall. In 1994, the altar area of the church was renovated. The parish began major upgrading and remodeling of its facilities in July 2006. Father Stephen Schack is the current pastor. Ministries and organizations include Catechetical Ministry, RCIA, Saint Vincent de Paul Society and Sacramental Preparation. Santa Teresita Parish currently serves 1,550 registered families.

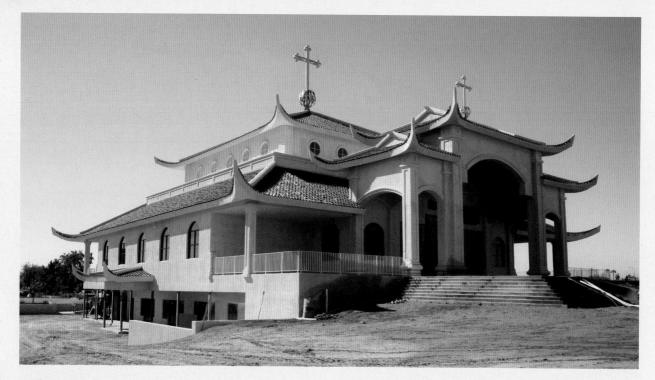

In summer 2001, the Vietnamese Community of Most Holy Trinity Parish in Phoenix learned that the long serving Dominican priests would be returning the parish back to the Diocese. At that time, the Vietnamese Community was one of three in the parish. The members of the lay council met with the Vietnamese assistant priest to discuss the future of the Vietnamese Community there. It was agreed that the Vietnamese Community should have its own mission. A letter was sent to Bishop Thomas J. O'Brien of Phoenix requesting the new mission in 2001.

Bishop O'Brien advised the community to form a committee and began the process of establishing Vietnamese Martyrs Parish in early 2002. Over the next two years, the committee worked hard to establish the mission. On March 22, 2004, Bishop Thomas J. Olmsted of Phoenix signed an agreement entrusting the mission to the Vietnamese Dominican Fathers. The Vietnamese Martyrs Mission was established by Bishop Olmsted on March 23, 2004. Just three months later, the mission became a parish. Vietnamese Martyrs Parish was established by Bishop Olmsted on July 1, 2004. It was established as a non-territorial parish serving Catholics of Vietnamese descent and their families who chose to affiliate with the parish in Phoenix.

Vietnamese Martyrs Parish has shared the facilities of Most Holy Trinity Parish for all of its activities and Masses since June 2003. Masses are held at the McHugh Hall. A new church is currently being built on West Northern Avenue in Phoenix. Father Joseph Nguyen, O.P., is the founding pastor of the parish. Vietnamese Martyrs Parish currently has 550 registered families.

MISSIONS

CAMPUS MINISTRIES

HIGH SCHOOLS

THE DIOCESE
of Phoenix

MISSIONS

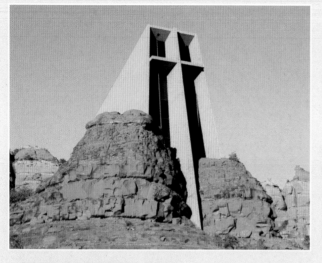

> CHAPEL OF THE HOLY CROSS
Sedona, Arizona

> HOLY FAMILY MISSION
Blackwater, Pinal County, Arizona
Canonically part of Saint Peter Parish
(Bapchule, AZ)

> GOOD SHEPHERD MISSION
New River, Arizona
Canonically part of Saint Rose
Philippine Duchesne Parish (Anthem, AZ)

> LA SANTISSIMA TRINIDAD MISSION
Littlefield, Arizona
Canonically part of Saint Mary Parish
(Kingman, AZ)

> GOOD SHEPHERD OF THE DESERT MISSION
Congress, Arizona
Canonically part of Saint Anthony of Padua
Parish (Wickenburg, AZ)

> MATER MISERICORDIAE MISSION
Phoenix, Arizona

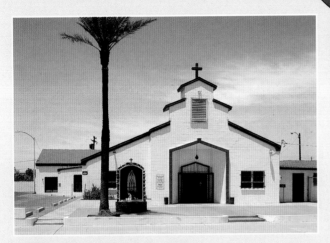

> OUR LADY OF FATIMA MISSION
Phoenix, Arizona
Canonically part of Saint Anthony Parish
(Phoenix, AZ)

> OUR LADY OF VICTORY MISSION
Sacaton Flats, Pinal County, Arizona
Canonically part of Saint Peter Parish
(Bapchule, AZ)

> OUR LADY OF GUADALUPE MISSION
Aguila, Arizona
Canonically part of Saint Anthony
of Padua Parish (Wickenburg, AZ)

> SAINT ANNE MISSION
Ashfork, Arizona
Canonically part of Saint Francis Parish
(Seligman, AZ)

> OUR LADY OF THE DESERT MISSION
Dolan Springs, Arizona
Canonically part of Saint Mary Parish
(Kingman, AZ)

> SAINT ANNE MISSION
Santan, Pinal County, Arizona
Canonically part of Saint Peter Parish
(Bapchule, AZ)

> SAINT ANTHONY MISSION
Sacaton, Pinal County, Arizona
Canonically part of Saint Peter Parish
(Bapchule, AZ)

> SAINT DOMINIC MISSION
Rio Verde, Arizona
Canonically part of Ascension Parish
(Fountain Hills, AZ)

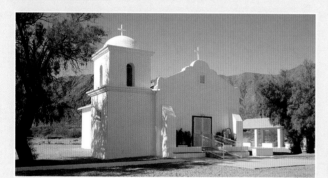

> SAINT CATHERINE MISSION
Santa Cruz, Arizona
Canonically part of Saint John the Baptist Parish
(Laveen, AZ)

> SAINT FRANCIS MISSION
Ak-Chin, Pinal County, Arizona
Canonically part of Saint Peter Parish
(Bapchule, AZ)

> SAINT CATHERINE LABOURE MISSION
Chino Valley, Arizona
Canonically part of Sacred Heart Parish
(Prescott, AZ)

> SAINT COLUMBA KIM MISSION
Mesa, Arizona
Canonically part of Queen of Peace Parish
(Mesa, AZ)

> SAINT FRANCIS OF ASSISI MISSION
Scottsdale, Pima-Maricopa Indian Community,
Arizona
Canonically part of Saint John the Baptist Parish
(Laveen, AZ)

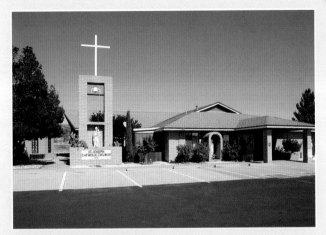

> SAINT JOSEPH MISSION
Mayer, Arizona
Canonically part of Saint Frances Cabrini Parish
(Camp Verde, AZ)

> SAINT PHILIP BENIZI MISSION
Black Canyon City, Arizona
Canonically part of Saint Rose Philippine
Duchesne Parish (Anthem, AZ)

> SAINT MARY MEDIATRIX MISSION
Yarnell, Arizona
Canonically part of Saint Francis of Assisi Parish
(Bagdad, AZ)

> SAINT PHILIP THE DEACON MISSION
Phoenix, Arizona
Canonically part of Saint Mark Parish
(Phoenix, AZ)

> SAINT PASCHAL BAYLON CHAPEL
Lehi, Arizona
Canonically part of Saint John the Baptist Parish
(Laveen, AZ)

> SAN LUCY MISSION
Gila Bend, Arizona
Canonically part of Saint John the Baptist Parish
(Laveen, AZ)

> ALL SAINTS CATHOLIC NEWMAN CENTER
Tempe, Arizona
Arizona State University

The Newman Club in Tempe was founded in 1932 when 25 Catholic students from Arizona State University (ASU) gathered in the basement of the Old Saint Mary Church. Originally known as the Tempe Newman Center under its first chaplain Father James Peter Davis (later Archbishop of San Juan de Puerto Rico and Archbishop of Santa Fe), the name was later changed to the All Saints Newman Center. In 1957, land was purchased by the center adjacent to the Old Saint Mary Church. Construction began in 1960 and the two-story facility was dedicated in 1962. In 1968, the old church, a National Historic Landmark, passed into the care of the Newman Center and has been restored several times in the past two decades. All Saints Newman Center is currently in the process of building a new chapel and student center near ASU's Tempe campus.

> HOLY TRINITY NEWMAN CENTER
Flagstaff, Arizona
Northern Arizona University

The first Newman Club was formed at Northern Arizona State Teacher's College (later Northern Arizona University) in 1930. Holy Trinity Newman Center was originally formed as a mission of Our Lady of Guadalupe Parish in Flagstaff during the 1950's and moved to the Northern Arizona University (NAU) campus in 1962. Holy Trinity Newman Center was merged with three Flagstaff parishes to form San Francisco de Asis Parish on July 1, 1997. The Newman Center is a Catholic student and faculty organization designed to help students through their journey at NAU and beyond. Weekday and Sunday Masses continue to be held for NAU students at the Holy Trinity Newman Center.

> JOHN PAUL II CATHOLIC NEWMAN CENTER
Mesa, Arizona
Arizona State University- Polytechnic campus

The John Paul II Catholic Newman Center was established in September 2006 by Bishop Thomas J. Olmsted of Phoenix to serve the Catholic students at Arizona State University's Polytechnic campus in Mesa. Father Michael Goodyear, L.C., was appointed as the founding chaplain. A vehicle, named the "Pope Mobile", was acquired by the John Paul II Newman Center to act as an office and raise visibility for the center in 2007.

> ## BOURGADE CATHOLIC HIGH SCHOOL
Phoenix, Arizona
Established 1962

Bourgade Catholic High School is named after the Most Reverend Archbishop Peter Bourgade who was the first bishop in Arizona. The school opened its doors in 1962 to students who were taught by the Marist Priests and Brothers, the Sisters of the Institute of the Blessed Virgin Mary, Sisters from the Congregation of the Humility of Mary, and several lay educators. In 1972, the Holy Cross Community of Priests from the University of Notre Dame assumed the administration of the school. Since 1988, the principal of Bourgade Catholic High School has been a member of the community of the School Sisters of Notre Dame, Sister Mary McGreevy. Bourgade High School currently has an enrollment of over 425 students.

> ## BROPHY COLLEGE PREPARATORY
Phoenix, Arizona
Established 1928

Brophy College Preparatory was founded in 1928 by Ellen Brophy in accordance with the Society of Jesus as a Jesuit Catholic all boys' school. The first school complex on the 19-acre Phoenix campus was completed for the opening on September 11, 1928, and included Regis Hall, the Chapel, and the Jesuit residence. During the Great Depression, the school struggled financially and was closed in August 1935. In the spring of 1952, the school was reopened. The school campus was expanded with the addition of Loyola Hall in 1959, the Robson Gymnasium in 1967, Charles Keating Hall and the Steele Library in 1986. In recent years, the major gifts campaign has allowed for the construction of the Ethel and Kemper Information Commons in 2001, Eller Fine Arts Center in 2003, McCain Colonnade in 2003, Piper Center for Math and Science in 2005, and the Harper Great Hall in 2006. Brophy College Preparatory has 1,270 students enrolled for the school year 2008-2009.

> ## NOTRE DAME PREPARATORY
Scottsdale, Arizona
Established 2002

Notre Dame Preparatory is the Diocesan Catholic High School located in north Scottsdale that opened in 2002. It was originally funded by a loan from a diocesan funding program and tax-exempt municipal bonds issued through the City of Scottsdale. Notre Dame student organizations include: Habitat for Humanity, Hands Across Borders, Special Olympics, and Saint Vincent de Paul Society. The Class of 2008 has also been awarded more than $ 3.1 million in college scholarships from prestigious universities nationwide. Notre Dame Preparatory has over 875 students enrolled for the 2008-2009 school year.

> ## SAINT MARY CATHOLIC HIGH SCHOOL
Phoenix, Arizona
Established 1917

> ## SETON CATHOLIC HIGH SCHOOL
Chandler, Arizona
Established 1954

> ## XAVIER COLLEGE PREPARATORY
Phoenix, Arizona
Established 1943

Saint Mary's High School was founded in 1917 by the Sisters of the Precious Blood and is the oldest Catholic high school in Arizona. The Sisters were able to set aside classroom space for 4 boys and 10 girls in Saint Anthony School. This was the beginning of Saint Mary's High School. In 1920, the school moved into its very first building located on East Monroe Street. All male students were transferred to Brophy College Preparatory School in 1928. The Depression caused Brophy to close in August 1935. Franciscan Fathers soon built a second Saint Mary's on Polk Street, to educate the boys displaced by the closure. Both schools were combined in 1958, making Saint Mary's coeducational once again. In 1988, the Polk Street campus was sold and the school moved to its present location at 3rd Street and Sheridan. The school built the Virginia G. Piper Education Center and it was dedicated on December 11, 2007. Saint Mary High School currently has an enrollment of 781 students.

Seton Catholic High School was founded in 1954 as a parish school by Father Joseph Patterson. It opened as a junior high school with grades 7-9. Through the next several decades, a majority of Seton Catholic's staff was composed of members of the Sisters of Charity of Seton Hill. It was named a diocesan school in 1973. A fire destroyed the original site of the school in 1980 and the campus was rebuilt at its current site in 1983. From 1984 until 1995, the Irish Christian Brothers operated the school. In 2002, 13 additional acres of land were purchased adjacent to the school. The first building of the new campus, the Saint Elizabeth Ann Seton Chapel, was dedicated on March 11, 2008, and efforts are underway for two new classroom buildings. Seton Catholic High School currently has an enrollment of 606 students.

Xavier College Preparatory was founded in 1943 by the Sisters of Charity of the Blessed Virgin Mary. There were 17 students enrolled that first year. Originally established as Saint Francis Xavier parish high school, Xavier later became a diocesan school in 1968. Over the last six decades, the Xavier campus has added Lutfy Hall, Brown Hall, the Activity Center, Virginia G. Piper Center for Science and Technology, and opened the Virginia G. Piper Performing Arts Center and Steele Educational Complex in 2003. In 2007, Xavier began the Legacy of Leadership Campaign, which includes construction of Founders Hall. Xavier is a four-year Roman Catholic college preparatory high school for young women in grades 9-12 and located in the heart of central Phoenix. Xavier College Preparatory currently has 1200 students enrolled.

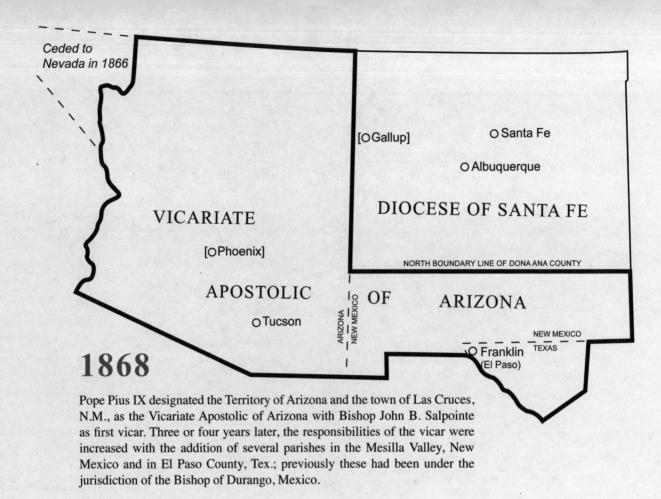

1868

Pope Pius IX designated the Territory of Arizona and the town of Las Cruces, N.M., as the Vicariate Apostolic of Arizona with Bishop John B. Salpointe as first vicar. Three or four years later, the responsibilities of the vicar were increased with the addition of several parishes in the Mesilla Valley, New Mexico and in El Paso County, Tex.; previously these had been under the jurisdiction of the Bishop of Durango, Mexico.

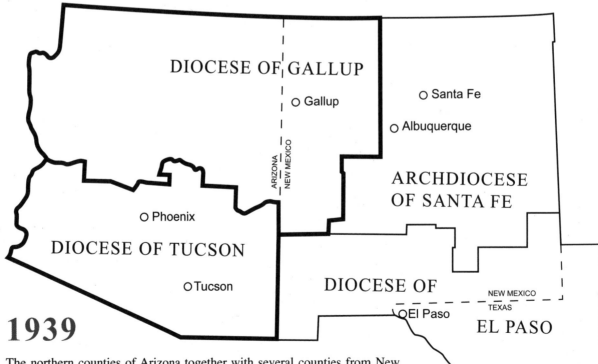

1939

The northern counties of Arizona together with several counties from New Mexico were formed into a new diocese with headquarters at Gallup, N.M. Bishop Daniel J. Gercke who had been Bishop of Tucson since 1923 continued as head of the southern Arizona diocese and Bishop Bernard Espelage, O.F.M. became the leader of the new diocese.